MW00830153

THE
END TIMES
MADE SIMPLE

*How Could Everyone
Be So Wrong About
Biblical Prophecy?*

Samuel E. Waldron

CALVARY PRESS PUBLISHING

1-800-247-6553
www.calvarypress.com

Book design and typography by Studio E Books
Santa Barbara, CA www.studio-e-books.com

Waldron, Samuel E.
    The end times made simple : how could everyone be so
wrong about biblical prophecy? / by Samuel E. Waldron.
    ISBN 1-879737-50-7
Suggested subject headings:
        1. Christianity—doctrines.
        2. Religion
        I. Title

10 9 8 7 6 5 4 3 2 1

Contents

Part III: *Next Question Please!*

Section 1: Questions Related to the Present Gospel or Church Age

Section 2: Questions Related to the Imminent Return of Christ

Section 3: Questions Related to the Resurrection

Section 4: Questions Related to the Eternal State

PART I
HOW OLD IS YOUR ESCHATOLOGY?

Chapter 1: Needed—
A Gospel Eschatology

THIS IS A BOOK about Christian prophecy, technically called *eschatology*, a word that means the doctrine or study of the last things. It is, thus, a book about what many call biblical prophecy. It is not a theoretical book. It is a book written out of several deep convictions: that eschatology is profoundly important, that the eschatological system of the Bible is basically simple, and that popular views of prophecy today are profoundly unbiblical.

More than two decades in Christian ministry (and a lifetime in evangelical churches) have convinced me that there are two prevalent attitudes toward eschatology or prophecy in our day. We may epitomize these two prevalent attitudes by two mythical (but very true to life) persons: Fascinated Fred and Practical Pam. Fascinated Fred represents all *the fascinated fans* of prophecy. Practical Pam stands for those *burned out and turned off* by eschatology. Fascinated Fred has read every one of the multi-volume series of novels on the last days that begin with the one entitled, *Left Behind*. He watches events in the Middle East and in the world with breathless excitement for signs of the onset of the last days and the tribulation. On the other hand, Practical Pam is of a more practical bent and fails to see much profit for Christian living in this fascination. Her attitude is, "Forget prophecy! Teach me something practical about the home or family!" Pam is a panmillennialist. (Everything will *pan out* allright in the end. So why worry about it?)

My conviction is that one and the same doctrinal problem has infected both Fred and Pam. It is responsible for both of their attitudes. This problem is the practical divorce of the gospel of Christ and eschatology in the popular, prophetic views of our day. The idea is (and I have heard this said): *We preach the gospel to get people saved. Once they are saved, and if they are interested in deeper, Christian doctrine, we can teach them about prophecy.* In such perspectives the divorce of the gospel and eschatology is plainly implied. No wonder with such ideas abroad that you end up with the *Fascinated Freds*, on the one hand, and the *Practical Pams*, on the other.

The fact is, however, that the popular eschatology widely taught in our day in evangelical churches really does have comparatively little to do with the gospel of Christ. Prophecy was often taught in the evangelical church in which I was raised. One of the things I keenly remember being taught was that the church age in which we live was a great parenthesis in biblical prophecy, a mystery-period unforeseen by biblical prophecy. It would end with the rapture of the church by the secret coming of Christ in the air before the tribulation period. Since this coming was imminent, that is to say, might occur at any moment, it would not be preceded by any prophetic events. Only with this secret rapture would the prophetic clock start ticking again. With the secret rapture of the church the important events of biblical prophecy would begin to unfold. They involved the appearance of the Antichrist and his world empire, the rebuilding of the temple in Jerusalem, a seven year tribulation, a glorious appearing of Christ, and a one thousand year reign of Christ on earth—all having to do with God's other, earthly people, the Jewish nation, not His heavenly people, the church. I remember feeling disappointed that I lived in such blank or vacant period with regard to biblical prophecy.

Now I was not the only one taught this system. It dominated evangelical churches then. Despite many critics, it retains its popularity. From best-selling novels to movies replete with amazing special effects, it still dominates the Christian imagination in our day.

Such a system of prophecy really does have little to do with the gospel of Christ. It is not surprising that the reaction of the Christian public to it is either fascination or irritation. If the church is a mystery parenthesis in world history, and if the prophetic clock only begins ticking again with the rapture of the church safely to the bliss of heaven, and if biblical prophecy is really about God's plan for the Jews, then the reaction of Christians can only be the fascination of the speculative, on the one hand, or the irritation of the practical, on the other.

This book provides a simple, but systematic presentation of Christian eschatology. It will show that this popular system is wrong and without biblical basis in all its distinctive characteristics. This may strike many readers as an incredible claim. But remember the little boy who exclaimed that the emperor's fine new ensemble was really not! If you will bear with me and give the Bible hearing, you may adopt the same opinion of the emperor's new clothes.

In contrast to the naked emperor, my hope in this book is to supply Christians with a biblical ensemble of eschatological clothing. This ensemble of prophetic clothing is not teaching that goes beyond the gospel or that is artificially attached to it. The Christian gospel has everything to do with eschatology, and eschatology has everything to do with the Christian gospel.

What I mean is briefly this: Jesus speaks of the goal of eschatology as "the regeneration" (Matt. 19:28). Peter speaks of it as "the restoration of all things" (Acts 3:21). Paul speaks of it as "the creation...set free from its slavery" (Romans 8:21). Eschatology has to do with the bringing of creation and mankind to its original God-intended destination. Eschatology has to do with the defeat of Satan's destructive purposes and the victory of God's redemptive purposes. Eschatology has everything to do, then, with the gospel that proclaims God's purpose to "reconcile all things to Himself having made peace through blood of His (Christ's) cross" (Col. 1:20). Biblical prophecy, then, is not about something other than the gospel of Christ. It has everything to do with Christ's cross, Christ's church, and Christ's coming.

That would be something, wouldn't it? A simple, gospel eschatology! Suppose the emperor really does have no clothes! Suppose prophecy really is about Christ, His cross, and His church! Listen to the little boy, look at the emperor, and examine the Bible for yourself.

Chapter 2: But How Could Everyone Be So Wrong?

I ENDED the first chapter by urging you to look again and carefully at what the Bible says about eschatology. Before, however, we can begin that study, the problem suggested by the heading to this chapter must be addressed. Many will wonder how so many earnest Christians could be so wrong.

Before I answer that question, let me make clear that I believe that many that hold the view of prophecy in question are Christians. I am not attacking the Christian character of those with whom I differ. I owe a great debt to many that hold the view I will be criticizing. The fact that they are Christians does not mean, however, that they are right or that our differences are unimportant. Some men's hearts are better than their heads. What is in their heads may still be dangerous to others.

Since I believe this, I must do a thorough job of convincing people of the error of the popular view. Of course, I must do this mainly through opening up the clear teaching of the Word of God. Before I do that, however, I must attempt to remove a prejudice in favor of the popular view and against what I will teach. The view I will criticize has been popular for the last few decades in the Christian church. This makes it seem to many to be the *historic* view of the Christian church. Anything else thus appears novel. Therefore, in order to test the validity of the claims for the popular, prophetic view of our day, we will have to study a little church history. We will study the history of eschatology in the church by responding to the question that titles this chapter, *How could everyone be so wrong?*

First Response:
Actually, the view popular today is only one of four views that have been held and are held by evangelical Christians.
The prophetic view popular today has a name. It is called *Dispensationalism,* or more fully, *Dispensational Premillennialism.*

DISPENSATIONAL PREMILLENNIALISM

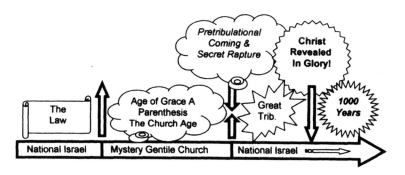

Dispensational Premillennialism (as this name suggests) is a form of premillennialism. Premillennialism is the view that Christ is to return before the millennium prophesied in Revelation 20:1–10. The term, millennium, is simply the Latin for 1000 years. The 1000 years of Revelation 20 is a time in which Christ reigns and Satan is bound. Premillennialists take this to mean a personal and physical reign of Christ on earth after He returns for a literal 1000 years.

Dispensational Premillennialism is the form of premillennialism that emphasizes that history is divided into different dispensations. Of course, all Christians—no matter their eschatological persuasion—allow that in some sense this is true. Dispensationalism is more specifically the view that God is pursuing alternating programs in these different dispensations. As the chart above suggests, God alternately pursues His plan for the Jewish nation, on the one hand, and His plan for the Gentiles and the church on the other.

Closely related to this Dispensational scheme of history and, in fact, built on it is the secret rapture theory of Christ's Second Coming. This theory (spectacularly popularized by the special effects of recent movies) is the view that Christ's return will be in two stages. The first of these two stages will be secret and will remove the church from the world prior to the Great Tribulation. The second will be glorious and will bring an end to the reign of the Antichrist and usher in the millennial reign of Christ with the Jewish nation over the world.

It is important to emphasize that the unique and distinguishing feature of Dispensationalism is the consistent separation between Israel and the Church that it maintains. This is called the Church-Israel distinction. It is this point that most clearly distances Dispensational Premillennialism from the next view to be described. That view is often called *Historic* or *Covenant Premillennialism*.

HISTORIC PREMILLENIALISM

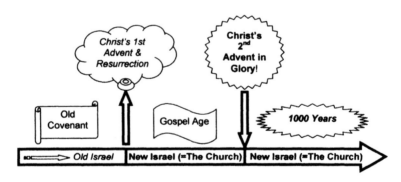

This view holds, in common with Dispensationalism, a premillennial view of Christ's return. Premillennialism, as just noted, is the view that says that Christ is to return before the millennium prophesied in Revelation 20:1–10.

The name, **Historic** Premillennialism, is, of course, loaded. It claims for this view that it is the *historic* premillennialism to be found earlier in the history of the church. It implicitly claims that Dispensationalism is not to be identified with the premillennialism to be found in the early centuries of church history. This claim will be examined later in this chapter.

This view has also sometimes been called Covenant Premillennialism. The name, *Covenant* Premillennialism, associates this form of premillennialism with Covenant Theology. This name emphasizes that this form of premillennialism does not separate Israel and the Church in the way that Dispensationalism does. Rather, it sees the Church as the New Israel of God and rejects the Church-Israel distinction of Dispensationalism. It follows that rejecting this distinction this form of premillennialism also rejects the secret rapture theory built upon it.[1] Note the table of differences below.

HISTORIC AND DISPENSATIONAL PREMILLENNIALISM
A Table of Differences

	Historic Premillenialism	Dispensational Premillenialism
The Church and Israel	*"The Church is the true and new Israel."*	*"The Church is distinct from Israel."*
The Second Coming	One return and post-tribulational	Two-stage return with secret rapture & pretribulational coming first.

Amillennialism literally means no millennialism. In one sense this name is accurate, and in another it is not. It is accurate in that the millennium has usually been defined as a great golden age of material blessing on earth before the eternal state in which evil is suppressed and righteousness is triumphant. It is true that in this sense amillennialism holds no millennium. Amillennialists, however, are Bible-believing Christians and view Revelation 20:1–10 as divine truth. Thus, they do believe in the millennium of Revelation 20 and associate this period of time with the gospel or church age between Christ's first and second advents. They teach, consequently, that Christ returns after this millennium is

AMILLENNIALISM

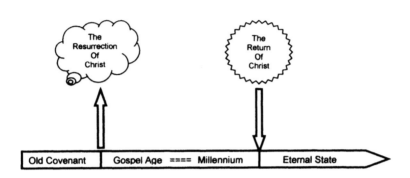

POSTMILLENNIALISM

completed. At His return the general judgment and general resurrection occur and the eternal state commences.

Postmillennialism, as the name indicates, teaches that Christ will come back after the millennium (Post is the Latin preposition for *after*). In contrast to amillennialism it does believe in a great, golden age of spiritual and material blessing on earth before the eternal state. In contrast to premillennialism, it believes that this great golden age is brought to pass through spiritual means before the return of Christ.

These are the four views of eschatology that have historically and are today held by Christians. These millennial views can be classified in different ways. They can be classified by their view of the relation of the return of Christ to the millennium. (Note that in this narrow sense amillennialism is in a sense post-millennial.)

PREMILLENNIAL	POSTMILLENNIAL
Dispensationalism	Amillennialism
Historic Premillennialism	Postmillennialism

They may also be classified by means of their view of the relation of the return of Christ to a future tribulation.

PRE-TRIBULATIONAL	POST-TRIBULATIONAL
Dispensationalism	Historic Premillennialism
	Amillennialism
	Postmillennialism

These views may also be classified by way of their view of the relation of the Church and Israel.

DISPENSATIONAL "The Church is Distinct from Israel"	HISTORICAL "The Church is the New Israel"
Dispensationalism	Historic Premillennialism
	Amillennialism
	Postmillennialism

Finally these views may be categorized by way of their view of a future millennium before the eternal state. Millennialism is sometimes called chiliasm.

CHILIASTIC OR MILLENNIAL	ANTI-CHILIASTIC
Dispensationalism	Amillennialism
Historic Premillennialsm	
Postmillennialism	

Now the main point of this brief overview is to show that Dispensationalism is not the only view held by evangelical Christians. The idea that, if the popular view is wrong, then the Christian church has been wrong, assumes something that is simply mistaken. Evangelical Christians today hold each of the above views.

Each of the views discussed above, with the exception of Dispensationalism, has been widely held by Christians in past centuries of the church. Granted, Dispensationalism is prominent in our day, but each of the other views has had its day in the church. Historic Premillennialism was quite prominent for a period in the early church. It was also prominent for a period in the 1800's. Amillennialism was actually dominant in the church from the time of Augustine (who died in 430) through the 1500's and the early Reformation period. Augustine, Luther, and Calvin were each amillennialists. Postmillennialism was widely held in the 1600's and 1700's by some of the great, evangelicals of the day like Jonathan Edwards. What is my point? Dispensational Premillennialism is not the only Christian alternative!

Second Response:
Actually, the Dispensationalism taught today is a quite recent development in church history.

Many have the impression that the Dispensationalism widespread today is the historic view of the Christian church. This impression is sadly mistaken and based on a remarkably nearsighted view of church history. It is true that Dispensationalists have made extraordinary claims with regard to premillennialism in the early church. The noted Dispensationalist, Dr. Charles Feinberg, has asserted, "The entire early church of the first 3 centuries was Premillennial almost to a man."[2] There are, however, three problems with Dr. Feinberg's claim.

First, even if his claim were true, it would do him little good. As we have noticed above, there is a great deal of difference between Dispensationalism and Historic Premillennialism. In fact, in a number of respects Historic Premillennialism has as much or more in common with Amillennialism and Postmillennialism, than it does with Dispensationalism. It is indisputable that the

Premillennialism found in the early church was *Historic* rather than *Dispensational* in character.

The proof of this is to be found in the first church father in whose writings we find premillennialism. This father is known as Justin Martyr. Justin's writings date from about the year 160. He was clearly a premillennialist. In his *Dialog with Trypho, the Jew*, he says:

> But I and others, who are right-minded Christians on all points, are assured that there will be a resurrection of the dead, and a thousand years in Jerusalem, which will then be built, adorned, and enlarged, [as] the prophets Ezekiel and Isaiah and others declare. (chapter 80, cf. chapters 76–81)

The difficulty with Justin's premillennialism for Dr. Feinberg is that in this very work he bears explicit and repeated testimony to his complete rejection of the essential feature of Dispensationalism, the Church-Israel distinction. One of the main themes of his *Dialog with Trypho the Jew* is that Christians are God's true Israel. The following statement from chapter 11 is representative of many.

> For the true spiritual Israel, and descendants of Judah, Jacob, Isaac, and Abraham...are we who have been led to God through this crucified Christ... (See for many more such statements chapters 11, 120, 123, 125, 135.)

None of the early premillennialists manifest any understanding or commitment to the crucial distinctive of Dispensationalism, the Church-Israel distinction.

Second, Dr. Feinberg's claim that the early church was premillennial almost to a man is simply false. We know that it is false for a number of reasons.

In what are arguably the two earliest references to premillennialism it is clear that some early Christians were not premillennial. The first reference has already been mentioned. In the same chapter cited above in which Justin Martyr affirms his premillenniialism, Trypho, the Jew, cross-examines Justin about his belief

that Jerusalem will be rebuilt during the millennium. Is he really
serious, asks Trypho, in affirming a doctrine held also by the
Jews? Justin replies:

> I am not so miserable a fellow, Trypho, as to say one thing
> and think another. I admitted to you formerly that I and
> many others are of this opinion, and [believe] that such will
> take place, as you assuredly are aware; but, on the other
> hand, I signified to you that many who belong to the pure
> and pious faith, and are true Christians, think otherwise.

In this amazing statement we learn that even in the early church
people that Justin viewed as genuine Christians (*many who are of
the pure and pious faith*) disagreed with him about the subject of
premillennialism.

The second reference of these two earliest references to
premillennialism is associated with the name of Papias who
claimed to be a disciple of John, the Apostle. Though none of Papias' books survive, excerpts of them are recorded in the church
history of Eusebius. (Eusebius lived from about 260 to 340.) Eusebius intersperses his own comments throughout his excerpts of
Papias. Eusebius' comment about Papias is relevant to our point.

> The same person, moreover, has set down other things as
> coming to him from unwritten tradition, amongst these
> some strange parables and instructions of the Saviour, and
> some other things of a more fabulous nature. Amongst
> these he says that there will be a millennium after the resur-
> rection from the dead, when the personal reign of Christ
> will be established on this earth.[3]

Eusebius' comment makes clear that he regarded Papias' premillennialism as beyond *strange* and actually *fabulous*. From this it is
clear that Eusebius himself was not a premillennialist. This is another clear indication that Feinberg's statement about the early
church being premillennial to a man in its first three centuries is
simply unwarranted. Clear and important evidence, then, flatly
contradicts Feinberg's claim.

The impropriety of Feinberg's claim is shown, thirdly, by the fact that it is Dispensationalism itself that is the novel in church history. Far from being the historic position of the church, there is clear evidence that the peculiar form of premillennialism known as Dispensationalism only developed in the first half of the 1800's. Here briefly is what happened.

Dispensationalism was born in the cradle of what is called *futurism*. This was a theory of the interpretation of prophecy and especially the Book of Revelation that assigned its events mainly to a future period of tribulation. (It is opposed to the *preterism* that sees prophetic events as mainly fulfilled in the destruction of Jerusalem in A.D. 70 and to the *historicism* that sees them fulfilled progressively in the events of church history.)

The genesis of futurism among Protestant premillennialists must be traced to the influence of Edward Irving. In 1826 Irving came into the possession of a book written by Emmanuel Lacunza, *The Coming of Christ in Glory and Majesty*. As might be expected from one converted out of a Jesuit background, the method of prophetic interpretation utilized by this author was futurism. Says Mark Sarver:

> As concerns the developments leading up to the emergence of dispensationalism, the primary significance of Lacunza's work lay in its futurism with reference to the interpretation of the book of Revelation (not only regarding the millennium of chapter 20 but also the tribulation of chapters 6 to 19).[4]

The futurism popularized by Irving is the backdrop and context of the development of the Dispensationalism of J. N. Darby. Though there were futurists who were not dispensational, yet Dispensationalism grew and could only grow on the futurist ground plowed by Irving. It seems clear that the secret or pretribulational rapture theory emerged from within the context of the revival of spiritual gifts in Irving's congregation.

THE SECRET OR PRETRIBULATIONAL RAPTURE THEORY

It is clear that this theory was given a considerable measure of acceptance at the Powerscourt Conferences in 1831 and 1833. Both Darby and Irving were present at these conferences.

Darby built Dispensationalism upon the foundation laid by Irving. Many of his emphases may be found in seed form in Irving. To defend the secret rapture theory of an any-moment pretribulational coming of Christ he emphasized the distinction between Israel and the church. This distinction was both novel and crucial to the defense of Darby's system. Iain Murray remarks:

At Albury and in Irving's London congregation a curious belief, practically unknown in earlier Church history, had arisen, namely, that Christ's appearing before the millennium is to be in two stages, the first, a secret 'rapture' removing the Church before a 'Great Tribulation' smites the earth, the second his coming with his saints to set up his kingdom. This idea comes into full prominence in Darby. He held that 'the Church' is a mystery of which only Paul speaks. She is Christ's mystic body and will be complete at the 'rapture'. The Jews and other Gentiles converted thereafter will never be Christ's bride: ' I deny that the saints before Christ's first coming, or after his second, are part of the Church.' With breath-taking dogmatism Darby swept away what had previously been axiomatic in Christian theology.[5]

Iain Murray records this humorous, but telling, statement of Charles Haddon Spurgeon who lived just at the time when the Church-Israel distinction was beginning to be proclaimed by Darby and his brethren. It bears witness to the novelty with which Dispensationalism struck the greatest Baptist preacher of the last century.

> Spurgeon declared: "we have even heard it asserted that those who lived before the coming of Christ do not belong to the church of God! We never know what we shall hear next, and perhaps it is a mercy that these absurdities are revealed one at a time, in order that we may be able to endure their stupidity without dying of amazement (Vol. 15, 8).[6]

With the emergence of what is known as Dispensational Premillennialism or simply Dispensationalism, a distinctly different form of Premillenialism and, indeed, a distinctly different system of eschatology had been brought to birth. It differed from Historic or Covenant Premillennialism in two respects: First, it separated or distinguished Israel and the Church. Second, it taught a secret, pretribulational return of Christ. Both these peculiarities were novel eschatological views. For Feinberg to claim any historic precedent in the earlier ages of the Christian church is completely inappropriate.

PART II
ESCHATOLOGY MADE SIMPLE!

Chapter 3: A Matter of Interpretation

WITH THIS CHAPTER we reach a turning point in our study. In the previous chapter we briefly surveyed the history of the church on the subject of eschatology. We briefly *listened in* on that great conversation about last things that has been going in the church for 20 centuries. My purpose in this 'holy eavesdropping' was to acquaint you with the basic questions, terminology, and options to be considered as we turn to a study of the Word of God. There is a downside to this study of the opinions of even Christian men. This brief survey of the history of eschatological discussion in the church could well be sub-titled *Eschatology Made Difficult (by Men)*. With this chapter, however, we turn from the complications and complexities of human tradition to the clarity and simplicity of divine revelation. I have entitled this part of the study, (I hope without too much audacity.) *Eschatology Made Simple*.

Of course, when we turn to the Word of God there are prophetic passages and detailed questions about the doctrine of last things that arouse our curiosity, provoke our interest, and may result (if we are not careful) in a sense of general confusion. If one unwisely sets out to explore such passages and questions *first*, the result may be general confusion.

It is important, therefore, to state at the outset several crucial principles of biblical interpretation that must guide one in the study of eschatology. There are three self-evident principles of biblical interpretation that ought to prevent us from setting out on such a misguided course. *The first principle is that we should study the clear passages before we come to the difficult passages.* To put this in other words, we should interpret difficult passages in light of clear ones. *The second principle is that we should study literal passages before we come to figurative passages.* Figurative passages should be interpreted within the doctrinal boundaries set by the literal passages. *The third self-evident principle of biblical interpretation is that general truths of eschatology should be grasped before we come to discuss the details of prophecy.* Clarity will be served by an attempt to grasp the big picture or the overall structure of prophecy. In order to do this we must remember that eschatology has to do with history in general as well as the goal of history. Before one can deal with the details of eschatology and properly interpret the numerous difficult and figurative passages, it is necessary to discover the broad or basic structure of history and eschatology.

Crucial Principles of Biblical Interpretation

In the interpretation of Bible passages related to prophecy we should study...

- *The Clear before the Difficult*
- *The Literal before the Figurative*
- *The General before the Detailed*

Each of these principles assumes that eschatology is not a subject confined to only certain prophetic books of the Bible (like Daniel and Revelation). Prophecy permeates the whole Bible. The doctrine of last things is a vital part of the gospel of Christ itself. For instance, the doctrine of Christ's bodily return, the bodily resurrection of the saints, the eternal and bodily punishment of the wicked—all these are truths vital to the gospel of Christ itself. Appropriately, they are truths confessed in the great confessions of the church from the simple creeds of its earliest days to the great confessions that followed the Reformation.[1] A broader understanding of the eschatological system of the Bible will illuminate many aspects of the Bible's teaching. One purpose of this study is to help you come to a clearer grasp of the Bible's teaching as a whole by providing you with a systematic understanding of its teaching about eschatology. Simply by keeping in mind these obvious and self-evident principles of biblical interpretation the whole subject can be delivered from mind-boggling confusion and reduced to divine simplicity. If we take the literal before the figurative, the clear before the figurative, and the general before the detailed, *eschatology will be made simple!*

There are three broad biblical categories of thought that enable us simply to understand the basic structure of eschatology. These considerations provide, so to speak, the basic floor-plan of the house of eschatology. If we impress upon our minds this basic floor-plan, we will be greatly helped when we come to look at all the different, prophetic furniture and fixtures found in the more difficult passages. We may, of course, still be somewhat puzzled by certain pieces of this furniture, but we will at least know that these furnishings must fit someplace in the basic floor-plan.

In the examination of these broad biblical categories of thought we will implement the principles of biblical interpretation mentioned above. We will be looking first at the clear, the literal, and the general passages. Later in the study of these categories we will examine some of the more important figurative and difficult passages in light of the literal and clear passages.

What are these broad, biblical categories of thought that will enable us to understand the floor-plan of the house of eschatology? In the following chapters we will consider:

- *The Bible's Own System—The Two Ages*
- *The Dividing Line—The General Judgment*
- *The Coming of the Kingdom—The Eschatological Kingdom*

Chapter 4: The Bible's Own System

THERE IS NO more basic or formative issue for our understanding of the structure of biblical eschatology and, indeed, of much else in biblical doctrine than the teaching of the Bible with regard to what I have called the two ages. In this and the following two chapters this formative issue will be examined under three headings:

- *The Biblical Terminology of the Two Ages*
- *The Basic Scheme of the Two Ages*
- *The Modified Scheme of the Two Ages*

The Biblical Terminology of the Two Ages

The Greek word for age (aion) refers not only to time, but also to space. It includes in itself both a temporal and a spatial dimension. Interpreters mingle these two meanings in their definitions. It is "a vast period of time marked by what transpires in it" or "the world in motion." The New Testament uses of this word confirm that it combines in itself the ideas of world and age. Perhaps the best way to convey its meaning would be by the hyphenated word, world-age. This can be seen in Gal. 1:4 which speaks of "this present evil age". Since it is not an evil age in heaven, the term, age, must refer to an age in this world's history. Similarly, in Luke 20:35 Jesus speaks of those "who are considered worthy to attain to that age". Again, the time reference of the word cannot be doubted, but the space dimension of this word is clearly assumed. The wicked do not cease to exist in the coming age. Rather, they do not inhabit the world in the coming age. The key terminology contrasts this world-age with the world-age to come.

The use of this unique word to refer to both the present and the future life makes an important fact clear. The Bible views future, eternal existence as endless existence in space and time. To put it differently, the Bible views eternity as *the age to come*, unending time. As creatures we will always live in space and time. Only God transcends these categories both now and forever. George Eldon Ladd has properly remarked:

> In biblical thought eternity is unending time. In Hellenism men longed for release from the cycle of time in a timeless world beyond, but in biblical thought time is the sphere of human existence both now and in the future. The impression given by the AV at Revelation 10:6, 'that there should be time no longer,' is corrected in the RSV, 'there should be no more delay.'[1]

Ladd is correct to say that the biblical idea of eternity for human beings is unending time. He is also right about Revelation 10:6. The word for time used there can mean a moment of time, occasion, or delay. In most modern versions of the Bible (including the New Kings James Version) the word is translated delay and not time.

This point exposes a flaw in many studies of eschatology. Many prophetic interpreters assume that if biblical prophecy predicts that an event will happen in space and in time that this means it must occur before the eternal state. They think that if the Bible predicts that something is to happen in history and on earth that it must happen before (what we call) the end of the world. A close reading of many prophetic manuals will reveal this flawed premise.[2] The Bible does not, however, share this faulty assumption. It views the eternal state as the world-age to come. Events predicted to happen in time and in space (in history and on earth) may be fulfilled in the unending or eternal world-age to come. One of the major themes of biblical prophecy is the glory of the world-age to come. The content of biblical prophecy is far from being fulfilled at the consummation of this world-age.

To give proper weight to the importance of the phraseology, *this age and the age to come*, it is important to overview the places where it occurs in the New Testament. Those uses will in various ways point us to closely related terminology that will further tend to vindicate the fact that the ideas embodied in this terminology are at the core of biblical teaching.

There are 16 places in the New Testament where this terminology or a distinctive part of it are used:

Matt. 12:32: *"And whoever shall speak a word against the Son of Man, it shall be forgiven him; but whoever shall speak against the Holy Spirit, it shall not be forgiven him, either in this age, or in the age to come."* This age and the age to come exhaust all time. Note how the parallel passage in Mark 3:29 confirms this: "but whoever blasphemes against the Holy Spirit never has forgiveness, but is guilty of an eternal sin".

Mark 10:30: *"but that he shall receive a hundred times as much now in the present age, houses and brothers and sisters and mothers and children and farms, along with persecutions; and in the age to come, eternal life."* This passage teaches that along with the blessings of being part of the Christian community persecutions will also be the lot of Christ's disciples in this age.

Luke 16:8: *"And his master praised the unrighteous steward because he had acted shrewdly; for the sons of this age are more shrewd in relation to their own kind than the sons of light."* The sons of this age are contrasted with the sons of light. This suggests that the age to come is the age of light. It also suggests that the sons of this age are children of light.

Luke 18:30: *"who shall not receive many times as much at this time and in the age to come, eternal life."* A synonym for *this age* is *this time*.

Luke 20:34–36: *"And Jesus said to them, "The sons of this age marry and are given in marriage, 35 but those who are considered worthy to attain to that age and the resurrection from the dead, neither marry,* *nor are given in marriage; 36 for neither can they die anymore, for they are like angels, and are sons of God, being sons of the resurrection."* The significant contrasts between this age and that age must later be examined in detail.

Rom. 12:2: *"And do not be conformed to this world, but be transformed by the renewing of your mind, that you may prove what the will of God is, that which is good and acceptable and perfect."* Here the duty of being transformed by the renewing of our minds is described negatively in the exhortation, "Do not be conformed to this age." It is the word, age (aion), in the original. The ethical contrast between the two ages is suggested by this exhortation.

1 Cor. 1:20: *"Where is the wise man? Where is the scribe? Where is the debater of this age? Has not God made foolish the wisdom of the world?"* The debater of this age is the advocate of the wisdom of this world.

1 Cor. 2:6, 8: *"Yet we do speak wisdom among those who are mature; a wisdom, however, not of this age, nor of the rulers of this age, who are passing away....the wisdom which none of the rulers of this age has understood; for if they had understood it, they would not have crucified the Lord of glory;"* Note the three uses of "this age" in this passage to refer once again to this world's wisdom and twice to its rulers. Both are devoid of the wisdom of God.

1 Cor 3:18: *"Let no man deceive himself. If any man among you thinks that he is wise in this age, let him become foolish that he may become wise."* Parallel to the previous passages in 1 Corinthians, this passage speaks of the man "who thinks that he is wise in this age".

2 Cor. 4:4: *"in whose case the god of this world has blinded the minds of the unbelieving, that they might not see the light of the gospel of the glory of Christ, who is the image of God."* The god of this age is Satan! The darkness of this age is contrasted with the light of the age to come, the light of the gospel of the glory of Christ.

Gal. 1:4: *"who gave Himself for our sins, that He might deliver us out of this present evil age, according to the will of our God and Father,"* Deliverance from "this present evil age" is the fruit of the death of Christ for our sins.

Eph. 1:21: *"far above all rule and authority and power and dominion, and every name that is named, not only in this age, but also in the* *one to come."* Christ is king already and will be forever: "not only in this age, but also in the one to come."

Eph. 2:2: *"in which you formerly walked according to the course of this world, according to the prince of the power of the air, of the spirit that is now working in the sons of disobedience."* "Walking according to the age of this world" is descriptive of the way of life dominated by "the prince of the power of the air" and "the lusts of our flesh" and characteristic of "the children of wrath".

1 Tim. 6:17–19: *"Instruct those who are rich in this present world not to be conceited or to fix their hope on the uncertainty of riches, but on God, who richly supplies us with all things to enjoy. 18 Instruct them to do good, to be rich in good works, to be generous and ready to share, 19 storing up for themselves the treasure of a good foundation for the future, so that they may take hold of that which is life indeed."* Here we have the contrast between the riches and life of "the present (now) age (and)...the one coming. (Life in the one coming is) life indeed."

Titus 2:12: *"instructing us to deny ungodliness and worldly desires and to live sensibly, righteously and godly in the present age..."* The present (now) age is to be lived in with an eye to the blessed hope of Christ's glorious appearing mentioned in verse 13. This blessed hope climaxes this age. Nevertheless, verse 11 teaches that the grace of God that brings salvation to all men has also already appeared in this age.

Heb. 6:5: *"and have tasted the good word of God and the powers of the age to come..."* The powers of the age to come are already operative in the world. This is in all likelihood a reference to the miraculous gifts of the Spirit of which the apostates were 'made partakers' at the time of their conversion. These supernatural powers or miracles are a projection of the supernatural future age into the present age.

Terminology in the New Testament closely related to the two-age phraseology is revealed by the foregoing overview. John in all of his New Testament writings never uses age (aion) in the way described above. World (cosmos) is used instead. While *this world* is a synonym for *this age*, world (cosmos) is never used of *the age to come* by John. The reason is probably that the term, world, conveyed an evil connotation for him (John 12:25, 31 and 16:11). *This time* is a synonym for *this age* (Mark 10:30; Rom. 8:18). *This time* in Romans 8:18 is contrasted with the glory that is to be revealed. The world (economy) to come is also parallel in Hebrews 2:5: "For He did not subject to angels *the world to come*, concerning which we are speaking." The reign of Christ is already inaugurated, but not yet consummated in Heb. 2:8–10. The phrase, consummation of the age, is parallel (Matt. 13:22, 39, 40, 49; 24:3; 28:20). There are textual variants in Matt. 13:22, 40 which read "the consummation of this age", rather than "the consummation of the age". This and concepts in Matthew 13 parallel to Luke 20:34–36 (see the next chapter) confirm that this terminology is also parallel. Both *this age* and *the age to come* are composed of many lesser ages which are not to be confused with the two ages. The many ages which compose *this age* are mentioned in 1 Cor. 10:11 and Heb. 9:26; and the many ages which compose *the age to come* are mentioned in Eph. 2:7. The exact identity and boundaries of these lesser ages remain undefined in these passages and does not appear to be of importance in biblical teaching.

Three practical conclusions are warranted by this survey of the two-age terminology in the New Testament.

First, this survey of the two-age terminology and related terminology plainly manifests how this terminology permeates the New Testament. The explicit phraseology is frequent and extends through most of the major writers of the New Testament. The closely related terminology supplements this terminology in the other writers of the New Testament. In this terminology, therefore, we have a truly foundational aspect of New Testament teaching. Here we touch the beating heart of the biblical scheme of redemptive history and eschatology.

Second, the passages surveyed above are not normally thought of as prophetic passages. They are, however, some of the plainest and most literal passages in the New Testament. It is clear, then, that it is not necessary to unlock the mysteries of Daniel and Revelation to obtain a basic grasp of the biblical doctrine of last things. The clear, literal, and general passages here overviewed will provide us with the basic floor-plan of eschatology.

Third, this language of the two ages (so crucial to biblical prophecy) permeates the teaching of the New Testament about almost everything. This is why a study of eschatology is so important. It helps us to understand more clearly the teaching of the Bible about many other things.

Chapter 5: The Bible's Own System— The Basic Scheme

THE BASIC SCHEME of the two ages can be simply explained by means of three statements or propositions.

Proposition 1:
This age and the age to come taken together exhaust all time, including the endless time of the eternal state.

The simplest way to underscore the truth of this first proposition is to compare two parallel passages in the gospels: Matthew 12:32 and its parallel Mark 3:29. Matthew 12:32 uses the terminology of the two ages. Mark 3:29, the parallel passage, uses different, but synonymous language to convey the same meaning. Notice the emphasized words in both passages below:

> Matthew 12:32 "And whoever shall speak a word against the Son of Man, it shall be forgiven him; but whoever shall speak against the Holy Spirit, *it shall not be forgiven him, either in this age, or in the age to come.*

> Mark 3:29 but whoever blasphemes against the Holy Spirit *never has forgiveness, but is guilty of an eternal sin."*

It is not necessary for our purposes to discuss the difficult issues related to the unpardonable sin. The important thing for the present purpose is simply that it is unpardonable. The unpardonable character of this sin is made plain in both passages, but in different ways. Matthew says that this sin will not be forgiven either in this age or the age to come. Mark specifies this very point when he conveys Jesus' meaning with the words, "*never has forgiveness, but is guilty of an eternal sin.*" Therefore, we learn that a sin that is not forgiven either in this age or in the age to come is never forgiven, but is an eternal sin. Clearly, the two ages are equivalent to all time. The two ages together exhaust all time including the endless time of the eternal state.

The same point is suggested by Mark 10:29 and 30.

> Mark 10:29 Jesus said, "Truly I say to you, there is no one who has left house or brothers or sisters or mother or father or children or farms, for My sake and for the gospel's sake, 30 but that he shall receive a hundred times as much now in the present age, houses and brothers and sisters and mothers and children and farms, along with persecutions; and in the age to come, eternal life.

The phrase, *in the age to come, eternal life*, clearly suggests that the age to follow the present age—the age to come—is as eternal as the life received in it. If eternal life is received in the age to come, the implication is that the age to come is itself eternal.

Another important passage is 1 Timothy 6:17–19.

> 1 Timothy 6:17 Instruct those who are rich in this present world not to be conceited or to fix their hope on the uncertainty of riches, but on God, who richly supplies us with all things to enjoy. 18 *Instruct them* to do good, to be rich in good works, to be generous and ready to share, 19 storing up for themselves the treasure of a good foundation for the future, so that they may take hold of that which is life indeed.

This passage teaches that there are the true riches and eternal life of *the future*. (The Greek behind this translation is literally *the coming (one)* and plainly refers to the coming age.) This is contrasted with the temporary life and uncertain riches of *the present world*. (The Greek here is literally *the now age*.) The implication is that these two ages exhaust all conceivable human conditions. The two kinds of life and the two kinds of riches correspond with the two ages. The implication is that this age and the age to come exhaust all human history unto the endless time of the eternal state.

Now what has been said so far suggests the answer to the related question, When did *this age* begin? The evidence examined so far certainly requires us to say that this age originated with the beginning of human history. Is there, however, more evidence that this is the case?

Yes, there is. The Bible teaches that *"this age"* originated at the beginning of human history at the time of the creation and fall of mankind. In other words, it begins in that complex of events recorded in Genesis 1–3. If this is true, then *"this age"* did not begin at the time of Christ's first advent, but was in existence even from the beginning.

The probable origin of the two-age terminology proves this. *"This age and the age to come"* was a terminology that systematized the Old Testament contrast between the present existing state of things and the future redeemed order. It probably originated with Rabbis of the Inter-Testamental period and was adopted by Jesus and His Apostles as an accurate way to state systematically the Old Testament's teaching. Thus, *"this age"* already must have been in existence in the Old Testament period.

Consistent with this, Jesus and the Apostles never teach that this present age is of recent origin. Rather, from the very beginning of his ministry Jesus assumes that *this age* is already in existence (Matt. 12:32; Mark 10:30).

The character of *this age* also points to the conclusion that it originated in the complex of creation-fall recorded in Genesis 1–3. Many phrases related to the two-age terminology point in this direction. It is the natural order of creation. Phrases like *"the sons of this age marry"* (Luke 20:34) and *"those who are rich in this age"* (1 Timothy 6:17) strongly imply this. It is the evil order produced by the fall. It is a *"present, evil age"* (Galatians 1:4), with Satan as its *"god"* (2 Corinthians 4:4).

We must conclude that this age originated with the events at the beginning of human history that shaped the world as we know it. *"This age* and *the age to come,"* thus, originated at the beginning of human history and exhaust all periods of human existence to all eternity. If the two ages exhaust all possible time, there is also, of course, *no possibility of a state intermediate between them.*

There is no period of human history before this age. It began with the beginning of human history. *There is no period between "this age and the age to come."* The one follows the other immediately. *There is no period after "the age to come."* It is eternal.

Proposition 2:
This age and the age to come are qualitatively different states of human existence and qualitatively different periods in the history of the world.

This age does not evolve or change through any natural or gradual process into *the age to come.* The difference is that between the natural and the supernatural order. The crucial passage here is Luke 20:34–36.

> Luke 20:34 And Jesus said to them, "The sons of this age marry and are given in marriage, 35 but those who are considered worthy to attain to that age and the resurrection from the dead, neither marry, nor are given in marriage; 36 for neither can they die anymore, for they are like angels, and are sons of God, being sons of the resurrection.

The theme of the surrounding context is plainly the resurrection of the dead. Jesus uses the two-age terminology to contrast this present age with the age of resurrection—the age to come. What are the differences between *this age* and *the age to come* according to this passage? They lie on the surface of this very clear and literal passage. The contrasts are marriage in contrast to no marriage, death in contrast to no death, mixed good and evil men in contrast to only good men, and natural men in contrast to resurrected men. These contrasts remind one very clearly of the parallel concepts found in the parable of the tares (Matt. 13:24–30; 36–43). In that passage is also found the contrast between mixed wheat and tares (good and evil men) in the present age and only the wheat (good men) in the age to come. There is also found the contrast between natural men in the present age and glorified men ("shining as the sun") in the age to come.

THE BIBLICAL CONTRASTS BETWEEN THIS AGE AND THE AGE TO COME

LUKE 20:27–40

This Age	The Age to Come
Marriage	No Marriage
Death and Dying	No Death and Dying
Natural Men	Ressurrected Men
Righteous and Wicked Co-exist	Only the Worthy (the Sons of God) Attain

MATTHEW 13:24–30, 36–43

Sowing	Harvest
Mixed Wheat ("sons of the kingdom") and Tares ("The sons of the evil one")	Only the Wheat ("sons of the kingdom")
Natural Condition	Glorified Condition ("shining as the sun")

Proposition 3:
This age and the age to come are divided by the judgment of the wicked and the resurrection of the righteous which end this age and inaugurates the age to come.

Massive support exists for this proposition in the New Testament. A sampling of it follows. First, Luke 20:35 teaches that attaining to that age is equivalent to attaining to the resurrection of the dead. The resurrection is the door out of this age, and into the age to come. When, however, does the resurrection occur? It occurs, according to the uniform and repeated teaching of the New Testament, at Christ's return (1 Cor. 15:22, 23, 50–55; 1 Thess 4:16). Second, Matthew 13:39–43 refers, as we have seen, to the same event as Luke 20:35. It is clearly a reference to the judgment of the wicked and the resurrection of the righteous which occur at the second coming of Christ as the Gospel of Matthew itself teaches (Matt. 24:30, 31; 25:31). Third, in the age to come, we receive eternal life (Mark 10:30). This occurs at Christ's second coming (Matt. 25:31, 46). Fourth, Titus 2:11–13 clearly implies that the second coming consummates *this age* and brings in *the age to come* in its fullness. That passage reads, *"For the grace of God has appeared, bringing salvation to all men, instructing us to deny ungodliness and worldly desires and to live sensibly, righteously and godly in the present age, looking for the blessed hope and the appearing of the glory of our great God and Savior, Christ Jesus."* Our hope in the present age is the appearing of Christ. Compare this with Matthew 28:20, *"teaching them to observe all that I commanded you; and lo, I am with you always, even to the end of the age. "* Here Jesus promises to be spiritually present with His people to the consummation of the age because at the consummation of the age He bodily returns. John 6:39 is relevant here, *"And this is the will of Him who sent me, that of all that He has given me I lose nothing, but raise it up on the last day."* The last day of this age is the day of Christ's second coming, and it is the first day of the age to come.

Here, then, are three plain truths about this age and the age to come. *This age and the age to come taken together exhaust all time, including the endless time of the eternal state.* This means that there is no period between or beside this age and the age to come. *This age and the age to come are qualitatively different states of human existence and qualitatively different periods in the history of the world.* There is the clearest contrast between them. *This age and the age to come are divided by the judgment of the wicked and the resurrection of the righteous.* These events conclude this age and inaugurate the age to come. Three practical observations are suggested by these three plain truths. They may be summarized in three words.

Simplicity

What could be simpler than this system? Only two ages, not 7, 10, 12, 21 or more. There could not be a simpler eschatology. Christians may put aside their assumptions that biblical eschatology is too complex for them. There are only two ages—one temporal and natural, the other eternal and supernatural, separated by the second coming, and resurrection. If one grasps this, one knows vastly more than most of the so-called *"prophetic teachers"* of our day. It is men who have made eschatology difficult, not God.

Of course difficulties of detail remain. Nonetheless, the basic scheme of the Bible is not obscured. The Bible teaches a clear-cut and even humiliatingly simple scheme. Is this one of the very reasons why so many have passed it by? Is the Bible's own system of prophecy like its teaching about salvation? Is it just too simple for sophisticated men?

Here in the basic scheme of the two ages there is a comprehensive system of prophecy. If this scheme is grasped, many of the details of biblical prophecy will be remarkably clarified.

Similarity

In our study of the systems of eschatology held by different Christians during church history, several views were distinguished. All of these views, we discovered, could be categorized as either premillennial or postmillennial in nature. In other words, they could be categorized by the relationship of the return of Christ to the millennium. If in a given view Christ was said to return before the millennium mentioned in Revelation 20, we categorized that view as premillennial. If in a given view, Christ was said to return after the millennium, we categorized that view as postmillennial. In this sense we noted that both Amillennialism (paradoxically) and Postmillennialism were *postmillennial*, while Dispensationalism and Historic Premillennialism were *premillennial*. There are, thus, basically two kinds of Christian views about the relation of the return of Christ and the millennium.

PREMILLENNIAL	POSTMILLENNIAL
Dispensationalism	Amillennialism
Historic Premillennialism	Postmillennialism

The question before us now is very simple. To which of these two kinds of eschatology is the basic scheme of the two ages similar? With which of these two views is it consistent?

The essence of premillennialism is, as we have just noted, that there is a thousand year earthly reign of Christ after His second coming and before the eternal state. According to every form of premillennialism this is and must be the meaning of Revelation 20:1–10. Upon any premillennial interpretation of that passage un-resurrected, evil men inhabit the millennial period along with un-resurrected righteous men after the return of Christ. Is the biblical doctrine of two ages consistent with this view which is essential to premillennialism? No. The doctrine of the two ages confronts premillennialism with an impossible dilemma. Where will premillennialism put the millennium within the scheme of the two ages? In *this age* or in *the age to come*? It cannot put it into this age. Why not? Because according to premillennialism the millennium occurs after Christ's second coming, and this age concludes with Christ's second coming. Neither, however, can it put the milllennium in the age to come. Again, why not? Because no wicked men in an un-resurrected condition remain in that age. As we have seen, there are only righteous men in a resurrected condition. Since there is no intermediate or other period beside the two ages, premillennialism cannot be reconciled with the biblical, two-age scheme.

Is one reason that biblical prophecy has been such a mystery to many because they have been taught false theories of prophecy that confront them with impossible questions on every page of their New Testaments? Premillennial brethren have, I suspect, problems and confusion about eschatology because of the system they have inherited. Premillennialism is confusing simply because it is impossible to make consistent with the clearest and simplest biblical passages.

Supernaturalism
Biblical eschatology involves an emphatic supernaturalism. No gradual process can bring the fulfillment for which the Bible teaches us to hope. The theory of evolution is of no help. There can be no evolution into the age to come. There is no naturalistic or materialistic explanation for the glory that shall be revealed. Even the improvements in men and in the world wrought by the preaching of the Word of God will never by themselves transform men into the glory of the resurrection. Biblical hope is and must be frankly supernatural in character. Only almighty, divine, and supernatural intervention can ever bring about the glory of the age to come—that is the Christian hope.

Chapter 6: The Bible's Own System— The Enhanced Scheme

MANY YEARS AGO, I had a friend with whom I had discussed eschatology a number of times, but with no success in changing his views. One day I became aware that he had come around to my way of thinking. Wondering what I might have said to help him, I asked him to tell me what Scripture or arguments had changed his mind. His answer was both humbling and instructive. It went something like this: "*In the system I had been taught I had a slot for every Scripture. There was a little drawer into which I could place every Scripture that someone might use against my old view of prophecy. One day, however, I finally faced the question whether my system with all its little slots and drawers was itself scriptural.*"

One of the most prevalent and yet subtle problems with biblical interpretation is the way in which people read their own views into the Bible. Instead of allowing the Bible to impose its views on them, people impose their views on it. All sorts of ideas and presuppositions that ought themselves to be examined in light of the Bible without serious reflection are imposed upon it. These views and ideas become the unexamined framework within which everything in the Bible is understood. These folks read their Bibles, but always through the spectacles of their unquestioned assumptions. They never consider taking these glasses off. They probably are not even aware that they are wearing them. They never think of testing these spectacles themselves in the light of Scripture.

My simple appeal in these chapters on the *Bible's Own System* is that you remove your doctrinal spectacles and allow the Bible to speak for itself. Allow it to sit in judgment on your assumptions. Consider whether the Bible has a system of its own. In this chapter we proceed to examine the Bible's own system in a little more detail.

The basic scheme of the two ages opened up in the three propositions of the last chapter may be enhanced and supplemented by other data in the New Testament. The United States uses high-tech spy satellites to keep watch on the missile bases of potential adversaries like China. Photographs that show the entire base may be computer enhanced to show particular details of interest in the missile base. Similarly, in this chapter we look in a little more detail at the biblical scheme of the two ages. This enhancement of the biblical doctrine of the two ages may again be presented via three assertions.

Proposition 1:
This age is **and always will be** *an evil age.*

The proposition here is, in other words, that the basic character of this age will always be morally evil. A number of the key passages where the two-age terminology is used require this conclusion. Luke 16:8 speaks of evil men as the sons of this *age* and contrasts them with the sons of light. Mark 10:30 teaches that those who have left all for Christ must always expect persecutions in this age. As long as this age lasts, then, persecution will be the lot of the true Christian. Romans 12:2 is Paul's exhortation to Christians not to be conformed to *this age*. Such language plainly assumes that this age will always be an evil age. It is asserted in 2 Corinthians 4:4 that Satan is *"the god of this age"*. It is, therefore, necessarily evil. Galatians 1:4 is Paul's description of this age as a *"present, evil age"* from which the elect are to be delivered by the death of Christ. Ephesians 2:2 describes the former, wicked lives of Ephesian believers as a *"walking according to the age of this world"*.

Such passages as these presuppose and assume that this present age is, and always will be, evil. If this were not the case, there might come a day when the persecution of Christians would cease, when it would not be wrong to be conformed to this age, when Satan would not be its god, when Paul's description of it as evil would cease to be true; and when one could walk according to the age of this world and be righteous. All this would defy, however, the plain implications of these passages.

Such passages confront postmillennialism with a serious difficulty. Postmillennialism teaches that good triumphs over evil in this age. Righteousness and peace in this age overcome unrighteousness and hatred according to postmillennialism. Postmillennialists may qualify their teaching by saying that they do not believe that this age will become perfect or that every single man will be converted. Still, nonetheless, their contention remains that in substance good triumphs over evil in this age. When the Bible, however, assumes that this age (that ends, as we have seen, only with the Second Coming of Christ) is and always will be evil, it teaches something that pointedly contradicts postmillennialism.

This Age = Evil	The Age to Come = Good
The Sons of This Age	The Sons of Light
Persecutions (for Christ's disciples)	Eternal Life (for Christ's disciples)
"Do not be conformed to this age"	"Be transformed by the renewing of your mind"
(Satan is) the god of this age	"The glory of Christ who is the image of God"
A Present Evil Age	(A Future Age of Righteousness)
Formerly Walked according to the age ofthis world	(Now Walk According to the Standards of the Coming Age

Proposition 2:
This age is in its last days.
A number of the passages that use the two-age terminology plainly convey that this age is in its last days. We see that 1 Corinthians 2:6 stresses this by its use of the present tense: "Yet we do speak wisdom among those who are mature; a wisdom, however, not of this age, nor of the rulers of this age, *who are passing away....*" This is parallel with the statement of 1 John 2:17: "And

the world is passing away, and *also* its lusts; but the one who does the will of God abides forever." Compare verse 8 of the same chapter: "On the other hand, I am writing a new commandment to you, which is true in Him and in you, because *the darkness is passing away, and the true light is already shining."* The same implication is present in Hebrews 9:26, "Otherwise, He would have needed to suffer often since the foundation of the world; but now once at the consummation of the ages He has been manifested to put away sin by the sacrifice of Himself." Likewise 1 Corinthians 10:11 says, "Now these things happened to them as an example, and they were written for our instruction, upon whom the ends of the ages have come."

Since the coming of Christ and His resurrection, this age has been in its last days. It is in the process of passing away. It is popular in some quarters to ridicule those Christians who continually declare that we are in *the last days.* Still, it is true that since the first advent of Christ this age has been in its last days. This reality is pressed upon Christians as having solemn, practical implications for their daily life. There is a danger in ridiculing those who misunderstand the New Testament at this point and teach extremist views of the imminence of Christ's return. We must ourselves take care not to lose a sense of the nearness of Christ's return. If we lose this sense, we lose an important practical emphasis of New Testament eschatology.

Proposition 3:
The great realities of the age to come have broken into and are already operative in this age.

The emphasis of the New Testament that most strikingly supplements or enhances our understanding of the two-age structure of redemptive history is that the great realities of the age to come have in some sense broken into and become operative in this age. The clearest passage here is Hebrews 6:4–6:

For in the case of those who have once been enlightened and have tasted of the heavenly gift and have been made partakers of the Holy Spirit, and have tasted the good word of God and *the powers of the age to come,* and *then* have fallen away, it is impossible to renew them again to repentance, since they again crucify to themselves the Son of God, and put Him to open shame.

The term, powers, used here is one of the technical terms in the New Testament for miracles. Thus, the reference here is to the miraculous sign gifts that accompanied the preaching of the gospel at the beginning of the gospel age. These sign gifts announced the coming of the kingdom and the breaking in of the age to come. There is, then, in the presence of these sign gifts an announcement of the inauguration of the age to come.

This suggests the equation: **The Age to Come = The Reign of Christ.** Since the reign of Christ has already begun (Heb. 2:9; Eph. 1:21), the age to come must in a certain sense also have begun.

Other New Testament emphases support this assertion. The age to come is the age of the resurrection (Luke 20:34–36). The resurrection has, however, already begun. Christ is the first fruits of the resurrection (1 Cor. 15:20–23).

20 But now Christ has been raised from the dead, the first fruits of those who are asleep. 21 For since by a man *came* death, by a man also *came* the resurrection of the dead. 22 For as in Adam all die, so also in Christ all shall be made alive. 23 But each in his own order: Christ the first fruits, after that those who are Christ's at His coming,

This is the explanation for the peculiar phraseology of Acts 4:2: "being greatly disturbed because they were teaching the people and proclaiming *in Jesus the resurrection from the dead.*" Another parallel biblical concept may be added here. As this age is the age of the old creation, so the age to come is the age of the new creation. In a qualified sense, however, the new creation has already been inaugurated.

2 Corinthians 5:17 Therefore if any man is in Christ, *he is* a new creature; the old things passed away; behold, new things have come.

Galatians 6:15 For neither is circumcision anything, nor uncircumcision, but a new creation.

THE OVERLAPPING OF THE AGES

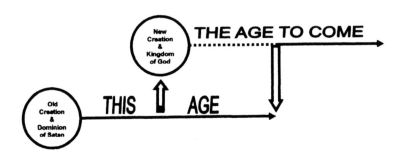

The chart above illustrates the overlapping of the ages.[1] The supplementary propositions studied in this chapter may seem to complicate the basic scheme of the previous chapter. An illustration may, however, clear up any difficulty. Think of a young couple who are married and looking forward to having children. After several years they become serious, but month after month brings no results. Finally after a trip to the doctor, the wife announces the great news, "Husband, I'm pregnant!" The future has come! But has it? A week goes by and nothing much changes. There is still that long period of gestation, before they can hold the little one in their arms. There are, of course, growing signs that something is happening: Baby's room is re-decorated. Mommy's tummy grows increasingly larger. Daddy's nervousness increases as the great day draws near. But despite all of this there is no visible reality. There is no cooing baby to hold in their arms. It is even so with the age to come and the kingdom of God. The age to come has come in certain subtle, but significant ways, but it has not come in outward, glorious reality. Just as there is an overlapping of the ages in the history of this family, so there is in the history of the world. Right now history is pregnant with the age to come.

This general perspective of the biblical doctrine of the two ages and especially the overlapping of the two ages has vast practical and doctrinal importance for Christians. In line with my call for a gospel eschatology in the first chapter, let me provide a few illustrations of practical, gospel significance of this framework for eschatology.

This framework explains so much about the two-stage character of salvation. It explains in other words why the Bible constantly speaks of salvation in terms of the *already and not yet.* Everywhere the Bible assumes the two-stage character of salvation: *Justification* (Romans 5:1; Matthew 12:37), *adoption* (Romans 8:14–16 with verse 23 of the same chapter and also Galatians 4:4–6 with Eph. 4:30), and *redemption* (Ephesians 1:7 with 4:30), *eternal life* (John 3:36; Matthew 25:46), *rest* (Matthew 11:29; Hebrews 4:9–11) with many other of the biblical realities associated with salvation can be spoken of both as past realities and future blessings. This is so because the age to come that brings salvation unfolds itself in two stages. There is an overlapping of this age and the age to come.

One of the many practical implications of this for Christians is to underscore the necessity of persevering in the Christian life unto eternal life. Most evangelical Christians do not understand the necessity of perseverance because they think of salvation only in terms of something they already have. It is also, however, according to the New Testament, something they are yet to receive. Thus, the exhortation comes to Christians (who have according to Matt. 11:28–30 already received Christ as their rest) that they must "be diligent to enter that rest, lest anyone fall through following the same example of disobedience" (Hebrews 4:11).

This framework also explains the ethical tension in the life of the Christian. So many Christians are taught to seek experiences which will deliver them from the tension of living in the period of the overlapping of the ages. They want in this age a higher life, or a deeper life, or a victorious life, or a second blessing, or a baptism of the Spirit that would in effect take them out of the contradiction, sorrow, and trial of this age. The only way, however, for a true Christian to escape the battle with sin and the experience of sorrow in this age is to depart this age. He must either die and go to heaven or enter at Christ's return into the age to come. The teaching that promises the cessation of conflict and trial in this life is no friend to the Christian. This biblical structure warns us that in this age there is no blessing not followed by trial, no joy not followed by sorrow; and no final victory over remaining sin.

Christians must beware of the mountain-top syndrome. There is no remaining always on the mountain top in this age. We must always rejoice with trembling. When Christians stop seeking an experience that the Bible never promises them in this life, they will be prepared properly to enjoy the blessings God gives them in this life and not look for something in these blessings that they will never find. They will also be prepared to face the reality of the Christian life squarely, fight the good fight of faith, finish their course, and run in such a way as to win.

This framework also explains much about the future of the church. We must not look for a golden age before Christ's return. This is a denial of the character of this age. But we must not be "pessimillenialists" either and see nothing but apostasy for the visible church. This is also a denial of the overlapping of the ages. The church is enlivened by the powerful realities of the age to come that have already broken into the world with the first advent of Christ. Those who tell people that they should not "polish brass" on the sinking ship of the church are tragically mistaken. Those who teach that this dispensation of the church (like every other dispensation) must surely end in failure and apostasy are wrong. They weaken the hands of true Christians in their God-ordained labor to build the church of Christ. Both the gloomy pessimists and the starry-eyed optimists have imbalanced views of the future prospects of the church. The biblical viewpoint understands the overlapping of the ages and balances these contrasting viewpoints in a realistic optimism.

Concluding Remarks

This exposition of the *Bible's Own System* began with the intention of showing that a study of the clear language, the literal passages, and the general truths of the Bible resolve many of the greatest difficulties and much of the deepest confusion about biblical eschatology. From the clear, the literal, and the general statements of the Bible we have learned a view of history and especially of future history that is simple in its nature and yet profound in its implications. This simple, biblical structure of redemptive history is inhospitable to both premillennialism and postmillennialism. It also arms the Christian churchman with a realistic, fighting optimism with which to fight the good fight of faith in this the overlapping of the ages. Finally, the *Bible's Own System* sheds amazing light on the meaning and teaching of the Bible on matters that go far beyond what are often thought to be the strict confines of eschatology. The reader must judge for himself, but the writer feels that the intention of these studies on the *Bible's Own System* has been fulfilled.

Chapter 7: The Dividing Line—
The General Judgment

THE DAY OF JUDGMENT is a vastly important and practical subject in the study of eschatology. It is an issue that is the subject of extensive revelation in the Bible. The term *"day"* as a reference to the day of judgment occurs 58 times in the New Testament. It is a fundamental point, an elementary principle, of Christian teaching (Heb. 6:1–3). Once more let me emphasize that to establish the biblical system of prophecy we are not going to the details of eschatology nor to marginal biblical issues.

The following treatment is, however, not intended as a comprehensive study of the day of judgment. Our interest is simply on how the general judgment clarifies the system of eschatology taught in the Bible. We are asking, How does this doctrine help us choose between the various eschatological systems that compete for our allegiance.

The thesis of this chapter is that there will be one judgment of all men living or dead, righteous or unrighteous, occurring at the second coming of Christ issuing in either eternal life or eternal punishment. This thesis has three points. The *scope* of the judgment is all men living and dead. The *timing* of the judgment is the Second Coming of Christ. The *issues* of this judgment are eternal life or eternal punishment.[1]

In the preceding chapters all of time was considered as we looked at the two ages. In this chapter, we narrow our focus to the dividing line between the two ages. If the thesis mentioned above can be established, it will have a tremendous clarifying impact on our system of eschatology. If the judgment occurs at the second coming, is absolutely universal, and issues in the eternal state, this will powerfully corroborate many of the conclusions to which we have come in preceding chapters.

Our methodology will not be an attempt to survey the vast, biblical materials, but to take up the three classic passages which most extensively deal with the subject.[2] Those passages are:

    I. *Matt. 25:31–46*
   II. *Rom. 2:1–16*
  III. *2 Pet. 3:1–18*

I. Matt. 25:31–46

31 But when the Son of Man comes in His glory, and all the angels with him, then He will sit on His glorious throne 32 And all the nations will be gathered before Him; and He will separate them from one another, as the shepherd separates the sheep from the goats; 33 and He will put the sheep on His right, and the goats on the left. 34 Then the King will say to those on His right, 'Come, you who are blessed of My Father, inherit the kingdom prepared for you from the foundation of the world. 35 'For I was hungry, and you gave Me *something* to eat; I was thirsty, and you gave Me drink; I was a stranger, and you invited Me in; 36 naked, and you clothed Me; I was sick, and you visited Me; I was in prison, and you came to Me. ' 37 Then the righteous will answer Him, saying, 'Lord, when did we see You hungry, and feed You, or thirsty, and give You drink? 38 'And when did we see You a stranger, and invite You in, or naked, and clothe You? 39 'And when did we see You sick, or in prison, and come to You?' 40 And the King will answer and say to them, 'Truly I say to you, to the extent that you did it to one of these brothers of Mine, *even* the least *of them*, you did it to Me.' 41 Then He will also say to those on His left, 'Depart from Me, accursed ones, into the eternal fire which has been prepared for the devil and his angels; 42 for I was

hungry, and you gave Me *nothing* to eat; I was thirsty, and
you gave Me nothing to drink; 43 I was a stranger, and you
did not invite Me in; naked, and you did not clothe Me;
sick, and in prison, and you did not visit Me. ' 44 Then they
themselves also will answer, saying, 'Lord, when did we
see You hungry, or thirsty, or a stranger, or naked, or sick,
or in prison, and did not take care of You?' 45 Then He will
answer them, saying, 'Truly I say to you, to the extent that
you did not do it to one of the least of these, you did not do
it to Me.' 46 And these will go away into eternal punishment, but the righteous into eternal life."

There can be no real doubt about the *timing* of the judgment described in this passage since verse 31 begins with the words,
"when the Son of Man comes in His glory, and all the angels with
Him." This is a clear reference to the second coming of Christ.
The entire preceding context of the Olivet discourse confirms this
reference to the second advent of Christ as its constant theme
(24:3, 14, 27, 30, 31, 37, 42, 46, 50; 25:6, 10, 13, 19).

The *issues* are clearly stated in verse 46. They are eternal life
and eternal punishment. This language in this context clearly refers to the permanent eschatological conditions of the eternal
state and assumes, of course, that both the righteous and wicked
are in a resurrected condition.

It is difficult to raise significant questions about either the timing or issues of the judgment of Matt. 25:31f. Alternative interpretations have labored, however, to suggest that this judgment
must be understood—not as general, but—as having a limited
scope. Of course, even here the language of the passage burdens
such interpretations with much labor. Matthew 25:32 seems clear
when it says that *all the nations will be gathered before Him*. Nevertheless, Premillennial interpretations have labored to limit some-
how the reference of *all the nations*.

Clearly, the key issue here is the meaning of the phrase, *all the
nations*. Does it include the Jewish nation or does it refer exclusively to the Gentiles? The phrase, *"all the nations."* must be understood, first of all, by means of its context in Matthew. The
word, *nations*, by itself used in the plural (as it is here) designates

the Gentile nations in Matthew and may even be translated *Gentiles* (6:32; 10:5, 18; 12:18, 21; 20:19, 25). The case is, however, very different with the terminology, *all the nations*. This occurs in three other places (Matt. 24:9, 14; 28:19). When Matthew 24:9 speaks of Christ's disciples being hated "by all the nations", there is good reason to regard this phrase as including the Jewish nation. The contextual emphasis on the destruction of Jerusalem and the apostate Jewish nation makes it extremely unlikely that we should exclude the Jews from those nations that hate and persecute the disciples of Christ. The phrase is used in Matt. 24:14 and 28:19 to designate the universal scope of the church's evangelistic mission. This scope certainly includes the Jews (Acts 1:8; Rom. 1:16, 17). Matt. 28:19's parallel passage, Luke 24:46–49, makes this fact explicit.

> Luke 24:46 and He said to them, "Thus it is written, that the Christ should suffer and rise again from the dead the third day; 47 and that repentance for forgiveness of sins should be proclaimed in His name to all the nations, beginning from Jerusalem. 48 "You are witnesses of these things. 49 "And behold, I am sending forth the promise of My Father upon you; but you are to stay in the city until you are clothed with power from on high."

In such passages as these—the true parallels of Matt. 25:32—the distinction between Jews and Gentiles sometimes designated by *nations* used by itself disappears. The phraseology, *"all the nations,"* therefore designates the world—both Jews and Gentiles—which is the object of the preaching of the gospel during the last days.

Matthew 25:31–46 is the final, triumphant stanza of a judgment-theme that runs throughout Matthew's gospel (Matt. 7:22; 11:20–24; 12:36–42; 16:26, 27 etc.). We must interpret Matt. 25:31–46 in line with such passages which always speak of a single judgment or day of judgment. They teach that ancient nations, cities of Jesus' day, "every man," and "all the nations" of all history will be there. Matt. 25:31–46 must be seen as in its scope absolutely universal.

II. Romans 2:5–16

5 But because of your stubbornness and unrepentant heart
you are storing up wrath for yourself in the day of wrath
and revelation of the righteous judgment of God, 6 who
will render to every man according to his deeds: 7 to those who
by perseverance in doing good seek for glory and honor
and immortality, eternal life; 8 but to those who are selfish-
ly ambitious and do not obey the truth, but obey unrighteousness, wrath and indignation. 9 *There will be* tribulation and distress for every soul of man who does evil, of
the Jew first and also of the Greek, 10 but glory and honor
and peace to every man who does good, to the Jew first
and also to the Greek. 11 For there is no partiality with
God. 12 For all who have sinned without the Law will also
perish without the Law; and all who have sinned under
the Law will be judged by the Law; 13 for not the hearers
of the Law are just before God, but the doers of the Law
will be justified. 14 For when Gentiles who do not have the
Law do instinctively the things of the Law, these, not having the Law, are a law to themselves, 15 in that they show
the work of the Law written in their hearts, their conscience bearing witness, and their thoughts alternately
accusing or else defending them, 16 on the day when,
according to my gospel, God will judge the secrets of men
through Christ Jesus.

This key passage on the judgment occurs in the larger section of
Romans that has for its theme, *the revelation of the wrath of God
against all men*, Romans 1:18–3:20. The section 1:18–2:16 deals
with the wrath of God against all men in general, while 2:17–3:8
emphasizes the wrath of God against Jews in particular; and 3:9–
20 states the general conclusion. The structure of this section of
Romans may be best illustrated by means of two concentric
circles.[3]

Again we will simply ask what this passages teaches about
the timing, issues, and scope of the judgment here in view.

Its *issues* are very clear. Positively, it is eternal life. Note the descriptions of verse 7: "glory, honor, immortality, eternal life" and verse 10: "glory, honor, peace". These words clearly describe the bliss of the eternal state and the resurrection.

Negatively, the issue of this judgment is also clear. It is eternal death or eternal punishment. The contrast with eternal life (v. 7) creates the strongest presumption that Paul is here describing eternal torment. This presumption is borne out by the language Paul uses—all of which characteristically refers to the torments of eternal punishment. This is true in verse 5 which speaks of "wrath" and the "righteous judgment of God.", in verse 8 which speaks of "wrath and indignation," in verse 9 which speaks of "tribulation and distress," and in verse 12 which speaks of those who "will also perish."

Paul's teaching on the *scope* of this judgment is also emphatic. In general the scope is "every man" (verse 6); "every soul of man who does evil" (v. 9); "every man who does good" (verse 10); and "all who have sinned without the law"; and "all who have sinned under the law" (verse 12). In particular the scope is both the righteous and the unrighteous (Note vvs. 7–10); both Jew and Gentile (Note vvs. 9–12 where the Greek speaks of the one without law.); and both the living and the dead (This is clearly implied in Paul's assumption that his contemporaries as well as those in the past would experience this judgment. Note the present tenses in vvs. 4, 5, 7–10).

The *timing* of this judgment is also clear, if not as emphatic. The following considerations clearly point to the time of this judgment as that of Christ's second advent. First, the parallels between verses 6 and16, and Matt. 16:27 show this. The language of these verses is clearly parallel to Matt. 16:27, but in Matt. 16:27, there is an explicit reference to Christ's second coming: "For the Son of Man is going to come in the glory of His Father with His angels; and *will then recompense every man according to his deeds.*"

Second, the parallel between the rewards mentioned here and the rewards given Christians at the Second Advent manifests this connection. Note verse 7 which speaks of *eternal life* and compare with Matt. 25:46. Note verses 7 and 10 which speak of *glory*, cf. Col. 3:4; 1 Cor. 15:43; Rom. 8:18. Note verse 7 which speaks of *immortality* and compare 1 Cor. 15:53.

Third, the explicit mention of the day when God will judge the secrets of men through Jesus Christ (vvs. 5, 16) also makes the timing of this judgment clear. This is the day of judgment taught in Paul's gospel (v. 16). *Day* for Paul is often a synonym of judgment (1 Cor. 4:3). The eschatological day is the time of Christ's second coming (1 Cor. 4:3–5; 2 Thess. 1:10; Rom. 13:12; 1 Cor. 1:8; 3:13; 5:5; Phil. 1:6; 2 Thess 2:2).

Again, our thesis has been plainly established. Romans 2:1–16 is plainly speaking of a general judgment that is absolutely universal in scope, that has for its issues eternal life or eternal punishment; and that takes place at Christ's second coming.

III. 2 Peter 3:3–13

3 Know this first of all, that in the last days mockers will come with *their* mocking, following after their own lusts, 4 and saying, "Where is the promise of His coming? For *ever* since the fathers fell asleep, all continues just as it was from the beginning of creation." 5 For when they maintain this, it escapes their notice that by the word of God *the* heavens existed long ago and *the* earth was formed out of water and by water, 6 through which the world at that time was destroyed, being flooded with water. 7 But the present heavens and earth by His word are being reserved for fire, kept for the day of judgment and destruction of ungodly men. 8 But do not let this one *fact* escape your notice, beloved, that with the Lord one day is as a thousand years, and a thousand years as one day. 9 The Lord is not slow about His promise, as some count slowness, but is patient toward you, not wishing for any to perish but for all to come to repentance. 10 But the day of the Lord will come like a thief, in which the heavens will pass away with a roar and the elements will be destroyed with intense heat, and the earth and its works will be burned up. 11 Since all these things are to be destroyed in this way, what sort of people ought you to be in holy conduct and godliness, 12 looking for and hastening the coming of the day of God, on account of which the heavens will be

destroyed by burning, and the elements will melt with intense heat! 13 But according to His promise we are looking for new heavens and a new earth, in which righteousness dwells.

2 Peter 3 is one of the richest and most interesting passages in the Bible with regard to the structure of eschatology. It presents its own unique perspective on the structure of redemptive history, while at the same time confirming the general thesis we are establishing with regard to the general judgment.

Verse 4 taken with verses 9 and 13 clearly shows that the theme of this passage is the certainty of the promise of Christ to come again. The term, *promise,* in each of these verses refers to the promise of the parousia, a Greek word which speaks of Christ's second coming as His arrival. It is to be noted here that the term, "the day of the Lord," is equivalent to and synonymous with Christ's parousia. Several considerations demonstrate this: (1) As has been seen, throughout the New Testament the day of the Lord Jesus Christ is the day of the Second Coming. (2) The term, *Lord,* designates Jesus Christ throughout this passage and in fact throughout 2 Peter without exception (3:2, 8, 9, 15, 18). (3) The connection between the mention in verse 9 of the Lord's "promise" and the substitution of the phrase, "day of the Lord", in verse 10 constrains the identification of the two events. Furthermore, the term, "day of God," in verse 12 is also a synonymous reference to the same event. (1) The connection demands this identification. (2) The designation, "God," may be a reference to Jesus Christ (2 Peter 1:1). The second coming of Christ, His parousia, is the permeating emphasis of this passage.

Simply in terms of itself and by itself, what is the eschatology of 2 Pet. 3:3–18? Peter clearly divides all of history into three worlds divided by two universal judgments (see the figure on the following page). Once this simple scheme is understood, it may be filled in with all sorts of detail provided by Peter.

The problem with certain false interpretations of this passage may be clearly seen in the way that they disrupt this simple but profound scheme.

The preterist interpretation of this passage is typically

THE ESCHATOLOGY OF PETER

Destruction By *Water*	Destruction By *Fire*

The Then World   The Now World   The New World

adopted by postmillennialists. This statement of J. Marcellus Kik epitomizes the preteristic and postmillennial misinterpretation of this passage:

> Perhaps the great stumbling block to the acceptance of the *postmil* position is the misunderstanding of the term "new heavens and new earth." Many look upon this as a material concept rather than a term descriptive of the gospel economy.... That the words are not inapplicable to a revolution of a moral and spiritual nature, we may learn from Paul's analogous description of the change wrought in conversion (2 Cor. 5:17; Gal. 6:15) and from Peter's application of this very passage, "Nevertheless, we, according to His promise, look for new heavens and a new earth wherein dwelleth righteousness" (2 Peter 3:13).[4]

Such interpreters understand *the new heavens and new earth* in a *spiritual*, i.e. non-material fashion, and as a reference to the gospel age after the destruction of Jerusalem. The New Testament in general and 2 Peter 3 in particular leave no room for this understanding. In 2 Peter 3 three considerations refute it. First, in this passage, the subject under consideration is the literal second coming of Christ. The *"promise of the parousia"* is likely a reference to Acts 1:11 among other passages. The reference is clearly not to a spiritual coming. Such a coming was not the subject that produced the mocking of verse 4. The mockers were denying the possibility of any supernatural interruption of the uniformity of natural law (v. 4). In 2 Peter 3:13 the text makes the new heavens and new earth an expectation we await "according to His promise"—and in this context the promise can be nothing other than the promise of the second coming of Christ. Second, in 2 Peter 3 a material destruction by fire of the world is in view. This destruction finds its analogy in the material destruction of the world by water in the flood (vvs. 6, 7, 10, 12). Third, the crisis in view in 2 Peter 3 brings not the conversion of the ungodly, but their destruction (vvs. 9–12).

A second false interpretation is exposed by the simplicity of Peter's scheme. Classic Dispensationalism as epitomized in the Scofield Bible teaches that the *day of the Lord* stretches from the second coming of Christ to the end of the millennium over 1000 years later.[5]

Besides the way in which this view distorts Peter's scheme of last things, there are two powerful objections to this theory. First, it is without exegetical basis. Its basis is simply the presuppositions of Dispensational Premillennialism and the necessity of justifying this scheme in the hostile atmosphere of 2 Peter 3:3–13. It is invented, that is to say, to make their scheme fit this passage. Second, this theory results in a forced and unnatural understanding of 2 Peter 3:3–13. Our objection is not that the *Day of the Lord* is literally a day of 24 hours, it is rather based on the following considerations:

(1) Verse 10 would have to read not "*in which*" but "*at the end of which*".[6] The natural significance of 2 Peter 3:10 is, however, that when Christ comes the world is immediately (not 1000 years later) destroyed.

(2) This understanding contradicts the clear implication of the pasage that the destruction of the *Day of the Lord* is swift destruction. The analogy of the flood implies (v. 6) swift destruction (Matt. 24:37–44; Luke 17:22–27). The analogy of the thief (v. 10) implies swift destruction (Matt. 24:42, 43; 1 Thess. 5:2ff.). A destruction that takes place over a period of 1000 years is anything but swift and sudden.

(3) This theory ignores the fact that in the New Testament and in 2 Peter 3:3–13 the *day of the Lord* is a synonym for the parousia. To affirm that the *day of the Lord* lasts over 1000 years is to affirm the same with reference to the parousia. Verse 9 makes plain that the alternative to repentance before the parousia is perishing. A 1000 year parousia or day of the Lord undermines the starkness of this alternative.

(4) The analogies of the flood and the day of the Lord undermine this theory. The day of the Lord, like the flood, is a catastrophic event not an age-long period of time.

We have been examining the subject of the general judgment via these passages. This passage certainly addresses this subject.

Clearly the *timing* of this judgment is the Second Coming of Christ. It has already been shown that the promise of Christ's Second Coming is the pervasive theme of this passage. The phrases, "day of the Lord", and, "day of God", also refer to this event as has been shown. Note especially the connection of verse 7 with the succeeding verses and see how Peter passes immediately from the day of judgment to the promise of His coming. Note also verse 10 where the day of the Lord "in which the heavens will pass away" is obviously a reference to the promise of His coming which has formed the theme of verse 9. This identification is confirmed by the statement that it *"will come like a thief"*. In Matt. 24:43 this very phrase is used of the coming of the Son of Man. Note also verse 12 as well where the *"coming of the day of God"* is the time at which the heavens and the elements will be burned up. Clearly, the day of God is equivalent to the day of the Lord and the coming of Christ. In verse 13 it is the *"promise"* of His coming which is regarded as precipitating not only the destruction of the present world, but the coming of the *"new heavens and a new earth, in which righteousness dwells."*

The *scope* of this judgment is plainly nothing less than universal. The world as a whole is destroyed (v. 7, "heavens and earth"; v. 10, "heaven and elements"; v. 12, "heavens and elements"). The parallel with the flood, found in verse 6, strengthens this statement of the universal character of this judgment. Further, the mention of the new heavens and new earth in verse 13 also plainly declares its universality.

The *issues* of this judgment are also not in doubt. There is the eternal destruction of the wicked. The eternal destruction of the wicked is implied by the universal destruction of the present world that the judgment brings. It is mentioned explicitly in the references to their destruction in these verses. Verse 7 speaks of the *"judgment and destruction of ungodly men"*. Verse 9 says that the unrepentant will *"perish"* at Christ's coming.

The eternal blessedness of the godly is also clearly a result of this judgment. Verse 13 asserts that this judgment will usher in the new heavens and the new earth. This is clearly a reference to the eternal state of the righteous (Rev. 21:1ff.).

General Conclusions

The three major New Testament passages affirm clearly that the *timing* of the coming judgment is the second coming of Christ, the *issues* of the coming judgment are eternal life and eternal punishment, and that the *scope* of the coming judgment is general or, in other words, absolutely universal. They are clear enough when considered separately. When considered together and in conjunction with the many other references to the general judgment in the New Testament, they are absolutely conclusive in favor of a general judgment at Christ's Second Coming that ushers in the eternal state.

The unavoidable implication of this is that premillennialism is excluded as the biblical scheme of last things. There is no room for a millennial kingdom inhabited by natural men, subsequent to Christ's second coming. Since every form of premillennialism requires just such a kingdom, premillennialism cannot be reconciled with this most foundational structure of biblical teaching about last things, its very doctrine of the final judgment.

Chapter 8: The Coming of the Kingdom Introduced

The Importance of the Kingdom

IT HAS BEEN my purpose in this book to build our understanding of the structure of biblical eschatology on what is central in biblical thought. Well, there should be no doubt that the "coming of the kingdom" in biblical thought is central. The Bible could very defensibly be entitled, as one scholar remarks, "The Book of the Coming of the Kingdom of God."[1] The coming of the kingdom of God and the broader concept of the universal reign of God pervades the Scriptures and are, indeed, arguably the very theme of the Scriptures.

The Concept of the Kingdom

One's concept of the kingdom of God will influence one's understanding of this subject in all sorts of ways. It is important, therefore, to review some of the basic biblical tensions which must be held together in order to have a balanced concept of the kingdom.

1. The Definition of the Kingdom:
The Kingdom—Reign or Realm?

The Kingdom of God is primarily God's royal sovereignty (His reign) and only derivatively a particular sphere or realm over which He rules. Reign, not realm, is the fundamental meaning of the biblical words for kingdom. A throne, not a piece of real estate, is the proper analogy. Psalm 103:19 illustrates this when it translates the Hebrew word for kingdom as sovereignty: "The LORD has established His throne in the heavens; And His *sovereignty* rules over all." Many other texts bear out this observation (Psalm 145:11–13; Matt. 3:2, cf. vvs. 7–12; Matt. 12:28 cf. context; Mark 9:1; John 18:36; 1 Cor. 4:20).

The idea of reigning or sovereignty is the root meaning of the biblical words for kingdom. This does not mean, however, that the word, kingdom, never refers to a realm over which a king rules. By derivation the word does come to mean the realm or sphere over which God reigns. Think of a tree trunk with several branches growing from it. The trunk is the idea of reigning. The branches are the secondary meanings derived from this root meaning.

Since the idea of reign is the fundamental idea, the idea of realm is secondary and derived. Thus, there is variation with respect to the precise realm in which this sovereignty is exercised. Often, of course, the realm over which God rules is the sphere of salvation (Luke 18:24, 25; John 3:5; Matt. 11:12). Yet in Matt. 13:41 the realm is the entire world and the unconverted are viewed as within Christ's kingdom until the end of the age. Matthew 13:41 reads, "The Son of Man will send forth His angels, and they will gather out of His kingdom all stumbling blocks, and those who commit lawlessness."

The fact that the idea of the reign or sovereignty of God is the fundamental meaning of the kingdom is very significant. When we remember that this is one of the central ideas of the Scriptures, it tells us that the sovereignty of God is a central concept of biblical revelation.

2. The Character of the Kingdom:
The Kingdom—Eternal or Eschatological?

We have said that the coming of the kingdom is central to both biblical and eschatological thought. Here we address the question, How can we speak of the coming of the Kingdom when God has always reigned over all things? Two balancing statements must be made here in order to bring out the whole of the biblical presentation.

a. God's Kingdom is eternal.

According to the Scripture, the fact is that God has always reigned over all things. This is the message of Psalm 103:19 cited earlier. Daniel 4:34–36 (cf. also Dan. 6:26–28) also underscores this reality:

> 34 But at the end of that period I, Nebuchadnezzar, raised my eyes toward heaven, and my reason returned to me, and I blessed the Most High and praised and honored Him who lives forever; For His dominion is an everlasting dominion, And His kingdom *endures* from generation to generation. 35 And all the inhabitants of the earth are accounted as nothing, But He does according to His will in the host of heaven And *among* the inhabitants of earth; And no one can ward off His hand Or say to Him, 'What hast Thou done?'

This eternal reign or sovereignty of God implies at least four things: (1) God has always possessed the royal right to all His creatures' allegiance. (2) God as sovereign Creator has always possessed the omnipotence to maintain such rights. (3) God has always maintained these rights in heaven, the throne of the universe. (4) God has always exercised a royal providence over all things so that everything occurs through and in accordance with His royal purpose and decree.

b. God's Kingdom is Eschatological

While God has always reigned in the senses stated above, the fact of sin and the defeat of the forces of evil makes necessary the prayer, "Thy Kingdom come" (Matt. 6:10). The Kingdom of God is, thus, also the eschatological goal of history (Dan. 2:44; Zech. 14:9) and not simply an ever-present reality. This coming has for its twin results the defeat of the enemies of God and the salvation of the world (1 Cor. 15:21–28).

3. The Coming of the Kingdom: The Kingdom—Past or Future?

Again, two balancing statements must be made in order to bring out the biblical perspective on this matter. The coming of the kingdom is yet future and awaits the return of Christ in glory (Matt. 5:3, 10, 20; 7:21; Luke 21:31; 22:15, 16). At the same time the Scriptures make clear that the coming has already taken place, and that the kingdom is a present reality.

The fact that the kingdom has come is the more surprising fact and the more debated issue, and we must be sure to note this. The Scriptures are, however, plain in their teaching on this subject. Alongside of the perspective of the future coming of the kingdom, the New Testament teaches that the kingdom has come in Jesus Christ. The following lines of evidence plainly show this: (1) The defeat of Satan means the presence of the kingdom (Matt. 12:28, 29). (2) The preaching of the kingdom means the presence of the kingdom (Luke 16:16; Matt. 11:11–14). (3) The entering of the Kingdom means the presence of the Kingdom (Matt. 23:13; Mark 10:15). (4) The presence of the King means the presence of the kingdom (Matt. 21:4, 5; John 18:36). (5) The preaching of the Apostles attests the presence of the Kingdom (Rom. 14:17; 1 Cor. 4:19, 20, 21; Col. 1:13; Heb. 12:28). (6) The enthronement of the King means the presence of the Kingdom (Acts 2:29–36; Eph. 1:20–23).

THE COMING OF THE KINGDOM

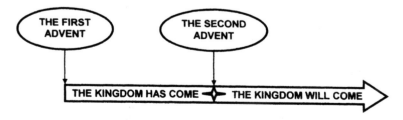

Many false theories with regard to the kingdom of God have in common that they misunderstand or ignore the biblical distinction between the present and future comings of the kingdom.

Some have put forward a distinction between the kingdom of God and the kingdom of heaven. There is, however, no biblical evidence for such a distinction. It also forgets that *heaven* is used in the phrase, *kingdom of heaven*, as a figurative way of alluding to God (Matt. 23:22). Yet more, it neglects the parallels of Scripture that use these two phrases interchangeably (Cf. Matthew 4:17 with Mark 1:15). Some have spoken of the kingdom as an exclusively future reality. The evidence examined above, however, makes clear that the kingdom is a present reality. Some have spoken of the kingdom as exclusively a present reality. This view, however, over-reacts to popular eschatological excesses and misses the balance and tension in the teaching of the New Testament. Taken to an extreme, it denies the central element in the teaching of the New Testament, the coming of the kingdom in supernatural power at the Second Coming of Christ.

Some have said that the kingdom was *postponed* because the Jews rejected their Messiah. Such language entangles itself in questions about the sovereignty of God and the necessity of the work of Christ. It also misses the fact that God's reaction to the unbelief of the Jewish nation is not to postpone the kingdom, but to transfer the kingdom. Matthew 21:43 declares, *"Therefore I say to you, the kingdom of God will be taken away from you, and be given to a nation producing the fruit of it."*

Some have admitted that in some sense Christ is already king on the throne of God, but have denied that He is on the throne of David. This view postulates an unbiblical distinction between the throne of God and the throne of David. In the Davidic Covenant God adopted David's sons as his own sons (2 Samuel 7:14). There is, therefore, no distinction between the throne of God and the throne of David's greater Son, Jesus the Messiah. Furthermore, the New Testament explicitly asserts that by His resurrection Jesus has taken His seat on the throne of David in fulfillment of prophecy (Acts 2:30, 31).

The Treatment of the Kingdom

In the following chapters we will study the coming of the kingdom by looking at three of the major passages that have this subject for their theme:

- *Matt. 13:1–58: The Coming of the Kingdom Revealed in Parables*
- *1 Cor. 15:21–28: The Coming of the Kingdom Proclaimed in Prose*
- *Rev. 20:1–10: The Coming of the Kingdom Seen in Vision*

Chapter 9: The Coming of the Kingdom in Christ's Parables

THE THEME OF the parables of Matthew 13 is indisputable. It is clearly the kingdom of God, and even more precisely the coming of the kingdom (vvs. 11, 16, 17, 19, 24, 31, 32, 44, 45, 52). These parables are rich in meaning and application. Brevity requires, however, that we focus exclusively on their central teaching—their teaching regarding the coming of the kingdom. This will be best brought out by examining two simple points: *Their Common Emphasis* and *Their Specific Emphases.*

Their Common Emphasis

These parables have a common emphasis because they all address the same question. This question was raised by the historical situation in which Jesus and His disciples found themselves. The Jews in general conceived of the coming of the kingdom as a glorious deliverance from all their troubles. Political and temporal expectations permeated the Jews' view of its coming (John 6:15; Acts 5:35–39). Even those Jews with a less carnal expectation (like John the Baptist) viewed its coming as involving the judgment of the wicked with irresistible might (Matthew 3:2–12). It was in such a context that Jesus came preaching the nearness and then the actual coming of the kingdom (Matt. 4:17; 12:28, 29).

John the Baptist gladly embraced Jesus as the one who would usher in the glorious and irresistible coming of the kingdom

(John 1:29). But when Jesus continued to preach the nearness of the kingdom and even preach the actual presence of the kingdom (Matt. 12:28f.) without the coming of the judgment of the wicked and the onset of the glorious consummation, John the Baptist began to have doubts. When John was arrested and imprisoned, the problem became acute. How could the kingdom have come already in Jesus while John was rotting in Herod's prison? Prison was the last place John expected to be after the coming of the kingdom! Thus, we read in Matthew 11...

> 2 Now when John in prison heard of the works of Christ, he sent *word* by his disciples, 3 and said to Him, "Are You the Expected One, or shall we look for someone else?" 4 And Jesus answered and said to them, "Go and report to John what you hear and see: 5 *the blind receive sight* and *the* lame walk, *the* lepers are cleansed and *the* deaf hear, and *the* dead are raised up, and *the poor have the gospel preached to them.* 6 And blessed is he who keeps from stumbling over Me."....
> 11 "Truly, I say to you, among those born of women there has not arisen *anyone* greater than John the Baptist; yet he who is least in the kingdom of heaven is greater than he.

How could Jesus say that the one who was least in the kingdom of heaven was greater than John? Verse 11 in speaking of the one "who is least in the kingdom" being greater than John the Baptist refers to John in his distinctive capacity as a prophet. That is the capacity in which John is being considered in this context as verses 12 through 14 make clear.

> 12 And from the days of John the Baptist until now the kingdom of heaven suffers violence, and violent men take it by force. 13 For all the prophets and the Law prophesied until John. 14 And if you care to accept *it*, he himself is Elijah, who was to come.

Prophets were distinguished for their knowledge of the mysteries of the kingdom. It is in this respect that Jesus ranks John as least in the kingdom. It is in his capacity as a prophet—the last

and greatest of the Old Testament prophets—that Jesus is referring to John. It is, therefore, at the point of insight with regard to
the mysteries relating to the coming of the kingdom that the one
who is least in the kingdom is greater than John.

To understand this we must confront a scriptural phenome-
non that may surprise us. Old Testament prophets and prophecy
had what we may call a flattened perspective about the future.
That is, the prophets were given little depth perception about the
future. Sometimes, therefore, events that were widely separated
in future time can be found predicted and mixed together in their
writings. Consider for example the prophecy of Micah about the
exile of Israel to, and their deliverance from, Babylon (Micah
4:9ff.) and how this is intimately connected to predictions of the
birth and glory of the Messiah (Micah 5:2ff.). It is for this reason
that the New Testament clearly teaches that prophets themselves
did not at times understand clearly the things they were prophe-
sying (1 Peter 1:10–12).

We learn from Matthew 11:2–6 that a godly and believing man
like the great prophet John the Baptist struggled with the seem-
ing inconsistency of Jesus' preaching of the kingdom and with
what the Old Testament itself had led the Jews to expect (Dan.
2:44). Can we think, therefore, that Jesus' disciples would be im-
mune to the same doubts? No, they would have to face the same
question. How could the all-conquering, glorious eschatological
kingdom of God be present in this former carpenter and His Ga-
lilean followers?[1] In other words, the question addressed in the
parables of the kingdom in Matthew 13 is how the kingdom
could be present in Jesus, His preaching, and His disciples.[2] The
common emphasis of these parables is the response to this question. This response is the theme of these parables. It is that the
kingdom has come and is present in a form unexpected by the
Jews, but that this present form anticipates its future, glorious
consummation. To put this in other words, the theme of these
parables is that the coming of the kingdom has two phases. It unfolds in two stages. It comes in a form unexpected by the Jews
(and even John the Baptist), before it comes in its final glorious
form.[3]

Their Specific Emphases

Each of the parables picks up this common emphasis and elaborates it in its own peculiar fashion.

The Parable of the Four Soils (Matt. 13:3–9, 19–23) teaches that the kingdom of heaven is present in the sowing of the Word of God. The fact that the kingdom is present in the world as the sowing of the gospel seed is expanded in two directions in this parable. We learn, first, that the presence of the kingdom is consistent with the rejection of the Word and its consequent fruitlessness in the lives of some that hear it. If the kingdom is present as sowing such fruitlessness is understandable and explicable. Even the best seed, the Jews well knew, does not always sprout and grow. We learn, second, that the presence of the kingdom is nevertheless indicated and vindicated by the amazing fruitfulness of the Word in those who receive it. In some it bears fruit thirty, sixty and even one-hundred fold.

The Parable of the Tares is found only in Matthew 13:24–30, 36–43. This parable expands on a truth implied in the Parable of the Four Soils. If the kingdom is present as sowing, then the kingdom of God comes in two stages. If it is to come as the eschatological harvest, then it must for that very reason come first as seed-time. This was surely an extraordinary thought for the Jewish mind. It meant that until the time of harvest good and evil men would co-exist in the world *even during the time of the kingdom and after the coming of the kingdom.* The coming of the kingdom does not mean the immediate destruction of the wicked. It is in this that the mystery of the kingdom in large part consists. The Messiah comes first as sower then as harvester. It is not His will that the wicked be immediately destroyed. That must wait until the kingdom comes as harvest.

The Parable of the Dragnet is the sister parable to the Parable of the Tares and is also found only in Matthew 13:47–50. This parable is the twin of the Parable of the Tares. The point of this parable is almost, if not completely, synonymous with that of the Tares. Not only in agriculture, but also in fishing, two distinct phases of activity must occur. If there is to be the sorting of good and bad fish at the end of the fishing trip, there must first be the casting of the net into the sea. Until the time of sorting and separation good and bad co-exist together in the net.

The Parables of the Treasure and the Pearl are found together and only in Matthew 13:44–46. Two related emphases are present in these twin parables. First, Jesus intimates that the kingdom is present in a hidden and unexpected form (v. 44, "treasure hidden in the field"; v. 45, "finding one pearl"). Second, Jesus declares that in order to possess this hidden kingdom there will be the need of total sacrifice. To a Jew with ideas of a glorious, earthly kingdom, possessing the kingdom meant glory, riches, fame, and honor. Jesus, however, says a flat "no" to such ideas. Possessing the kingdom means rather the total sacrifice of this world's possessions.

The Parables of the Mustard Seed and Leaven are found in Matthew 13:31–33. The main emphasis of these parables is again that the kingdom comes in two phases. More especially, Jesus is affirming that the present, apparent insignificance of Himself and His followers is no reason to doubt that they are the present manifestation of that kingdom which would one day attain supreme dominance. Jesus' answer to the problem of the present apparent insignificance of the kingdom is first the mustard seed, then the huge plant or tree. First the absurdly small bit of leaven in over a bushel of meal and then the whole leavened.[4]

Another emphasis is also present in these parables. The parables of the mustard seed and leaven not only contrast the small beginning and the great consummation of the kingdom, but also teach that there is a process of astonishing growth which occupies the period between the small beginning and the great consummation. Many questions surround this growth aspect of these parables. These problems will be addressed in detail later when we deal with the Bible's teaching about the earthly prospects of the kingdom of God during this age. Suffice to say here, that the idea of a process of growth in the kingdom need imply neither postmillennialism nor evolutionary theory.

In previous chapters, I pointed out that the coming of the kingdom is according to the Bible both past and future for the Christian today. I did not, however, comment upon how these two stages in the coming of the kingdom were different. From these great parables of the kingdom taken together, however, we receive an expanded understanding of the two-stage coming of the kingdom.

With respect to the prospects of the kingdom during this age, both pessimism and unalloyed optimism must be rejected. A realistic optimism is, however, warranted by these parables. Growth and progress will occur, but not such growth or progress as will supersede the problems that confronted the early followers of Jesus and their faith. In the case of many, the Word will continue fruitless. Good and evil will continue to co-exist in the world. Sacrifice will always be necessary during this first stage of the kingdom for those who would possess the kingdom. Yet, in many, the Word will cause extraordinary and fruitful effects and over-all growth will continue.

The Christian must look to the future phase of the coming of the kingdom for the final fulfillment of all his hopes and the final deliverance from all his trials. The consummate kingdom brings the separation of the righteous and the wicked, the punishment of the wicked, the glory of the righteous, and the bringing of the nations of the world under the dominion of the kingdom of God.

THE COMING OF THE KINGDOM IN THE PARABLES OF MATTHEW 13
(An Expanded Picture)

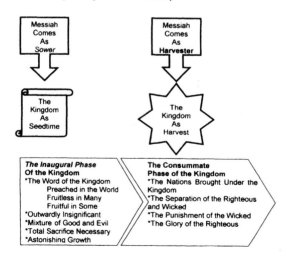

Chapter 10: The Coming of the Kingdom in Paul's Prose

MATTHEW 13 treats the coming of the Kingdom via parables. As we will see, Revelation 20 treats it in vision form, while 1 Corinthians 15:20–28 treats the same theme in ordinary prose. Since literal language (prose) is more easily interpreted than the figurative language of parable and vision, this passage has a special importance and normative significance. Here is the text of this crucial passage:

20 But now Christ has been raised from the dead, the first fruits of those who are asleep. 21 For since by a man *came* death, by a man also *came* the resurrection of the dead. 22 For as in Adam all die, so also in Christ all shall be made alive. 23 But each in his own order: Christ the first fruits, after that those who are Christ's at His coming, 24 then *comes* the end, when He delivers up the kingdom to the God and Father, when He has abolished all rule and all authority and power. 25 For He must reign until He has put all His enemies under His feet. 26 The last enemy that will be abolished is death. 27 For *he has put all things in subjection under his feet.* But when He says, "All things are put in subjection," it is evident that He is excepted who put all things in subjection to Him. 28 And when all things are subjected to Him, then the Son Himself also will be subjected to the One who subjected all things to Him, that God may be all in all.

The Contextual Setting of the Passage

This passage is part of Paul's response to the heretical denial of the resurrection. In verses 1 through 11 Paul without specific reference to the heretical denial of the resurrection has laid the foundation for this rebuttal. With considerable detail he has established that the prophetic and apostolic gospel proclaims the resurrection of Christ. This is the presupposition of his entire argument. In verses 12 through 28 Paul proceeds to prosecute his argument via two devastating lines of thought. In verses 12 through 19 he argues that the denial of the resurrection is a denial of the gospel itself. Deny the resurrection, and you deny the gospel itself with all the terrible implications such a denial of the gospel entails. In verses 20 through 28, Paul proceeds to argue that the resurrection of Christ requires the resurrection of Christ's people as a whole. Christ's resurrection as firstfruits (vvs. 20, 23) necessarily entails the resurrection of His people. Several important points for the understanding of this passage become clear from this overview.

The first point of importance has to do with *the relevance of this passage* to the subject at hand. However we explain it, it is clear from the reference to the kingdom of God in verses 24 through 28 that Paul regards the subject of the resurrection as intimately related to the subject of the kingdom of God. When we turn to this passage we are, indeed, studying one of the most important New Testament passages with regard to the coming of the kingdom.

The second point of importance has to do with *the theme of the passage*. This passage is found in the midst of Paul's argument for the resurrection of Christ and believers. This clearly suggests that its theme is governed by the two events of the resurrection of Christ and the resurrection of His people.

The third point of importance has to do with *the scope of the passage*. No place in this context does Paul clearly take up, mention, or consider the resurrection of unbelievers. That event is taught in the Bible, but it is never mentioned in 1 Corinthians 15. Here Paul is interested only in that resurrection which is in the deepest sense of the word a giving of new life, that resurrection that is part of the salvation of Christ's people.

The fourth point of importance has to do with *the thrust of the passage.* Why does Paul proceed in such a context to bring in the matter of the kingdom of God? Paul's point is to underscore the utter and irresistible necessity of the resurrection of believers. Since the kingdom of God must come and the coming of this kingdom demands the resurrection of believers, their resurrection is an irresistible result and certainty. Christ *must* reign until He has put all His enemies under His feet. Death is the ultimate enemy of Christ's kingdom and Christ's people. It must, therefore, be abolished. The presupposition of verse 26 is that death is destroyed via the resurrection of believers.

The Plain Teaching of the Passage

The kingdom in this passage has reference to Christ's reign of conquest mentioned in verses 24 and 25: "then *comes* the end, when He delivers up the kingdom to the God and Father, when He has abolished all rule and all authority and power. For He must reign until He has put all His enemies under His feet." Two straightforward questions enable us to ascertain the teaching of this passage concerning the coming of the kingdom. When does Christ's reign of conquest begin? When does Christ's reign of conquest end? The following chart illustrates these questions and suggests the direction in which they should be answered.

When does Christ's reign of conquest end?
Verses 24 through 26 teach that the end of this reign of conquest comes when Christ defeats the last enemy. The last enemy is death. Thus, the abolition of death marks the end of Christ's reign of conquest. The crucial question is, therefore, When does the abolition of death occur? Both the previous and subsequent contexts clearly answer this question. The previous context, as we have seen, points clearly to the resurrection of believers as that which marks the defeat of death. Verses 22 through 24 are clear on when death is defeated and the reign of conquest ended: "For as in Adam all die, so also in Christ all shall be made alive. But each in his own order: Christ the first fruits, after that those who are Christ's at His coming, then *comes* the end...." The subsequent context, especially verses 50 through 58, spells this out in

unavoidable clarity. Verses 54 and 55 especially make this plain: "But when this perishable will have put on the imperishable, and this mortal will have put on immortality, then will come about the saying that is written, "Death is swallowed up in victory. 'O Death, where is your victory? O Death, where is your sting?'"

If the end of the reign of conquest occurs with the resurrection of believers at the parousia, this reign must begin prior to this. Since its beginning must come before the second coming of Christ, context by itself suggests that it is to be associated with Christ's first advent and Christ's own resurrection.

When does Christ's reign of conquest begin?

Several independent lines of evidence conclusively confirm this suggestion and show that Christ's kingdom or reign began at the time of His resurrection. There is, first of all, the evidence of the passage itself. Verse 27 speaks of the enthronement of Christ in the past tense. The second line of evidence involves the other quotations of Psalm 8 in the New Testament. Ephesians 1:20–22a and Hebrews 2:9 both cite Psalm 8 and both regard Christ's reign of conquest as already begun in His resurrection. A third line of evidence that powerfully favors this exposition of the beginning and ending of Christ's reign of conquest is that this view of the reign of conquest is in perfect harmony with the contextual emphasis on the resurrection of Christ as the firstfruits and the resurrection of believers at Christ's parousia. The beginning and the ending of Christ's reign of conquest in the view here propounded correspond to the resurrection of Christ and the resurrection of Christ's people.

CHRIST'S REIGN AND THE RESSURECTION

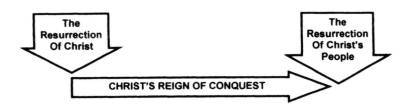

The Resurrection Of Christ

The Resurrection Of Christ's People

CHRIST'S REIGN OF CONQUEST

The Necessary Conclusions

Premillennialism will not hold up to examination in light of this passage. Two considerations rule out premillennialism. First, the resurrection of believers at Christ's parousia (v. 23) concludes Christ's reign of conquest. The *last* enemy is death. After death's abolition through the resurrection of believers no enemy remains to be abolished. It is plain, however, that Rev. 20:1–10 speaks of a 1000 year reign in which many enemies are not yet abolished. In light of 1 Cor. 15:21–28 a premillennial interpretation of Rev. 20:1–10 is impossible. The millennium of Revelation 20 must occur prior to the destruction of the last enemy at Christ's second coming. Second, the end of the reign of conquest at the second coming ushers in the ultimate consummation. Verse 28 speaks of it in the most ultimate terms conceivable. Since the end of the reign of conquest occurs at the parousia, the parousia ushers in the eternal state—not a millennium.

Verses 24 through 26 speak of the reign of conquest in terms which indicate a progressive and growing measure of victory. A process characterized by increasing victory is associated with the reign of Christ. The victory over the last enemy, death, is viewed as the last in a series of victories over Christ's enemies.

Paul's view of the coming of the kingdom is markedly identical with that of Jesus. The same peculiarity of a two-phase coming of the kingdom, which bounds a distinctive interim reign, occurs in both Matthew 13 and 1 Corinthians 15. This distinctive feature of New Testament eschatology—interestingly enough—re-occurs in Rev. 20:1–10.

Chapter 11: The Coming of the Kingdom in John's Vision

Revelation 20:1–10: Principles of Interpretation

THERE IS NO more important issue in the church today than how the Bible should be interpreted. The study of biblical interpretation is called *hermeneutics*. No matter how correct one's doctrine of the Bible is, if one's way of interpreting it is wrong enough, it will completely destroy biblical authority. Harold Camping has an adequate doctrine of biblical inerrancy, but his allegorical and spiritualizing method of biblical interpretation enabled him to predict that the Christ would come in 1994.[1] Many people claim to believe without qualification in biblical authority and yet would impose feminism and the erasure of the difference between male and female roles on the church. Why? Inadequate methods of biblical interpretation! Many cults hold high views of Scripture and yet destroy the gospel of Christ through their bad hermeneutics. Remember the warning of the Apostle Peter in 2 Peter 3:16 that in the writings of Paul "are some things hard to understand, which the untaught and unstable distort, as *they do* also the rest of the Scriptures, to their own destruction." Many people followed Paul to their own destruction because they distorted the meaning of his writings. What was the problem? Deplorable hermeneutics!

The avowed purpose of these studies is to follow better and more biblical hermeneutics. By studying the clear before the difficult, the literal before the figurative, and the general before the detailed, I have attempted to build a prophetic scheme from what is clear and indisputable in the Scriptures. With this chapter, however, I am forced finally to move from studying the clear to the difficult, from studying the literal to studying the figurative, and from studying the general truths of God's Word to focusing on the detailed interpretation of one portion of God's Word. I am forced to do this because no study of biblical prophecy could pretend to be complete unless it took up Revelation 20:1–10. This passage may claim the title of the most disputed passage in the Bible on the subject of biblical eschatology. Thus, this passage has been so disputed in the history of the church that it must be studied. Furthermore, its interpretation is also so crucial and pivotal for the premillennial interpretation of Scripture that it cannot be ignored. No premillennialist would take this book seriously—and justly so—if it failed to attempt the exposition of this portion of Scripture. The constant attack on premillennialism in the previous chapters fairly raises the question: *What, then, is the meaning of Revelation 20? How do you explain Revelation 20?*

Here is the passage in dispute:

1 And I saw an angel coming down from heaven, having the key of the abyss and a great chain in his hand. 2 And he laid hold of the dragon, the serpent of old, who is the devil and Satan, and bound him for a thousand years, 3 and threw him into the abyss, and shut *it* and sealed *it* over him, so that he should not deceive the nations any longer, until the thousand years were completed; after these things he must be released for a short time. 4 And I saw thrones, and they sat upon them, and judgment was given to them. And I *saw* the souls of those who had been beheaded because of the testimony of Jesus and because of the word of God, and those who had not worshiped the beast or his image, and had not received the mark upon their forehead and upon their hand; and they came to life and reigned with Christ for a thousand years. 5 The rest of the dead did not come to life until the thousand years were completed.

This is the first resurrection. 6 Blessed and holy is the one who has a part in the first resurrection; over these the second death has no power, but they will be priests of God and of Christ and will reign with Him for a thousand years. 7 And when the thousand years are completed, Satan will be released from his prison, 8 and will come out to deceive the nations which are in the four corners of the earth, Gog and Magog, to gather them together for the war; the number of them is like the sand of the seashore. 9 And they came up on the broad plain of the earth and surrounded the camp of the saints and the beloved city, and fire came down from heaven and devoured them. 10 And the devil who deceived them was thrown into the lake of fire and brimstone, where the beast and the false prophet are also; and they will be tormented day and night forever and ever.

The purposeful avoidance of difficult and figurative passages thus far in this study has permitted us to put off a consideration of principles of biblical interpretation or *biblical hermeneutics*. When we confront a disputed and difficult passage like Revelation 20, biblical hermeneutics must take center stage and precede the detailed study of the passage. I want to point you to five features of the passage and develop those principles of biblical interpretation crucial in the interpretation of Revelation 20.

Feature 1: The Historical Context of the Vision

The first and most basic principle of biblical interpretation is known as *grammatical-historical interpretation*. Simply stated this fundamental principle says that the Bible must be interpreted in terms of the normal grammatical meaning of the language and in a way that makes sense in light of the historical context of the passage. The original sense of the words for the original author and readers is the true sense.

Of course, this strict attention to the grammatical-historical interpretation of the passage must be supplemented by an appreciation of its theological interpretation. The Bible is a divine–human document. Each of its parts has both a human author

(Isaiah the Prophet or John the Apostle) and a divine author (the Holy Spirit). Each part of the Bible, then, has both a specific grammatical-historical meaning because of its human author and a larger theological significance because of its divine author. To put this another way, each part of Scripture is intended by the Holy Spirit as the canon (or rule of faith and life) of the church and has, therefore, a significance for the whole church.

These two sides of Scripture do not contradict one another. The human authorship of Scripture does not make it less divine. On the other hand, its divine authorship does not mean that we can ignore either the peculiar language or the historical situation of the human author. Rather the theological interpretation always is consistent with and, in fact, grows out of the grammatical-historical interpretation of the passage.

Now what has all this to do with Revelation 20? It means that the historical context of its visions cannot be ignored in its interpretation. The exact date of the writing of the Book of Revelation is disputed. What ought not to be disputed is that it was originally written by John the Apostle exiled to Patmos for his faith to local churches in the Roman province of Asia also suffering more or less for their faith (Revelation 1:9; 2:2, 3, 10, 13; 3:9, 10). Interpretations that forget that these visions were recorded by a suffering apostle for a suffering church defy the principle of historical interpretation. A credible interpretation must exhibit a clear line of connection with this historical context. Since the premillennial interpretation of this passage asserts that this passage has to do with a drastically different and far distant period of time after the return of Christ, it faces up front a problem with the principle of historical interpretation.

Feature 2: The Apocalyptic Genre of the Literature

When I speak of the *apocalyptic genre* of Revelation 20, I have used two words that I need to explain. The adjective, *apocalyptic*, comes originally from the Greek word that means revelation. It may also be derived more immediately from the name of the Book of Revelation. In some traditions it is called the Apocalypse. In the present context the word, apocalyptic, has reference to the

highly symbolic and dramatically figurative language characteristic of the Book of Revelation and also of some parts of the Book
of Daniel. For instances of this sort of language compare Daniel
8:1–27 and Revelation 13:1–4.

The word, *genre*, is a word of French origin that refers to a
kind, type, or sort of literature. Thus, the apocalyptic genre of
Revelation 20 refers to the fact that it is a kind of literature that
utilizes highly symbolic and figurative language. It is not ordinary, literal prose.

Now the principle of biblical interpretation that is relevant
here is that biblical literature must be interpreted in a way appropriate to its genre. *Genre analysis* is, therefore, crucial if the Bible is
to be properly interpreted. R. C. Sproul has these helpful comments on the subject of genre analysis in biblical hermeneutics.

> Genre analysis involves the study of such things as literary
> forms, figures of speech and style. We do this with all kinds
> of literature. We distinguish between the style of historical
> narratives and sermon, between realistic graphic descrip-
> tions and hyperbole. Failure to make these distinctions
> when dealing with the Bible can lead to a host of problems
> with interpretation. Literary analysis is crucial to accurate
> interpretation.[2]

Now the relevance of all this to Revelation 20 should be obvious.
Revelation 20 is clearly written in the apocalyptic genre and
should be interpreted in a way that takes this into account. The
opening words of Rev. 20:1, "and I saw," inform us of the vision-
ary and thus symbolic or apocalyptic character of the passage.
It must not, therefore, be interpreted *literally*. It must rather be
interpreted figuratively and symbolically in accord with its apocalyptic genre or form. Dan. 7:2–8 provides an example of such literature, while Dan. 7:16 shows that such language must be interpreted figuratively and not taken literally. "I approached one of
those who were standing by and began asking him the exact
meaning of all this. So he told me and made known to me the interpretation of these things...." These words make clear that the
visions seen by the inner eye of the prophet or apostle are not to

be interpreted literally, but figuratively. Their meaning is not immediately obvious like literal language or prose. Daniel has to inquire as to its interpretation, because as apocalyptic language its meaning is not immediately obvious to him.

All this leads to a further, important question. *How should such symbolic, apocalyptic, or figurative language be properly interpreted?* Several common sense answers can be made to this question.

Apocalyptic passages must be interpreted in a way that is consistent. They ought not to be suddenly interpreted literally at the whim of the interpreters. For instance, there is no good reason to exclude indications of time (i.e., the 1000 years) from the overall symbolic or figurative character of Revelation 20.

Biblical symbols must be interpreted, if they are not explained in the immediate context, by means of their biblical origin, background, and usage. Great help can be derived in interpreting New Testament symbols by studying Old Testament passages from which such symbolism is derived. The reference, for instance, to *the birds of the air* in Luke 13:19 is illuminated by a study of the use of this phrase in two Old Testament passages (Ezekiel 17:22–24; Daniel 4:12, 21, 22).

The interpretive principle known as the analogy of faith must also be applied here. No interpretation inconsistent with the analogy of Scripture is tenable. The Westminster and 1689 Baptist Confession agree in asserting that *the infallible rule of interpretation of Scripture is the Scripture itself* (Chapter 1, paragraph 9). The Bible is inerrant and infallible. No interpretation is acceptable that creates internal conflict in the meaning of Scripture.

One plain and important application of this principle is noted in the further statement of the old Confessions in the same paragraph: *"and therefore when there is a question about the true and full sense of any Scripture (which is not manifold, but one), it must be searched by other places that speak more clearly."* The application of this to the highly figurative and disputed language of Revelation 20 is manifold.

The symbolic language of Revelation 20 must be searched out in light of other and plainer Scriptures. The paramount question: When is Satan bound? must be answered on the basis of the teaching of the rest of Scriptures.

Furthermore, no interpretation of a highly symbolic passage that contradicts the plain meaning of straightforward, prose passages is acceptable. Plain passages must be given priority over and must interpret obscure passages. Given the considerations brought forward in previous chapters, a premillennial interpretation of Revelation 20:1–10 certainly contradicts these principles. To give only one example, the general judgment according to the clear teaching of Scripture occurs at Christ's second coming (Romans 2:1–16; 2 Pet. 3:3–18; Matt. 25:31ff.). In Rev. 20:11–15—subsequent to the millennium of verses 1 through 10—the general judgment is depicted. If Rev. 20:11–15 is regarded as chronologically subsequent to Rev. 20:1–10 (as it is by premillennialists) then the analogy of faith demands that the "1000 years" and "little season" precede the second coming of Christ.

These considerations are particularly crushing to premillennialism when we remind ourselves of the state of the doctrinal question about the millennium. The interpretation of Revelation 20 is absolutely crucial to the premillennialist. He must prove that Revelation 20 teaches a future millennium and that no other interpretation is possible. If there is another feasible interpretation of this passage, then premillennialism is left without its central exegetical pillar.

Feature 3: The Non-Consecutive Structure of the Book of Revelation

The Book of Revelation is not a consecutive, chronological, prophecy of history. Some interpreters (for example, those of the historicist and futurist schools) have begun with chapter four and assumed that each prophecy occurs in consecutive, chronological order in history right through chapter 22. The seven seals, seven trumpets, and seven bowls, for instance, occur in consecutive chronological order in history. Whatever one's conclusion on the structure of the Book of Revelation, this view must be immediately rejected. There are clear instances of repetition or recapitulation in the Book of Revelation. For instance, Rev. 11:18 speaks of the final judgment, while the immediately following passage (cf. 12:3, 5) returns to the period of Christ's first advent. This clearly shows that recapitulation must be taken into account in the interpretation of the Book of Revelation and that systems of interpretation (like that of historicism) which insist on a consecutive, chronological interpretation of the Book cannot be seriously entertained.

The significance of this for our present discussion is this. Simply because Revelation 20 follows the description of (what is apparently) the second advent of Christ in chapter 19, this does not demand that the historical fulfillment of the visions in Revelation 20 be chronologically subsequent to the historical fulfillment of the visions in chapter 19. Just as Revelation 12 takes us back to the beginning of the gospel age, so also may Revelation 20 do the same. The following chart compares the two views:

Feature 4: The Kingdom-Theme of Revelation 20

The millennial reign of Christ is clearly the theme of Revelation 20 (Note vvs. 2–7). Like Matthew 13 and 1 Corinthians 15:20–28, therefore, the theme of Revelation 20:1–10 is the coming of the kingdom of God. This points us to the normative importance of less figurative passages like Matthew 13 and 1 Corinthians 15:20–28 for the interpretation of Revelation 20:1–10. When a comparison is made with those passages, the similarities and parallels are striking. The significance of this observation against premillennialism is obvious, because it demands that the millennial reign be placed prior to Christ's second coming. The following chart attempts to show the striking character and significance of these parallels.

THE COMING OF THE KINGDOM

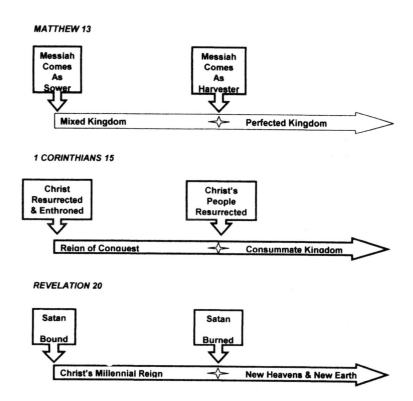

MATTHEW 13

Messiah Comes As Sower — Mixed Kingdom — Messiah Comes As Harvester — Perfected Kingdom

1 CORINTHIANS 15

Christ Resurrected & Enthroned — Reign of Conquest — Christ's People Resurrected — Consummate Kingdom

REVELATION 20

Satan Bound — Christ's Millennial Reign — Satan Burned — New Heavens & New Earth

Feature 5: The Internal Structure of Revelation 20:1–10

Any proper interpretation of a passage of Scripture involves an honest evaluation of its own structure and development. This evaluation of the structure and development of a passage begins with the identification of its theme. Thankfully, both the theme and the development of Revelation 20 are in their essential features clear.

The common theme of these verses is the millennial reign of Christ. The 1000 years both as the period of Satan's binding and the period of Christ's reign is mentioned six times in the passage: once each in verses 2, 3, 4, 5, 6, and 7. These verses clearly divide themselves into three major sections: verses 1 through 3, verses 4 through 6, and verses 7 through 10. From one point of view the arrangement of these verses is chronological:

Verses 1–3   *The Inauguration of the Reign*
Verses 4–6   *The Continuation of the Reign*
Verses 7–10 *The Completion of the Reign*

From another point of view an alternating structure may be discerned:

Verses 1–3   *The millennial reign on earth*
Verses 4–6   *The millennial reign in heaven*
Verses 7–10 *The millennial reign on earth*

The full justification for saying that verses 4 through 6 deal with the millennial reign in heaven must await the following exposition. Even at the outset, however, it is clear that the subject matter of verses 4 through 6 is clearly distinct from that of verses 1 through 3 and 7 through 10. Verses 4 through 6 deal with the *"souls"* who reign with Christ, while verses 1 through 3 and verses 7 through 10 deal with Satan and the nations. The outline of the following exposition is derived from this analysis of the passage. We will look first at *The Millennial Reign on Earth* (vvs. 1–3 and 7–10) and then at *The Millennial Reign in Heaven* (vvs. 4–6).

Chapter 12: The Coming of the Kingdom In John's Vision
Revelation 20:1–3, 7–10
The Millennium on Earth

THE ASSERTION that we are in the millennium now is in most quarters today liable to earn you a sympathetic smile. Who would not feel sorry for someone so deluded that he can believe an evident falsehood? I hope to show in this chapter that such an assertion is not so far-fetched as many to think. We have divided our study of Revelation 20 into two divisions: the millennium on earth and the millennium in heaven. In this chapter we take up the first of these divisions.

The millennium on earth in Revelation 20 is treated in verses 1 through 3 and again in verses 7 through 10. These verses deal respectively with Satan bound and Satan loosed.

Verses 1 through 3: Satan Bound

Several questions regarding the binding of Satan must be answered. In the last chapter we argued that we must interpret the figurative or apocalyptic language of the Bible on the basis of the clear teaching of the rest of the Bible. The clear and literal passages of the Bible set limits and give guidance for the interpretation of the obscure and figurative. Often the figures of the Bible are drawn from other places in the Bible where they are used. The use of such figures of speech in those places may wonderfully clarify the meaning of figurative passages that at first seem difficult.

When Was Satan Bound?

The teaching of the rest of the New Testament on when Satan was bound may be catalogued under three headings:

The Gospels contain at least three passages that are of clear relevance to the question of when Satan was bound. Christ in several places refers to the effect of His first advent on the power of the evil one. Speaking of His mighty power in casting out demons, He says in Matt. 12:28 and 29: "But if I cast out demons by the Spirit of God, then the kingdom of God has come upon you. Or how can anyone enter the strong man's house and carry off his property, unless he first binds the strong *man*? And then he will plunder his house." Here the binding of the strong man is associated with the coming of Christ's kingdom at His first advent. These same two ideas are, of course, associated in Rev. 20:1–3. The Greek word translated, binds, is the same word used in Rev. 20:2. These parallel concepts and this identical root present powerful reasons for finding here a parallel passage to Revelation 20:1–3. Luke 10:17–19 describes Satan's falling from heaven as an effect of the preaching of the coming of the kingdom (Luke 17:9): "And the seventy returned with joy, saying, "Lord, even the demons are subject to us in Your name." And He said to them, "I was watching Satan fall from heaven like lightning. Behold, I have given you authority to tread upon serpents and scorpions, and over all the power of the enemy, and nothing shall injure you." One of the great effects of Christ's first advent is the worldwide preaching of the gospel. This text suggests that if we had spiritual eyes we might see Satan falling from heaven again and again. John 12:31 and 32 explicitly associate the time of the "casting out" of Satan with Christ's being lifted on the cross: "Now judgment is upon this world; now the ruler of this world shall be cast out. And I, if I be lifted up from the earth, will draw all men to Myself." The word translated, cast out, is derived from the same root used in Rev. 20:3 to refer to the "casting" of Satan into the pit. Two ideas associated in Revelation 20:1–3 are also associated here: the curtailing of Satan's power and the blessing of the nations with a day of salvation. Again, the parallels with Revelation 20:1–3 are too obvious to be denied.

In *the Epistles* a number of passages teach the destruction of

Satan's power by the events of Christ's first advent. Colossians 2:15 for example speaks of the disarming or spoiling or disrobing[1] of the rulers and authorities as a completed result of Christ's death and resurrection: "When He had disarmed the rulers and authorities, He made a public display of them, having triumphed over them through Him." Hebrews 2:14 and 15 in bold language speaks of the destroying or rendering powerless of the devil by Christ's death. "Since then the children share in flesh and blood, He Himself likewise also partook of the same, that through death He might render powerless him who had the power of death, that is, the devil; and might deliver those who through fear of death were subject to slavery all their lives." We also see that 1 John 3:8 speaks of the destructive power of the first advent on the kingdom of Satan: "The one who practices sin is of the devil; for the devil has sinned from the beginning. The Son of God appeared for this purpose, that He might destroy the works of the devil."

The Book of Revelation contains at least one passage that is closely parallel in thought to Revelation 20:1–3. Chapter 12:5–10 has already been mentioned as one proof that the recapitulationist view of Revelation is correct. It also impacts on the view we take of the binding of Satan in Revelation 20:1–3. Revelation 12:5–10 speaks in figurative language of casting of Satan out of heaven. Clearly, this language is parallel to that of Rev. 20:1–3. This casting of Satan out of heaven is, however, associated with the birth and ascension of the Christ to the right hand of God.

This recitation of the biblical evidence proves conclusively that any interpretation of the passage that professes to interpret it in accord with the rest of Scripture must conclude that Satan was bound by the events of and at the time of Christ's first advent.[2] Only the interpretation that sees Satan bound in Christ's first advent is supported by the analogy of faith. A future, provisional binding of Satan is unknown elsewhere in Scripture and is, therefore, purely speculative and conjectural. Its sole exegetical basis is the premillennial interpretation of Rev. 20:1–10 here being challenged. A binding of Satan at Christ's second coming cannot be adopted without defying the most obvious applications of biblical hermeneutics to Revelation 20.

For How Long Was Satan Bound?

The passage plainly says that Satan was bound for 1000 years. The question is whether the 1000 years of Revelation 20 is to be understood literally or figuratively. The answer to this question must again be determined by an application of the principles of biblical interpretation explained in the last chapter. One of those principles was that each passage of Scripture must be interpreted in a way appropriate to its literary genre. Genre analysis must be practiced. We determined in the same chapter that Revelation 20 was written in the apocalyptic genre. This is a highly symbolic and dramatically figurative kind of literature. It is inconsistent with the apocalyptic or symbolic character of Revelation 20 to conclude that the 1000 years is intended as a literal period of time. Such a number occurring in such a passage must be taken figuratively.

These verses speak of the imprisonment of Satan. The language connected with Satan's imprisonment is clearly symbolic in other respects. The prison chain, the prison key, and the prison itself (the abyss) are all symbolic. If the *prison itself and everything associated with it is symbolic,* by what rationale can the *prison sentence* (the 1000 years) be dogmatically asserted to be literal? The presumption at least must be that it is figurative. In this passage it is not only permissible and reasonable to take the 1000 years as symbolic, it is necessary. The 1000 years is symbolic of an age-long, but definitely limited period of time.

Why Was Satan Bound?

One of the premier objections to the interpretation followed so far is that it seems to imply that Satan is completely unable to impact life here on earth at all during the present age. Does Satan's binding imply his total inactivity during the 1000 years? If this were the case, Satan could not be bound during the present, gospel age, since the New Testament clearly witnesses to his continuing activity (1 Peter 5:8; 2 Cor. 4:4). There are several reasons to reject the idea that Satan's binding means his total inactivity during the 1000 years and the conclusion that he cannot be bound in this present age.

First, it is necessary to remember that the language of Revelation 20 is that of vivid, apocalyptic symbol. Such language is not adapted to making fine distinctions. It is intended to give great and general impressions. Just as we may not press the details of Christ's parables beyond reason, so also our interpretation of apocalyptic language must be moderate. It is possible that the language of Revelation 20 means nothing more than that Satan's activity during the 1000 years has been restrained in some important respect.

Second, if we adopt the kind of mentality that presses the binding of Satan to mean his complete inactivity during the present age, we will be forced to object to other clear assertions of the New Testament about Satan. Hebrews 2:14 and 15 asserts that he is rendered powerless or destroyed by the cross of Christ. Colossians 2:15 asserts that the evil powers are disarmed and disrobed. John 12:31 and 32 asserts that the ruler of this world has been cast out. Will the objector complain that, if these passages were true, it would contradict the plain indications of the New Testament that Satan and his hosts continue to exercise great power during the present age? We hope not. We hope that the objector would realize that he is missing the forest for the trees.

Third, when we examine Revelation 20 clear statements are made which indicate the specific purpose of this restraint. That purpose is: "that he should not deceive the nations any longer, until the 1000 years were completed." The *un-deceiving* of the nations has often been equated with their salvation. This is a misconception which is corrected (if by nothing else) by the fact that this un-deceiving is temporary! Salvation is, of course, not temporary!

What, then, does this un-deceiving of the nations designate? The un-deceiving of the nations may be understood in terms of its opposite. This opposite—the deceiving of the nations—is explained in Rev. 20:7–9. What is the un-deceiving of the nations in verses 7 to 9? It is their being roused through the activity of Satan to a unified and concerted effort to destroy the church. Satan, therefore, is not bound today from deceiving individuals— many individuals—to some degree or another. He is bound or restrained from so deceiving the nations that they make a concerted, unified, intense, and prolonged effort to destroy Christianity in the world.

Think in terms of the big historical perspective. Satan's power was so complete until his binding, that he could easily have done this. Why didn't Satan (with Rome as his instrument) destroy the small, unprotected church? Clearly, Rev. 20:1–10 provides the answer.[3] He was bound!

Though the un-deceiving of the nations through Satan's binding does not mean that they are saved, this binding is closely related to the preaching of the gospel and the consequent salvation of men. It provides the context in which the eschatological preaching of the gospel and the salvation of men may occur.

Verses 7 through 10: Satan Loosed

The Period of His Loosing

Verse 3 speaks of Satan's loosing as a short time. This short time is subsequent to the 1000 years occurring immediately upon its conclusion. Its length is to be judged by comparison with the 1000 years. It is brief in comparison with the 1000 years. It is, therefore, a brief, but definite period of time that occurs immediately subsequent to the 1000 years.

The Result of His Loosing

As a result of Satan's loosing, the nations are deceived and are brought together to attack the *"camp of the saints."* The brief period after the 1000 years is, therefore, a period of severe persecution for the church. The distinctive feature of this persecution is the worldwide scope of this attack (v. 8).

This last great attack is called "the war" or "the battle." The use of the article (the article of previous reference as the Greek grammarians call it) tells us that John has previously mentioned this battle. This previous reference is to "the battle" mentioned in 19:19 and 16:14–16. (It is the same Greek phrase in both texts.) This clear reference of 20:8 to the battle of 19:19 and 16:14–16 identifies the battles in all these texts as one and the same. Premillennialists concede that these other references to *the battle* are a reference to a battle that takes place at Christ's second coming. Thus, this reference to *the battle* shows that the time period in view in Revelation 20 is that period immediately preceding the second coming.[4]

The Parallels to the Loosing

Hendriksen points to chapters 11 and 12 through 14 of Revelation as containing parallels to the "short time" in Chapter 20. In both, a long period of protection is succeeded by a brief period of intense persecution (11:1–13, esp. vvs. 3,9 and 12:1–13:10, esp. vvs. 12:10, 14; 13:5–7). These parallels seem accurate. Even more instructive, however, in my opinion is the parallel with 2 Thessalonians 2:1–12. The two passages combine to illumine each other remarkably. Look at the following chart of comparisons.

Revelation 20	2 Thessalonians 2
"Satan bound, vvs. 1–3 by *angel*".	"The Mystery of Iniquity, Coming of Man of Sin, activity of Satan restrained by restrainer" (vvs. 6, 7).
Short time of loosing after Millennium (vvs. 3, 7–9).	Restrainer taken out of the way and the man of lawlessness revealed shortly before the second advent (vvs. 2, 3, 8).
During this period nations are deceived (vvs. 7–9).	Those who are perishing believe a lie (vvs. 9–11).
Satan and the nations destroyed(vvs. 9, 10).	Man of sin and those who believed the lie judged by Christ's second Advent (vvs. 8, 12).

Two conclusions are warranted by these parallels. First, these parallels confirm that Rev. 20:1–10 is a reference to the present, gospel age. Second, these parallels confirm an element hitherto unmentioned in this study. A short period of intensified persecution for the church will precede the second coming of Christ.

Taken together these passages teach that there will be a brief period before Christ's second advent marked by: (1) the intensified activity of Satan (2) the appearance of a personal antichrist and a terrible apostasy (3) the concerted world-wide persecution of the church (4) the preservation of the church by the second advent of Christ destroying the wicked.

Several important practical lessons come out of this study. *First, there is much here to enlighten us.* Men and women all around us are in complete darkness as to what is going on in the world and where it is going. Their hearts fail them for fear of what is coming on the world. They walk in darkness and do not know at what they stumble. They are like people in a rowboat on a shoreless sea! They row, but have no idea where they are going, or why they should go there, or even if there is some place to go. Glorify God because by His Word He has delivered you from that!

There is much here to embolden us. Satan has been definitively restrained from so blinding the minds of his subjects as to block the missionary outreach of the church. Christ's servants have no reason to live in fear of Satan or his schemes. Though we must not (in the words of Paul) be ignorant of His schemes, we must never allow a sense of His power to paralyze us. Satan is a defeated and chained foe. In the words of Carey this should make us attempt great things for God and expect great things from God.

There is much here to entrench us. Satan is not so bound that he is prevented from going about as a roaring lion. He will be loosed in the future so as to bring a worldwide persecution on the church. Forewarned is forearmed. There is no Christianity where there is no willingness to suffer for Christ's name. An *Easy Christianity* which expects God to deliver us from all present and future tribulation and is unwilling to endure such persecution for His name is a false Christianity.

Chapter 13: The Coming of the Kingdom In John's Vision
Revelation 20:4–6
The Millennium in Heaven

MANY HAVE THE opinion that prophecy, while fascinating, is comparatively impractical. It has to do, they think, only with the distant future or only with future dispensations having little to do with the Christian. Given the popular system of prophetic interpretation, this attitude is understandable. Even the most disputed prophetic passages, however, when properly interpreted, are of enormous practical value. The subject of the present chapter provides a wonderful illustration of this reality. In it we come to one of the most difficult prophetic passages, but one that has glorious encouragement in it for the believer. The passage is Revelation 20:4–6. I have assumed in the outline of Revelation 20:1–10 presented in a previous chapter that, while verses 1–3 and 7–10 deal with *the millennium on earth*, verses 4–6 unfold *the millennium in heaven*. The diagram on the following page elaborates this interpretation and fits it into the two-age structure of biblical eschatology.

John's Narration of His Vision

A literal translation of John's narration of his vision will lay a helpful foundation for our study of these verses.

> And I saw thrones, and they sat upon them, and judgment was given to them, and the souls of those who had been beheaded on account of the testimony of Jesus and the word

THE MILLENNIUM OF REVELATION 20

of God and the ones who did not worship the beast neither the idol of him and did not receive the mark on the forehead and on the hands of them, and they lived* and they reigned with the Christ a thousand years. The rest of the dead lived* not until the thousand years were completed.[1]

This vision may be expounded by means of three questions.

What did John see first? John saw thrones. In the book of Revelation the throne of God, Christ, and His people are at present in heaven (Rev. 3:21; 4:2; 5:6; 12:5). Only in the New Heavens and New Earth does the throne of God come down to dwell with men on earth (21:3, 22; 22:1). These parallel mentions of thrones in Revelation provide the first indication that the scene of verses 4–6 is heaven and that these verses deal with the millennial reign of Christ and His people in heaven.

Who are the occupants of the thrones? The construction of the passage effectively raises the question as to who occupies these thrones. Thrones and those who sat on them are mentioned, but the occupants of these thrones are not identified. Only in the fourth clause of the passage is the identity of those who sit on the thrones specified.

John specifies their identity in a twofold way. He tells us, *first,* that souls who are in a condition of having been beheaded occupy the thrones. Though *souls* in the Scriptures may occasionally refer to whole persons and not disembodied spirits, the context demands the meaning of a disembodied soul. The Greek verb translated, beheaded, is in the perfect tense. This demands a translation something like this: "souls who remain in a condition of having been beheaded." The perfect tense plainly informs us that the effects of their being beheaded continue into the present. Further, Rev. 6:9 clearly uses *soul* of disembodied souls. He tells us, *second*, that those who did not worship the beast occupy the thrones. It was, of course, because of their refusal to worship the beast that these souls were beheaded. These martyrs represent all Christians as those who will reign with Christ because they have suffered with Him and for Him here on earth (Romans 8:17; 2 Timothy 3:12).

What is the nature of their reign? It is a living and reigning with Christ for 1000 years from which the rest of the dead are excluded. The statement that the rest of the dead did not come to life until the end of the 1000 years does not imply that they come to life after the thousand years. In fact, since the rest of the dead probably refer to the wicked dead, the wicked dead never come to life in this sense at all. The word, *until*, simply states that for the entire thousand years the wicked never share in this living and reigning with Christ. This meaning for *"until"* is clearly attested in the New Testament. It is borne out in the near context by Revelation 17:17: "For God has put it in their hearts to execute His purpose by having a common purpose, and by giving their kingdom to the beast, *until* the words of God should be fulfilled." Here *until* does not imply that *after* the Words of God are fulfilled the ten kings take their kingdom back from the beast and give it to Christ. The ten kings are in fact destroyed with the beast. *Until* only means that right up until the final fulfillment of God's Words the ten kings give their kingdoms to the beast.

John's Comments on His Vision

Again a literal translation of these comments will lay a helpful foundation for our study of these verses.

> This is the first resurrection. Blessed and holy (is) the one having a part in the first resurrection: over them the second death has no authority, but they shall be priests of God and of Christ and they shall reign with Him the 1000 years.

By way of exposition of John's comments, we will look at its designation of the vision and its interpretation of the vision.

Its Designation (v. 5b)

The vision found in Rev. 20:4–6 here has a name or title given to it. It is entitled, *the first resurrection*. This vision of the souls of the righteous reigning with Christ is designated the first resurrection because it is via sharing in the resurrection glory of Christ, who is the first fruits, that these *"souls"* reign. The first resurrection is Christ's resurrection that issues in His triumphant millennial reign. The passage in 1 Corinthians 15:20–23 suggests the reason for this designation.

> 20 But now Christ has been raised from the dead, the first fruits of those who are asleep. 21 For since by a man *came* death, by a man also *came* the resurrection of the dead. 22 For as in Adam all die, so also in Christ all shall be made alive. 23 But each in his own order: *Christ the first fruits*, after that those who are Christ's at His coming,

The contrast in this passage is between the first resurrection and the second death. This is stated in verse 6: "Blessed and holy (is) the one having a part in the first resurrection: over them the second death has no authority." The contrast is between those who have a part in the first resurrection and are, therefore, saved; and those on the other hand who do not have a part in it and over whom the second death does have power.

The Interpretation of the Vision (v. 6)

The blessings of the first resurrection seem related to the promises to the overcomers of Revelations 2 and 3 (Note Rev. 2:11, 26; 3:5, 12, 21). The promises to the overcomers in those chapters have a (at least partial) fulfillment in the intermediate state. (Compare Rev. 3:5 with 6:11; Rev. 2:7 with Luke 23:43 and 2 Cor. 12:4; also Rev. 3:12 with Rev. 6:11). This clear connection between Rev. 20:6 and the promises to the overcomers is, then, very significant. When it is put together with the fact that the promises to the overcomers have a fulfillment in the intermediate state, it is a strong indication that Rev. 20:4–6 is speaking of the glory of the intermediate state in heaven.

This interpretation fits well with the historical context in which John was writing down these visions. Do you see how relevant the glory of the state in heaven after death would have been to the persecuted early church? What a triumphant scene! The Romans thought they had killed these Christians. They thought they had put an end to any power or influence they might have. They had treated them as unworthy of presence in human society. But their most terrible persecutions had only accomplished exalting them to a truer life, a glorious reign with Christ, and a place of holy service not in the presence of mere men, but in the presence of the holy God. Their deaths gave them a share in the *first resurrection*. Those who capitulated to the beast, on the other hand, though they lived, were doomed to the *second death*.

Conclusion

At the beginning of this study, it was shown that Revelation 20 is crucial for premillennialism. Without it, the basic evidence for a premillennial viewpoint disappears from the New Testament. It is necessary for premillennialists to establish that only their interpretation of this passage provides an acceptable understanding of it. The above exposition has shown that there is another interpretation of this passage that is not only equally possible, but also far superior to the premillennial interpretation.

Chapter 14: What Does the Bible Say About Heaven?

Prefatory Remarks:

WITH THIS CHAPTER we commence the third and final part of this book. For popular purposes I have entitled this part of the book, *Next Question Please!* This part of the book is dedicated to addressing special questions of practical interest regarding the different periods in biblical eschatology. Previous chapters have already made the point that the *eschaton* or the last days began with the first advent of Christ. The age to come has already been inaugurated and broken into history in the events of Christ's first advent. The present era of history—often called the gospel or church age—is, therefore, a part of eschatology.

In answering the special questions raised about eschatology, it is convenient to arrange those questions chronologically. Since the first period of eschatological history is the present, gospel or church age, this chronologically ordered treatment of the remaining questions related to eschatology begins with questions related to the present age. In order we will deal with:

Section 1: Questions related to the Present, Gospel or Church Age
Section 2: Questions related to the Imminent Return of Christ
Section 3: Questions related to the Resurrection
Section 4: Questions related to the Eternal State

The structure by which we will deal with questions related to the present age is suggested by the exposition of Revelation 20 in the immediately preceding chapters. There are questions related to the church and the world of living men on earth. There are questions related to heaven and hell, what theologians call *the intermediate state*. In the chapters dealing with questions related to the present age, we will deal with the intermediate state first.

The intermediate state is mysterious even compared to other eschatological issues. It is one in which we must be careful to be especially on our guard against error. In this chapter it is my intention, therefore, to provide an introduction to the subject that will familiarize us with the views of our Reformed and Puritan forefathers. My hope is that an examination of their classic statement on this issue will provide a shield against innovation, novelty, and error.

In this chapter we focus on the happy subject of the intermediate state of the righteous. The scriptural teaching will be opened up through *A Catechism On The Intermediate State Of Believers*.

Question 1: *Where do the spirits of believers go at death?*
Answer: *They go to be with Christ (Phil. 1:19–24; 2 Cor. 5:6–9; Luke 23:43; Heb. 12:23, 24; Rev. 14:13).*

The foundational assurance of the primitive faith of Old Testament believers was that death could not break their relationship with their covenant God (Gen. 5:24; 2 Kings 2:1–14; Psa. 23:6; 73:24 [Ps. 16:9–11, 49:15]). The content of these Old Testament passages is very basic. They reveal that Jehovah is the master of death and may so order the destinies of some of His people that they do not even die. The passages in the Psalms do not clearly distinguish between the state of man after death and the resurrection. The basic confidence of the Psalms about the after life is, however, quite clear. *The God of covenant love who I have come to know and who has so displayed His care for me in life will not forsake me in death.*

This basic assurance of the Old Testament is brought to full revelation and sharp focus in the New Testament. Just as the covenant God is fully revealed in Jesus Christ, so also the confidence of the Christian in death is brought to sharp focus. This sharp focus is the confidence that "death" shall not "be able to separate us from the love of God which is in Jesus Christ our Lord" (Rom. 8:37, 39). Believers die in the Lord (1 Thes. 4:14, Rev. 14:13). It is Christ's will that where He is, there His people may also be (John 14:2). Therefore, when they die, they go to be with Christ (Luke 23:43; 2 Cor. 5:6–8; Phil. 1:23; Heb. 12:23, 24).

Life with Christ and for Christ is inseparable from confidence in death. Where there is no personal knowledge of, and no practical relationship with, the Living God, there can be no biblical confidence in death. There is reason, therefore, to think that your confidence in death will be related to the closeness of your walk to Jesus Christ.

The chief blessing and the source of all other blessings for believers after death is being with Christ where He is. Only love for Christ and a desire to be with Him will make death desirable to us. The popular, but carnal, interest in the after-life (and near-death experiences) so common today is alien to the message of the Bible.

Question 2: *Where is Christ?*
Answer: *Christ is highly exalted in heaven (John 16:28 with Matt. 6:9; Acts 3:21; Heb. 1:3; Eph. 4:10).*

The Bible makes clear in various ways that Christ is in heaven. In John 16:28 Jesus affirms that He is going to the Father. He teaches in Matthew 6:9, however, that our Father is in heaven. In Acts 3:21, Peter asserts that heaven must receive Christ until the period of the restoration of all things. In Hebrews 1:3, the writer affirms that Christ is at the right hand of the majesty on high. In Ephesians 4:10, the Apostle affirms that Christ ascended far above all the heavens.

Question 3: *What is heaven?*
Answer: *Heaven is the special dwelling of God where he peculiarly manifests His glory (Ps. 23:6; 1 Kings 8:27–49; Isa. 63:15; 66:1).*

Though heaven in the Bible is frequently used of the physical universe visible to us in the skies above, it is also used of that place invisible to us which is the special abode of God and His angels. This has given rise to the popular distinction between three heavens: the airy (atmospheric) heaven, the starry (celestial) heaven, and the heaven of God. Biblical precedent for such a distinction is given when Paul speaks of "being caught up to the third heaven," (2 Cor. 12:4) and because the biblical usages of heaven are easily classified in terms of these three meanings. The heaven of God may be defined as the special dwelling of God where He peculiarly manifests His glory. Though God is everywhere present, He is peculiarly present in certain places. W. M. Smith remarks, "Although it is true that the Scriptures teach that `the heaven of heavens cannot contain' God (1 Kings. 8:27 ASV), and that God is everywhere present in the universe, nevertheless, they clearly affirm that heaven is in a particular way the habitation of God."[1]

In 1 Kings 8, the dedication of the earthly temple built by Solomon is described as God's earthly house. Solomon, however, repeatedly reflects here upon God's heavenly house typified in the earthly structure (vvs. 10–13, 27, 30, 32, 34, 36, 39, 43, 45, 49). (Note also Ps. 23:6; Isa. 57:15; 63:15; 66:1). Heaven is the place of God's special presence, where His glory, His attributes, are peculiarly revealed. It is the most exalted and holy place in the universe.

Question 4: *Is heaven, then, a place?*
Answer: *Yes, the bodily state of Enoch, Elijah, and especially our Lord who are now in heaven assures us that heaven is a physical place (Gen. 5:21–24; 2 Kings 2:10–18; Luke 24:36–43; Acts 1:1–11; John 19:40ff.; Heb. 12:24).*

Heaven is a locality with spatial dimensions. It takes up space. It is as real a locality as London, Manila, or New York City. That heaven is a place that takes up space is proven by the fact that there are things there that take up space. The living bodies of Enoch, Elijah, and our Lord are in heaven (Gen. 5:21–24; 2 Kings 2:10–18; Luke 24:36–43; Acts 1:3, 4, 9–12; 3:21; John 19:40–20:17; Hebrews 2:14–18; 4:14; 15; 6:20; 8:1; 9:24; 12:22–24).

Question 5: *Is there time in heaven?*
Answer: *Yes, since only God transcends time, the created beings who dwell in heaven experience the limitations not only of space, but also of time (1 Tim. 1:17; Rev. 6:11; 20:4–6; Eph. 1:20; 2:7).*

Since God is "infinite, eternal, and unchangeable in His being," He is not subject to the limitations of space and time. According to 1 Tim. 1:17 He is not the subject of time, but (according to a literal translation) the "King of the ages." Due to the influence of Greek, and especially Platonic, philosophy and against all biblical reason, this attribute of God has often been transferred to heaven and its inhabitants. That, however, there is time in heaven is proven by several considerations.

(1) Since only God transcends time, the only possible way in which any creature could escape time would be to be deified. The Bible, however, never teaches this heresy. Whatever may be properly meant by the phrase "entering eternity," it must not be made to mean that we become eternal like God.

(2) The Bible plainly teaches that the souls of the righteous in heaven are subject to time (Rev. 6:11). Furthermore, Christ's ascension into heaven marks a new era, epoch, or time in the history of heaven.

(3) Time exists in the eternal state. That state is called the age or ages to come (Mark 10:30; Luke 20:34, 35; Eph. 1:21; 2:7). This word means world-age and actually implies that the eternal state is both a spatial and a temporal existence. Since the heavenly condition and the eternal state are both popularly conceived to be timeless, showing that the eternal state is not timeless suggests that heaven is also not timeless.

(4) The idea that there is no time in heaven or in the eternal state is often buttressed by an appeal to Rev. 10:6 which is translated in the KJV as follows, "that there should be time no longer." It is sufficient rebuttal of this appeal to note that the NIV, NASV, NKJV, Amplified Bible, and the major Greek lexicons understand this verse to mean that there should no longer be *delay* in the execution of God's purpose. Note also that the Greek root used here is *chronos*. In its verb form (the noun is used in Rev. 10:6) it often means "delay" (Matt. 24:48; 25:5; Luke 1:21; 12:45; Heb. 10:37).

All of this impresses upon us one main point: the reality of the glory of heaven. Heaven is in truth a place where men with bodies live. Enoch, Elijah, and our Lord live there. If you were there, you could see and touch your Savior. Of course, this biblical truth must not be distorted. The Bible teaches that heaven is a place, but it does not reveal where that place is. We must not set out on a quest to locate the coordinates of heaven in the galaxy. The biblical balance is simply this. We know that heaven is a place, but we do not know where this place is.

Question 6: *How is heaven described in the Bible?*
Answer: *It is described as the city of God and the paradise of God (Heb. 12:22–24; Gal. 4:24–31; Luke 23:43; 2 Cor. 12:2–4).*

Though this answer may not take into account the complexity in the biblical presentation of heaven most of the biblical descriptions of heaven are summarized in the two mentioned in this answer. The two descriptions mentioned in this answer are the most frequent descriptions of heaven in the Bible.

Heaven is the city of God (Heb. 12:22–24; Gal. 4:24–31). As God's city it is the place where His temple and His throne are. The frequent, biblical descriptions of heaven as God's temple and God's throne may be included under the description of heaven as God's city. It is important to note, however, that heaven is not just any city. It is Jerusalem! Jerusalem was the biblical capital of the promised land, Canaan (Heb. 11:16).

Heaven is the paradise of God. The word literally designates a beautiful park or garden. The Bible calls upon two examples to describe heaven as a beautiful park or garden. In Rev. 2:7 paradise is reminiscent of the Garden of Eden where was the tree of life. There man had fellowship with God in perfect righteousness and happiness. Heaven is a return of the Garden of Eden.

Closely related is the example of the promised land of Canaan, the rest promised to the people of God (Heb. 11:16; 3:18–4:1; Rev. 6:11; 14:13). The Canaan rest, the land flowing with milk and honey, was the great promise to which Israel looked during the weary years in the burning wilderness. Heaven is the inheritance to which Christians look. Much insight as to the nature of heaven can be gleaned from meditation on this imagery.

The description of heaven as the city of God and the paradise of God raises a question. Are not these two images used to describe the eternal state also? Of course, (Rev. 21:1–4; Heb. 13:14; 9:15)! This brings to view an important principle with regard to the doctrine of the intermediate state. The intermediate state anticipates the eternal state. Heaven is the present anticipation of our future hope. The Christian does not have two hopes. That hope is the return of Christ, the resurrection of the dead, and the eternal inheritance to be received at that time. He has one hope. But this one hope is anticipated in the heavenly existence of the spirits of believers.

Question 7: *What is the blessed condition of the spirits of believers in heaven?*

Answer: *They are made unchangeably and perfectly holy and happy in themselves (Heb. 12:23; Luke 23:43; 2 Cor. 5:8; Phil. 1:23; Rev. 14:13).*

This answer asserts four things about the condition of believers in heaven. *It asserts, first, that it is unchangeable.* This follows from the all-important fact that salvation is the outgrowth of the sovereign purpose of God. "The gifts and the calling of God are irrevocable" (Rom. 11:29). The blessing attained in the heavenly city is, thus, irreversible. If free will were the source of salvation, then one could apostatize even from the glory of heaven. Since, however, salvation is dependent on God, the glory of heaven is permanent. This city "has foundations" and its "architect and builder is God" (Heb. 11:10). The city of God is a place of security—ideally what all cities were intended to be (Ps. 48:3,8). It is also implied in that the spirits of believers are "perfected" according to Heb. 12:23.

The word used literally means *brought to the goal.* This goal as the goal of the sovereign God is irreversible and unchangeable. *It asserts, second, that it is a condition of perfect holiness.* Three considerations demand this conclusion. *Firstly,* the explicit statement of Scripture in Heb. 12:23 demands this conclusion. That verse speaks of "the spirits of righteous men made perfect." The implication is that they are made perfect precisely in their character as righteous men. That the spirits of the righteous are made perfect in holiness is necessitated, *secondly,* by their location. They are in the holy city and the paradise of God. Existence there, however, requires perfect holiness (Rev. 21:27 and Gen. 3). Man was expelled from the Garden of Eden when he fell into sin. He cannot be admitted back into the very presence of God until he himself is restored to ethical perfection. To dwell in that city that is bathed in the unveiled light of the glory of the God who dwells there demands moral perfection (Heb. 12:23). The ethical perfection of the spirits of believers is demanded, *thirdly*, by their companion. They go to be with Christ. In some sense at death they no longer walk by faith, but by sight (2 Cor. 5:6–8). But to see Christ is to be made like Him, 1 John 3:1–3. *It asserts, third, that it is a condition of perfect happiness.* Anyone who lives in the paradise of God, the city of God, and with the Son of God must be perfectly happy. *It asserts, fourth, that it is an incomplete condition.* It is only *in themselves* that they are perfectly happy and holy, that is to say, in their spirits.

Question 8: *What do these spirits do in heaven?*
Answer: *(1) They rest in the heavenly Canaan. (2) They commune with their fellow-citizens in the heavenly Jerusalem. 3) They reign with Christ. (4) They behold God and the intercession of the Lamb in the true temple where they serve as priests and worship God (Rev. 14:13; 6:11; Luke 23:43; Heb. 12:23; Rev. 20:4–6, w/3:12, 21).*

(1) They rest in the heavenly Canaan (Rev. 6:11; 14:13). Canaan was the rest of God's people, the land where they could serve God without the oppression of Pharaoh and without the dangers of the wilderness experience. They would rest from the trouble and toil of their previous experience. This idea of cessation from trouble is clearly present in Rev. 14:13. They rest from their *labors*. The word is plural. In the world it was necessary to persevere in keeping God's commands and believing in Jesus. Perseverance implies opposition in their endeavors to serve Christ. The context identifies this opposition as primarily the world and the devil. Their own flesh also, however, made obedience to God a labor. The rest of heaven means the cessation of such battles, the ability to worship and serve God without such hindrances, and the preliminary enjoyment of God's reward for their faithful labors. What Canaan was to Israel, what the day of rest is to a weary Christian, that and much more will heaven be to the spirits of believers.

(2) They commune with their fellow-citizens in the city of God. Will we know each other and communicate with each other in heaven? The very description of heaven as the city of God demands the idea of fellowship and communication with the other

inhabitants of the city. A city in the Scriptures is a society. A society by definition assumes communication and personal relationships. Heaven as the city of God is such a society. That we will know and communicate with others in heaven is further confirmed by the basic truth of the intermediate state, that we will be with Christ. This "being at home with Christ" surely includes communicating with Him. If it is clear that we shall know and communicate with our Lord, then it is reasonable to think that we shall know and communicate with the spirits of the righteous.

(3) They reign with Christ. Already Christians are legally seated with Christ in the heavenly places. That is to say, in virtue of our union with Christ we already participate in His glorious reign (Eph. 2:6; Col. 3:1–3). But what we have now legally, we will experience personally when at death we depart to be with Christ. Then our spirits will go to be with Him where He reigns at the right hand of God (Phil. 1:23). This is, furthermore, the direct statement of the Scriptures in its climactic teaching regarding the intermediate state (Rev. 3:21; 20:4–6).

(4) They behold God and the intercession of the Lamb in the true temple where they serve as priests and worship God (Rev. 3:12; 20:6). One Puritan remarks that here on earth we have only dark apprehensions of Christ's intercession, but that there we shall see him at His work. Certainly this must make deep, suitable, and glorious impressions on the spirits of believers.

Question 9: *When do the spirits of believers enter heaven?*
Answer: *The spirits of all believers immediately enter heaven at death (Luke 23:43; Phil. 1:23; 2 Cor. 5:6–8).*
The key word is "*all.*" This question and answer raises the issue of purgatory. The doctrine of purgatory is completely without any biblical support. It also presupposes many of the false doctrines of Rome such as the distinction between mortal and venial sin.[2] Thus, there is no scriptural alternative for the abode of the departed spirits of believers other than heaven. On the other hand, the positive argument is that every passage that identifies the abode of departed spirits of believers identifies it as heaven. Two passages are of special relevance here. The first is Luke 23:42, 43. Some who oppose the immediate entrance of believers

into heaven translate this verse as follows: "Truly I say to you today, you shall be with Me in Paradise." They put the comma after
the word, today, and connect it with the phrase, "Truly I say to
you." There are at least three things wrong with this rendering.
First, it makes Jesus utter trite nonsense. When else beside today
would Jesus be saying it? Second, it violates the natural meaning
of the passage. The thief has asked that Jesus remember him
when he would come in His kingdom. Jesus' response is, "Today,
you shall be with Me in Paradise." Third, it ignores the context
that emphasizes in the immediately succeeding verses that Jesus
died that very day (vvs. 44–46). The second passage is 2 Cor. 5:6–
8. Paul here states his confidence that his death will mean being
at home with the Lord in heaven. Two things heighten the significance of this passage and imply that what is true for Paul is
true for all believers. Paul uses the pronoun, we, throughout the
passage. This means that he expected that his fellow-workers
would experience the same blessing. The way that Paul repeats
the formula "at home in the body, absent from the Lord," (vvs. 6,
8, and 9) implies the idea that these are the only two, possible
alternatives. The many references to the fact that departed believers are in heaven (Phil. 1:21–24; Heb. 12:23; Rev. 6:9–11; 14:13;
20:4), further confirm this conclusion. The thief on the cross, Paul,
his fellow-workers, the spirits of righteous men made perfect,
martyrs, the dead who die in the Lord, all without exception are
in heaven. If all these are in heaven, if no other abode for the spirits of believers is revealed; if all Christians are equally in union
with Christ, equally forgiven, and equally joint-heirs of glory,
then we must conclude that the spirits of all believers when they
die immediately enter heaven.

Question 10: Is the blessedness of these spirits complete?
Answer: *No! In the Intermediate State the goal of redemption has not
been achieved. Their blessedness is incomplete, therefore, in five ways:
1) They have not received the redemption of their bodies. 2) Their brethren, the elect people of Christ, are yet partially unredeemed. 3) Their inheritance, a redeemed creation, is not yet theirs. 4) They have not yet
been publicly vindicated by the final judgment. 5) Their enemies have
not yet been judged (2 Cor. 5:1–8; Rev. 6:11; 21:1).*

Previously we saw that the intermediate state is an anticipation or preliminary fulfillment of the blessedness of the eternal state. Thus, there is a certain continuity between the intermediate state and the eternal state. Under the answer to Question 8, however, I intimated that there is a balancing reality with reference to the intermediate state. The intermediate state, though a state of perfect holiness and in one sense a state of perfect happiness, is from another perspective a state of incompleteness. Two passages intentionally reflect on the deficiency of the intermediate state. Some may think that the Bible never reflects negatively on the intermediate state of believers. It is important to realize, however, that the Bible never idealizes a disembodied condition and always holds up an historical consummation that is both earthly and bodily as the true hope of believers.

In Rev. 6:9–11, several unsatisfactory aspects of the intermediate state are revealed. The most prominent is the lack of vindication that the souls of the righteous feel because their enemies have not yet been judged. Two other unsatisfactory aspects are referred to more implicitly. The description, "the souls of those who had been slain," in verse 9 alludes to the disembodied condition as disquieting. The mention in verse 11 of "their fellow-servants and their brethren who were to be killed" reminds us of the unity of the elect people of God. The blessedness of the spirits of believers must be incomplete as long as their brethren are yet subject to the hostility of a cruel world.

The second passage is not found in the highly figurative surroundings of Revelation, but in the more commonplace atmosphere and language of 2 Corinthians. This passage also specifically reflects on the unsatisfactory aspects of the intermediate state. When Paul speaks in 2 Corinthians 5 of being "naked" (v. 3) and "unclothed" (v. 4), he is alluding to the intermediate state entered at death and the bodiless condition it entails. Furthermore, these verses explicitly state Paul's desire not to be naked or unclothed, but rather, if possible to put on the transformed body over his mortal body. That is to say, he hopes not to die, but to put on his resurrection body over his living body. In both verse 2 and again verse 4, Paul uses a form of the verb, to put on, which literally means to put on over. It is not precisely the same verb used in 1 Cor. 15:53–54 of the resurrection of the dead which simply means to put on. In these ten brief questions and answers is the heart of the Bible's teaching about heaven. Though the subject of the intermediate state is not elaborated at length in the Scriptures, it does say enough to provide us a clear basis for our faith with regard to the questions we have asked and answered.

Chapter 15: Sheol, Hades, and Hell

IN THIS CHAPTER we turn from the glory of the intermediate state of believers to the gloomy and dreadful prospect of the intermediate state of the wicked. Though this study is unpleasant, it is very necessary. For us as believers both our delight in Christ's salvation and the urgency of our concern for the lost is related to the dark reality of hell. If it is true that at the moment of death unbelievers enter hell with no second chance for salvation, then how tender a Christian's love for Christ must be and how urgent our concern for the lost must be!

The statement of *The 1689 Baptist Confession* about hell provides a helpful preview to this study:

> and the souls of the wicked are cast into hell; where they remain in torment and utter darkness, reserved to the judgment of the great day; besides these two places, for souls separated from their bodies, the Scripture acknowledgeth none.

This historic statement tells us three things about the condition of the wicked in the intermediate state: its location (hell), its circumstances (torment and darkness), and its expectation (the judgment of the great day). A thorough appreciation of the biblical basis for these assertions requires an examination of two matters: *The Basic Biblical Words relating to the Condition of the Wicked* and *The Basic Biblical Texts Discussing the Condition of the Wicked.*

1. The Basic Biblical Words relating to the Condition of the Wicked

No treatment of the intermediate state of the wicked would be complete which did not discuss the meaning of the term, *sheol*, in the Old Testament and its New Testament equivalent, *hades*. In the Greek version of the Old Testament (called the Septuagint) in use at the time of Christ sheol was usually translated by hades.[1] Uncertainty, confusion, and error surround the meaning of sheol.

The False Views of Sheol

The Jehovah's Witnesses assert that sheol means oblivion or non-existence. The sufficient rebuttal of this is that it makes nonsense of many passages of Scripture where oblivion and non-existence cannot possibly be the meaning (Deut. 32:22.)

Modernism and some Evangelicals influenced by Modernism think that sheol refers to a shadowy netherworld or underworld. According to this idea, the Jewish view of the after-life was profoundly influenced by the nations around them. The popular idea of the day was that all men both good and bad went to a gloomy netherworld. This view that both the righteous and the unrighteous go to sheol is based on those texts which teach or imply that all men go to the same place, sheol, when they die (Eccl. 2:14; 3:19; 6:6; 7:2; 9:2; 3, 10; Gen. 37:35; 2 Sam. 12:23). This view involves the faulty assumption that sheol always refers to same thing. This assumption is groundless. This view also fails to do justice to those texts that teach that there is a distinction in the experience of the righteous and the wicked after they die (Prov. 14:32). There is clear evidence in the Old Testament that the righteous experience a blessed after-life, while the wicked one of punishment.

Inter-testamental Judaism theorized that sheol contains two different compartments, one for the righteous and one for the unrighteous. Buis gives this account of the view just mentioned. "The main development in this period comes from the fact that sheol is now divided into two compartments: one for the good, called Paradise; the other for the evil, called Gehenna."[2] The Old Testament taught that all men go to sheol, but it also taught a distinction between the righteous and the unrighteous in death. The solution of the Jews to this dilemma was to suppose that there were two compartments in sheol, one of torment for the unrighteous, and one of blessedness for the righteous. This has seemed a logical theory to many since the time of Inter-testamental Judaism. Some early church fathers and modern Dispensationalists adopted this theory and elaborated it from a Christian point of view.

The objections to this theory are many. The first is that the Old Testament contradicts this teaching by asserting that believers even in the Old Testament went to heaven (Gen. 5:24; 2 Kings 2:11; Ps. 23:6; Ps. 73:23, 24). Second, and as we have seen previously, paradise in the New Testament is identified with heaven (2 Cor. 12:4; Rev. 2;7; Luke 23:43). Third, this theory is not consistent with Luke 16:22. The rich man is not in gehenna, but hades. Hades is the Greek equivalent to sheol. Paradise, Abraham's bosom, is contrasted not with gehenna, but with hades or sheol. Paradise is, therefore, not a part of sheol, but a different place than sheol.

The last and best rebuttal of this theory is a proper understanding of the biblical meaning of *sheol*. We now turn to a consideration of this:

The Proper Understanding of Sheol
There is a crucial premise or starting-point in the interpretation of sheol that is ignored by each of the false interpretations already mentioned. This crucial premise is that sheol (and hades) do not always refer to the same thing when used in the Bible. Each of the false views agree in thinking that sheol always refers to the same thing. It may be non-existence, the underworld, or the compartmentalized sheol of the Jews, but each of the false views agree in making sheol always refer to one and the same reality. The biblical word, death, a closely related word, provides a helpful analogy here. It has several different references in the Bible (i.e., physical death, spiritual death, eternal death). Thus, it is unnecessary to assume that sheol always refer to the same reality. A word study of the use of sheol in the Old Testament will quickly prove that this word does not always have the same meaning.

The exact derivation of the word, sheol, is uncertain, but its general meaning in the Scriptures is unclear. Though sheol refers to different things in the Bible, it has one general meaning. The first six passages where sheol is used in the Bible each convey this general meaning clearly (Gen. 37:35; 42:38; 44:29–31; Num. 16:30, 33; Deut. 32:22; 1 Sam. 2:6). Sheol, whatever more specific reference it may have, is *the place below*.

This general meaning suggests a helpful analogy that will clarify the meaning and usage of sheol in the Bible. If sheol is that which is below, what is the word that refers to that which is above? It is the Hebrew word, *shamayim*, translated heaven or heavens. Just as sheol is that which is below, so also shamayim is that which is above. This contrast becomes clear in Job. 11:8; Psa. 139:8; and Amos. 9:2.

Especially of interest is the fact that shamayim may also have different references in the Old Testament. Three heavens, in fact, are distinguished in the Bible: the airy heavens, the starry heavens, and the heaven of God (2 Cor. 12:1–4). Given the parallel between the word, shamayim, and the word, sheol, this certainly suggests that sheol also could refer to diverse things. The visible heavens are that which is above. Hence, they are associated with God and symbolize the place of his abode and of blessedness. Sheol, that which is below, is, thus, associated with that which is the antithesis of God and blessedness. It, therefore, symbolizes the place of woe and torment which is devoid of the divine presence and blessing. Sometimes, therefore, it is used of the grave, but in other instances of hell, because death and the grave is a symbol of divine judgment.

The key evidence for this interpretation of sheol is that this word is, in fact, used both of the grave (Gen. 37:35; 42:38) and of hell, the place of punishment for the wicked after death (Deut. 32:22; Job. 21:13; 24:19; 26:6; Psa. 9:17; Prov. 5:5; 9:18; 15:24; 23:14). That these Old Testament texts refer to the place we call hell is confirmed by a number of things. First, the statement of Prov. 14:32 (*The wicked is thrust down by his wrongdoing, But the righteous has a refuge when he dies.*) requires that something more than the grave be in view. Second, the fact that even the righteous go to the physical grave seems to demand much more than mere physical death and the grave as the just punishment of the wicked in these texts. Third, the literature of Inter-testamental Judaism shows that the Jews did see something more in such texts than physical death and the grave. Fourth, the use of hades in the New Testament, the Greek equivalent of sheol, demonstrates that sheol meant hell for the inspired authors of the New Testament. The use of hades to mean hell in the New Testament is indisputable (Matt. 11:23; 16:18; Luke 10:15; 16:23). Fifth, the Old Testament teaches that the righteous are delivered from sheol, in spite of the fact that in one sense the righteous die and go to sheol, the grave (Prov. 15:24; Ps. 49:14, 15). This requires us to distinguish between sheol as a place of punishment in the after-life (from which the righteous are delivered) and the grave (which symbolizes it and from which the righteous in general are not delivered till the last day).

The evidence for the existence of hell is not a matter of two or three or even ten proof-texts in the Bible. Hell is woven into the very fabric of the way that the Bible looks at the universe. The very words used in the Bible to describe the condition into which we enter at death are words which remind us that death is a divine judgment. Sheol may mean the grave, but that is because it points us to the opposite of all that is divine and blessed. Thus, it also means hell. Earthly existence with its obituaries, funeral homes, and cemeteries is a constant reminder that all mankind lives under the constant threat of divine wrath.

2. The Basic Biblical Texts Discussing the Condition of the Wicked

There are four key texts in the New Testament that speak directly to the issue of the intermediate state of the wicked. The first and perhaps the most important is ...

Luke 16:23–26
23 And in Hades he lifted up his eyes, being in torment, and saw Abraham far away, and Lazarus in his bosom. 24 And he cried out and said, 'Father Abraham, have mercy on me, and send Lazarus, that he may dip the tip of his finger in water and cool off my tongue; for I am in agony in

this flame.' 25 But Abraham said, 'Child, remember that during your life you received your good things, and likewise Lazarus bad things; but now he is being comforted here, and you are in agony. 26 'And besides all this, between us and you there is a great chasm fixed, in order that those who wish to come over from here to you may not be able, and that none may cross over from there to us.'

Three truths about the intermediate state of the wicked appear to be plainly conveyed in the words of Jesus in verses 23 through 26. First, the intermediate state of the wicked is clearly a conscious condition. Abraham and the rich man are pictured as speaking to one another. Second, the intermediate state of the wicked is a tormented condition in the place we call Hades. The rich man plainly says, "I am tormented in this flame." We must allow Jesus the poetic liberty of referring to the bodiless condition by means of the familiar bodily terms with which we are familiar. Yet, this does not disguise the fact that the bodiless condition is one of terrible and conscious torment. Third, the intermediate state of the wicked is an inescapable condition. There is great chasm fixed so that none can leave hell to enter heaven, and none can leave heaven to enter hell. These truths drive home the terrible danger of the Pharisees in their complacent rejection of the rebuke of Jesus. They constitute a dreadful warning to them.

Acts 1:25
"to occupy this ministry and apostleship from which Judas turned aside to go to his own place."

The Bible graphically describes the circumstances of Judas' death. Compare the above text with Matt. 27:3–10 and Acts 1:16–19. The circumstances of Judas' death probably symbolized in the minds of the biblical writers the place of which Acts 1:25 speaks, but they are not to be identified with it.

Two places are contrasted in Acts 1:25. The text may be literally translated from the Greek as follows: "to take the *place* of this ministry and apostleship from which Judas turned away to depart to his own *place*." This text asserts that Judas left a *place* of privileged office and ministry and went to his own *place*, the place peculiarly prepared for him by his sin and God's justice. Since he was the son of perdition (John 17:12), we know that the place he went to was perdition, a word that means loss, ruin, and destruction.

The doctrine clearly taught in Acts 1:25 is that each lost man has a place peculiarly prepared for him in hell when he dies. God's retribution is exact. Each has *his own* peculiar place. This implies differentiation in the divine judgment. Such differentiation involves two distinct ideas. There is the idea of gradation of punishment or degrees of torment in hell (Luke 12:47 and 48). There is also the idea of fitness or suitability. In other words, God's punishment will precisely and even ironically suit each man's peculiar wickedness. The Scriptures emphasize that there is propriety and irony in the judgments of God upon the wicked (Acts 12:22, 23; Rev. 16:5, 6). A further truth taught here is that this life is determinative of the after-life. Conduct in this life, in other words, fixes one's condition in the after-life. The sin of the wicked in this life produces according to the vengeance of God their exact place in the next.

1 Pet. 3:19
19 in which also He went and made proclamation to the spirits *now* in prison....

Many understand this verse to mean that after His death Christ personally descended into hell and announced salvation to the spirits there. Often it is used as a proof text for the idea that Old Testament saints were delivered from hades by Christ's death and brought at that time from hades to heaven. We have seen that this contradicts Scripture. Furthermore, it is not supported by the teaching of this passage since the spirits preached to here were not saints, but the rebellious and damned contemporaries of Noah. Certain cults teach from this text a second probation (or opportunity to be saved) after death. This teaching, however, is antithetical to the whole tenor of biblical teaching (2 Cor. 5:10).

The False Interpretation of 1 Peter 3:19

Stated:
Christ after his death personally descended into hell and announced salvation to the spirits there.

Refuted:
- The spirits of the righteous were not in Hades.
- The spirits preached to here are identified as the damned contemporaries of Noah.
- To announce salvation to the spirits of the damned is pointless unless one adopts the false doctrine of a second probation.

We are shut up, therefore, to the common Protestant interpretation of this verse. It is best commended by its clear explanation. This interpretation states that Christ went and preached *by His Spirit in Noah's day and through Noah* to men who were *by the time of Peter's day* "spirits in prison," because they had disobeyed the Spirit-empowered preaching of Noah while they were alive. A careful inspection of verse 18 will show that it does not assert that Christ personally preached to the spirits in prison, but that he preached to them in (or by) His Spirit. The instrumentality of Noah's proclamation of the Word of God is implied in verse 20. The word, disobedient, in its connection with the days of Noah clearly implies their disobedience to the preaching of the Word of God through Noah. This preaching of Noah is explicitly mentioned by Peter in his second epistle (2 Pet. 2:5 and Gen. 6:3). Other mentions are made in Scripture of preaching by Christ which He did not perform personally and bodily but through His Spirit (Eph. 2:17 and 1 Peter. 1:12). The words, "in prison," must, therefore be understood as the NASB does by adding the word, "now." They are Peter's comment on the result of these spirits' disobedience in Noah's day. The result of that is that "now" they are in prison.

The Proper Interpretation of 1 Peter 3:19

Stated: Christ went and preached by His Spirit in Noah's day and through Noah to men who were by the time of Peter's day "spirits in prison",

Supported:

- Verse 18 asserts that Christ preached to the spirits in prison by His Spirit.
- The instrumentality of Noah's proclamation of the Word of God is clearly implied in verse 20.
- This preaching of Noah is explicitly mentioned by Peter in his second epistle (2 Pet. 2:5 and Gen. 6:3).
- There are other mentions in Scripture of preaching by Christ through His Spirit that took place through the instrumentality of others (Eph. 2:17 and 1 Peter. 1:12).
- The words, "in prison," must, therefore be understood as the NASB does by adding the word, "now."

This text, therefore, teaches that the intermediate state of the wicked is a condition of divine imprisonment. This thought conveys at least three important ideas about hell. First, hell is a place from which you cannot escape. Escape from God's prison is inconceivable. Second, hell is a place of punishment. Though a prison in biblical times was not the place of ultimate punishment, the Bible is clear that hell is a place of preliminary punishment. Third, hell is a place where men are reserved for the Day of Judgment. Prisons in biblical times were places where men were held until their sentences could be decided or executed (Acts 12:4–6; 22:19). Hell is a place where men are held until the Day of Judgment when their final sentence will be announced publicly and executed.

2 Pet. 2:9

9 *then* the Lord knows how to rescue the godly from temptation, and to keep the unrighteous under punishment for the day of judgment,

The statement of Peter in 2 Peter 2:9 forms his conclusion from the three previous examples of divine judgment he has cited in verses 4 through 6. It specifically alludes to verse 4 by repeating the verb, *to keep*, used there. This suggests that Peter likens the condition of all the unrighteous after their deaths to that of the angels that sinned. The angels are right now kept for judgment in a place of punishment. So also are all the unrighteous dead, says Peter.

Confirming this reference to the intermediate state of the wicked is the grammar of the passage. The KJV misses the point when it translates: *The Lord knoweth how to deliver the godly out of temptations, and to reserve the unjust unto the day of judgment to be punished.* The verb meaning, "punish," is a present passive participle which should be translated, "while being punished." This is the translation of the NASB, the NIV, and the NKJV. Literally this phrase reads, "but unrighteous unto day of judgment while being punished to keep."

The teaching of this passage is, thus, that the wicked after death and while awaiting the Day of Judgment are kept and punished. In the first place, they are kept or guarded—literally—*by the Lord.* There is, therefore, no escape from their condition or from their judgment. In the second place, while being so guarded, they are punished. The implication of the passage is that they are punished in a way and in a place similar to that in which the angels who sinned are punished: a place described as "pits of darkness" (2 Pet. 2:4) and "eternal bonds under darkness" (Jude 6).

Conclusions

Several practical conclusions follow from this examination of the Biblical teaching in these four key passages on the intermediate state of the wicked. (1) It is a place of conscious torment and punishment. This torment is described as being in darkness, being chained, being burned. (2) It is a place that is entered by men and prepared for men because of their sin described variously as covetousness, scoffing at Jesus' words, disobedience to the preaching of God's Word, being unrighteous like Noah's generation and Sodom and Gomorrah, and selling Jesus for silver. So intimately related to the wickedness of men is this place that each one seems to have a unique punishment fitted to his sins. (3) It is a place from which there is no escape. This is demonstrated by a number of different considerations in these texts. There is a great gulf fixed so that none go from hades. It is described as a prison in which the Lord is the keeper. There is, therefore, consequently, no escape from this place. It is a man's place in the after-life. As his unique abode prepared for him there is no escape from it.

A Final Issue

Is there a second chance for men after death to be saved? The wicked are kept in this prison from which there is no escape for the specific purpose of arraigning them in the Day of Judgment. Besides the considerations flowing out of the texts already mentioned, there are other biblical considerations that demand this conclusion. We observe that 1 Pet. 3:20 implies that God's patience ended with the death of Noah's wicked contemporaries. In John 8:21 and 24 there is a similar note of finality in the words of Jesus, "you shall die in your sins." To die in sin is clearly a dreadful thing, but why so dreadful if there is a second chance? The Scriptures also teach that the final judgment proceeds on the basis of the earthly life of men. There is always a reference to the earthly life of men as the exclusive basis of judgment (2 Cor. 5:10; Rev. 14:13; 1 Tim. 5:25; Matt. 10:32, 33; Heb. 9:27). There is never any reference to any possible change due to behavior in the after-life.

The Question Stated:
 Is there a second chance for men after death?

The Answer Given:
 There is no second chance for salvation after death!
 - The wicked are according to these four key passages kept in a prison from which there is no escape.
 - 1 Pet. 3:20 implies that God's patience ended with the death of these men.
 - John 8:21, 24 contains a note of finality in the words of Jesus, "you shall die in your sins."

- The Scriptures teach that the final judgment proceeds on the basis of the earthly life of men (2 Cor. 5:10; Rev. 14:13; 1 Tim. 5:25; Matt. 10:32, 33; Heb. 9:27).
- There is never in the Scriptures any reference to any possible change in status after death due to an after-life repentance.

A Closing Word

If the teaching of the Bible about hell is what we have shown in this chapter, then what manner of men ought we to be? How thankful we ought to be for the salvation that has delivered us from such an awful destiny! How concerned we should be for the lost! How intensely should we pray for them! How carefully we should look for opportunities to share the gospel with them! If someone reading this chapter is not certain that he will go to heaven—and not hell—when he dies, how single-minded he should be in seeking salvation before it is eternally too late.

Chapter 16: The Prospects of the Church During the Gospel Age—Tribulation?

IN THIS CHAPTER we continue to deal with questions related to the present gospel age. Chapters 13 through 15 dealt with the intermediate state where we looked at the invisible world of heaven and hell. In this chapter we turn our attention to the visible world and consider the *Prospects of the Church during the Gospel Age*.

In both postmillennialism and premillennialism the negative and positive perspectives about the prospects of the church have often been divided and set at odds with one another. Generally, postmillennialism has concentrated on the positive perspective about the prospects of the church and its expansion, and minimized the negative perspective about the prospects of the church having to do with its tribulations. Premillennialism (especially that form of premillennialism prevalent today) has generally taken the opposite approach and emphasized the negative aspects of the church's prospects and minimized the positive. In my opinion both these approaches are faulty.

The proper approach is provided by the balancing parable of the kingdom known as the "Parable of the tares." The appropriate words of Jesus are, "Allow both to grow together until the harvest...." (Matt. 13:30). Jesus reveals here that it is God's decretive or secret will that both the good seed (later identified as "the sons of the kingdom" in v. 38) and the tares (later identified as "the sons of the evil one" in v. 38) are to be permitted by divine

FAULTY VIEWS OF THE CHURCH'S PROSPECT
DURING THIS AGE

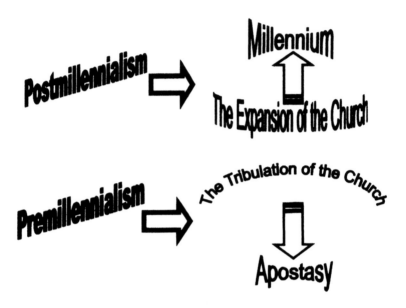

providence to grow (develop, mature, and have enlarging prominence, stature, and influence) until the judgment at the end of the age. The dual growth here predicated by Jesus has appeared contradictory to most types of eschatological thought. Postmillennialists have argued that if the wheat grows, it will crowd out and destroy the tares. Premillennialists have argued that if the tares grow, they will stunt and stop the growth of the wheat. Paradoxical though it may seem to our logic, according to Jesus both wheat and tares—good and evil—grow together until the harvest. It is not my purpose to explain in detail this paradox. Suffice to say that one of the profound truths implied in this paradox is that the very interaction of good and evil leads to the maturation of both the good seed and evil seed in their respective development. The main point that we must learn from Jesus' words is that there is both a negative and a positive perspective to be seen and balanced in any discussion of the prospects of the church in the gospel age.

THE BIBLICAL VIEW OF THE CHURCH'S PROSPECTS DURING THE GOSPEL AGE

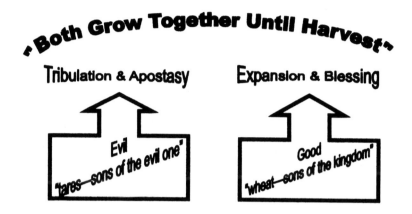

We may conclude with the words of John Murray with regard to the prospects of the church during the age intervening between Christ's two advents, "...interadventual history is characterized by tribulation, turmoil, strife, perplexity, wars and rumours of wars. Contemporaneous with this, however, is the universal expansion of the church."[1]

Chapter 17: Are Israel and the Church Distinct Peoples of God?
The Unity of, and Continuity Between, the Church and Israel

ARE ISRAEL and the church distinct peoples of God? This question raises the issue of *the church/Israel distinction*. This is the teaching of Dispensationalism that says that the church and Israel are two distinct peoples of God with whom God deals alternately in the history of the world. Popular, prophetic speculation about the Palestine and the nation of Israel is squarely based on the idea that the church is not a fulfillment or continuation of Israel (the new or the true Israel of God). Thus, ethnic Israel is thought to be the center of God's prophetic purpose. If, however, the church and Israel are not distinct, if the church is God's new Israel, than most of the prophetic speculation about the Middle East and the nation of Israel is simply groundless speculation.

One's understanding of the relation of Israel and the church is perhaps the single most important issue with reference to the question of Dispensationalism. Dr. Charles Ryrie has done everyone a favor by pointedly answering the question, "What is the *sine qua non* of dispensationalism?" His answer has three parts, but it is in its first part that in my opinion the most essential characteristic of Dispensationalism is stated: *"A dispensationalist keeps Israel and the Church distinct...a man who fails to distinguish Israel and the Church will inevitably not hold to dispensational distinctions."* [1]

There are two positions with reference to the issue of the relation of the church and Israel.[2] There is the position of classic Dispensationalism. This states that God has two distinct peoples, Israel and the church. These two must be kept separate. Thus, the promises made to Israel are fulfilled to Israel, not the church.[3]

There is the position of historic Christianity. This is that God has only *one people* in all ages. The promises made to Israel are fulfilled to the New Israel, the church.

I have called this position the historic position of the church.[4] I recognize that this might seem a somewhat prejudiced way of stating the matter. This description is warranted and may be supported by several facts of church history.

(1) The premillennialism that flourished among the early fathers in the early centuries of the church did not involve such a distinction. In fact, it would have been forthrightly rejected. Justin Martyr again and again speaks of the church as the Israel of God. Justin's testimony as one of the first two Christian writers who are demonstrably premillennial is very significant. Here is one representative statement among many:

> For the true spiritual Israel, and descendants of Judah, Jacob, Isaac, and Abraham (who in uncircumcision was approved of and blessed by God on account of his faith, and called the father of many nations), are we who have been led to God through this crucified Christ, as shall be demonstrated while we proceed. [5]

(2) The eschatological viewpoint that dominated the church through the Middle ages after the demise of the early premillennialism in the 4th century was not even premillennial. Obviously, the church/Israel distinction characteristic of Dispensational Premillennialism was rejected by such a viewpoint.

(3) Premillennialism itself did not find its way into any of the creeds resulting from the Reformation. As for the church/Israel distinction of Dispensationalism, the Westminster Confession of Faith and its daughter confession the 1689 Baptist Confession have parallel statements positively hostile to it.[6]

> The catholic or universal church, which (with respect to the internal work of the Spirit and truth of grace) may be called

invisible, *consists of the whole number of the elect, that have been, are, or shall be gathered into one, under Christ,* the head thereof; and is the spouse, the body, the fulness of him that filleth all in all.

(4) The revival of premillennialism in the 17th century did not necessarily entail the church/Israel distinction. Famous premillennialists have rejected it. Iain Murray provides extensive evidence that Charles Haddon Spurgeon, for instance, did not accept this distinction. Murray provides the following interesting specimen:

We have even heard it asserted that those who lived before the coming of Christ do not belong to the church of God! We never know what we shall hear next, and perhaps it is a mercy that these absurdities are revealed one at a time, in order that we may be able to endure their stupidity without dying of amazement.[7]

(5) As the above quotation implies, the church/Israel distinction was developed during the 19th century by such men as J. N. Darby.[8]

The answer to the question: "Are Israel and the church distinct peoples of God?" is of great practical importance in many respects. A strict church/Israel distinction means that much of the Bible is not "for the church" in its primary reference. Often application to the Church is not deemed appropriate.[9] The church/Israel distinction has had a practically antinomian effect on the 20th century church. The logical consequent of this perspective is to demand the reiteration and re-institution of the ethical norms of the Old Testament Scriptures before allowing their relevance to New Testament believers. "The redeemed of the present age are not under the law."[10] The relegation of the church to a less important status in the plan of God is the result of this distinction. It must share the stage with Israel. It is not the culmination of God's historical purpose. This carries with it a depreciation of the urgency of the church's mission and robs it of the confidence derived from the fact that it alone is God's instrument for the accomplishment of God's purpose and the evangelization of the world. Redemption in Christ is also depreciated by the church/ Israel distinction. It no longer is the center of God's world purpose. This point is made clear enough by the statement of Ryrie to the effect that Dispensationalists assert that God's purposes center in His glory, rather than the "single purpose of salvation".[11] Further, there is the inevitable tendency, though long-resisted and frequently denied, for the church/Israel distinction to have the logical result of teaching a different way of salvation for Israel.[12]

For all these reasons, it is crucial that we explore the teaching of the Bible on this important point. A balanced approach will be provided by studying two balancing, biblical perspectives in this chapter and the next.

- *The Unity of and Continuity between the Church and Israel*
- *The Superiority of the Church to Israel*

The Unity of and Continuity between the Church and Israel

Under this heading two questions must be answered. Is the church one with Israel and the continuation of Israel—in other words—the New Israel of God? Having answered that question with an emphatic yes, the second question will have to be addressed, How can this be? Thus, we must first *demonstrate* and then *defend* the unity of the church and Israel.

The Unity of the Church and Israel Demonstrated

Six lines of argument prove that the church is the true and new Israel of God.

First, the term, church (ekklesia), is used to describe the congregation of Israel. The evidence for this is twofold. *Ekklesia* is used in the Septuagint (the Greek version of the Old Testament in use at the time of the writing of the New Testament) to translate QAHAL. QAHAL, the Hebrew word for assembly, is translated by *ekklesia* approximately 70 times in the Old Testament. The following are representative specimens:

Deuteronomy 31:30 Then Moses spoke in the hearing of all the *assembly* of Israel the words of this song, until they were complete:

1 Kings 8:14 Then the king faced about and blessed all the *assembly* of Israel, while all the *assembly* of Israel was standing.

Micah 2:5 "Therefore, you will have no one stretching a measuring line for you by lot in the *assembly* of the LORD.

It is also used in the New Testament to describe the congregation of Israel.

Acts 7:38 This is the one who was in the *congregation* in the wilderness together with the angel who was speaking to him on Mount Sinai, and *who was* with our fathers; and he received living oracles to pass on to you.

Hebrews 2:12 saying, *"I will proclaim Thy name to my brethren, in the midst of the* congregation *I will sing Thy praise."*

Since the same term is used to describe God's people in both Old and New Testaments, this argues forcibly for the unity of God's people. It certainly refutes the strange statement often heard from Dispensationalists that *the church is not in the Old Testament.* This does not mean, of course, that we should simply equate the church in the New Testament with the church in the Old Testament or Israel. It does suggest, however, that they are not two distinct and separate peoples of God.

Second, the constitutive principle of Israel is the same as that of the church. The people of God become the people of God by God's electing, redeeming, covenant-making activity. It was in this way that Israel was constituted the people of God (Deut. 5:2, cf. Exod. 19:5; Deut. 7:6ff.; 13:5; 14:2; 21:8). The church became God's people by being elected, redeemed, and covenanted in Christ. How many elections, redemptions are there? Ultimately, there is just one (Rom. 3:25; Acts 4:12). The election and redemption of Israel were typical of the election and redemption in Christ. There can, then, be ultimately only one people of God. The election of Israel is typical of the election of the church. If that which constituted Israel the people of God was in its character typical and preparatory, Israel itself can scarcely be other than typical in character. The typical relation of Israel to the church confirms, however, the unity of the people of God. It confirms, in other words, that there is ultimately only one people of God.

Third, the New Testament directly asserts that the church is the true Israel of God. Five passages will be cited at this point.

1 Corinthians 10:18 calls us to "Behold Israel after the flesh." Hodge's comments are appropriate: "Israel after the flesh, i.e. the Jews, as a nation, as distinguished from Israel *after the Spirit*, or the spiritual Israel or true people of God. As Israel was a favorite term of honor, Paul rarely uses it for the Jews without some such qualification."[13]

Romans 2:28 and 29 are very clear about who the true Jews are:

> 28 For he is not a Jew who is one outwardly; neither is circumcision that which is outward in the flesh. 29 But he is a Jew who is one inwardly; and circumcision is that which is of the heart, by the Spirit, not by the letter; and his praise is not from men, but from God.

Some wish to restrict the terminology used in these verses to physical Jews who have become spiritually circumcised. The following considerations contradict this line of thought. (1) The statements of verses 26 and 27 assert that the uncircumcision of the Gentile will be regarded as circumcision if he meets the spiritual qualifications. (2) The absoluteness of Paul's statements also exclude this understanding: "He is not a Jew who is one outwardly.... He is a Jew who is one inwardly...by the Spirit, not by the letter." This absolutism precludes the insertion of another national qualification for Jewish-ness. (3) The subsequent statements by Paul in Romans (now to be considered) also preclude this understanding.

Romans 9:6–8 is also straightforward on this issue:

> 6 But *it is* not as though the word of God has failed. For they are not all Israel who are *descended* from Israel;

7 neither are they all children because they are Abraham's descendants, but: "through Isaac your descendants will be named." 8 That is, it is not the children of the flesh who are children of God, but the children of the promise are regarded as descendants.

Some also attempt to limit this verse to spiritually circumcised, physical Israelites. The statement of verse 8 prevents this. "The children of the promise are regarded as descendants." Who are the children of promise? Clearly, they are Christians, all Christians, even Galatian Gentile Christians (Gal. 4:28).

Philippians 3:3 also makes clear that the qualifications to be the new and true circumcision are not physical: "for we are the *true* circumcision, who worship in the Spirit of God and glory in Christ Jesus and put no confidence in the flesh..." Paul is here countering the claims of the Judaizers he has mocked in verse 2. They are "the mutilation" as he has called them in that verse. We, Christians, he asserts, are the circumcision. (The word, *true*, is added by the NASB.) Thus, the Christian community is seen as the Israel of God. Several things confirm this understanding. According to Acts 16 there was no Jewish synagogue in Philippi. Thus, the Philippian believers were not in the main converted Jews, but saved Gentiles. "Circumcision" is synonymous with "Israel" (Eph. 2:11 and Rom. 3: 29, 30). In the phrase, *put no confidence in the flesh* (and the succeeding verses), Paul denies that fleshly (physical) qualifications are in any way relevant to being one of the true circumcision. The conditions, therefore, for being identified as the true circumcision are exclusively spiritual.

Galatians 6:16 describes the church as the Israel of God: "And those who will walk by this rule, peace and mercy be upon them, and upon the Israel of God." Some have interpreted the Israel of God as equivalent to believing Jews. This interpretation, however, contradicts the entire context of this statement. The whole letter is a rebuttal of the Judaizing thought which demanded in addition to Christ Jewish-ness. Will Paul now at the end of such a letter implicitly require ethnic Jewish-ness for membership in the Israel of God? This is unthinkable. There is a total, spiritual devaluation of ethnic Jewish-ness in this epistle (Gal. 3:29; 4:26; Gal.

5:6; 6:15)! I once had a professor in seminary who said that you can only make spiritual Israelites out of physical Israelites, spiritual Englishmen out of physical Englishmen, and cooked carrots out of raw carrots. Paul would not have agreed. He believed that the gospel could make spiritual Jews out of physical Gentiles.

Fourth, the characteristics and privileges of Israel are assumed by the church. The massive evidence for this is easily summarized by way of the following table.

Old Israel or Church	New Israel or Church
1. Saints (Num. 16:3; Deut. 33:3)	1. Saints (Eph. 1:1; Rom. 1:7)
2. Elect (Deut. 7:6, 7; 14:2)	2. Elect (Col. 3:12; Titus 1:1)
3. Beloved (Deut. 7:7; 4:37)	3. Beloved (Col.3:12; 1 Thess 1:4)
4. Called (Isa. 41:9; 43:1)	4. Called (Rom. 1:6, 7; 1 Cor.1:2)
5. Church (Ps. 89:5; Mic. 2:5 (LXX) Act. 7:38; Heb. 2:12)	5. Church (Eph. 1:1; Acts 20:28)
6. Flock (Ezek. 34; Ps. 77:20)	6. Flock (Luke 12:32; 1 Pet. 5:2)
7. Holy Nation (Exod. 19:5, 6)	7. Holy Nation (1 Pet. 2:9)
8. Kingdom of Priests (Exod.19:5, 6)	8. Kingdom of Priests (1 Pet. 2:9)
9. Peculiar Treasure (Exod. 19:5, 6)	9. Peculiar Treasure (1 Pet. 2:9)
10. God's People (Hos. 1:9, 10)	10. God's People (1 Pet. 2:10)
11. Holy People (Deut. 7:6)	11. Holy People (1 Pet. 1:15,16)
12. People of Inheritance (Deut. 4:20)	12. People of Inheritance (Eph. 1:18)
13. God's Tabernacle in Israel (Lev. 26:11)	13. God's Tabernacle in Church (John 1:14)
14. God walks among them (Lev. 26:12)	14. God walks among them (2 Cor. 6:16–18)
15. Twelve Patriarchs	15. Twelve Apostles
16. *Christ married to them* (Isa. 54:5; Jer. 3:14; Hos. 2:19; Jer. 6:2; 31:32)	16. Christ married to them (Eph. 5:22, 23; 2 Cor. 11:2)

Fifth, the classic passages that speak to the relation of the church and Israel clearly teach the unity and the continuity between them. Here I would like to point out three passages in which Paul pointedly addresses the relation of the church to Israel.

Galatians 3:29 is the first passage: "And if you belong to Christ, then you are Abraham's offspring, heirs according to promise." Paul's main contention in verses 15 through 29 is that the promise of the Abrahamic covenant is more ultimate in the history of redemption than the Law. This points to the fact that it is promise, rather than law, which is the determining factor in God's covenant dealings. Paul points out that the Abrahamic covenant's promise was made with Abraham's Messianic Seed, verses 16 and 19. In verses 23 through 29 Paul points out the implication of all this by introducing the concept of union with Christ by faith. We are united with this Messianic Seed if we believe, no matter our nationality. In virtue of this, the church also is Abraham's seed. Paul tells the Gentile, Galatian Christians in verse 29 "you are Abraham's seed."

Here Paul takes that which was the boast of the Jews—that they were Abraham's seed—and transfers that title of honor to the church (John 8:33, 39). More importantly he regards the Messianic Seed and those in union with Him as the one, ultimate, eschatological fruition of this Abrahamic covenant.

Romans 11:16–24 is the second passage that plainly addresses the relation of the Church to Israel.

16 And if the first piece *of dough* be holy, the lump is also; and if the root be holy, the branches are too. 17 But if some of the branches were broken off, and you, being a wild olive, were grafted in among them and became partaker with them of the rich root of the olive tree, 18 do not be arrogant toward the branches; but if you are arrogant, *remember that it is not you who supports the root, but the root supports you.* 19 You will say then, "Branches were broken off so that I might be grafted in." 20 Quite right, they were broken off for their unbelief, but you stand by your faith. Do not be conceited, but fear; 21 for if God did not spare the natural branches, neither will He spare you. 22 Behold then the kindness and severity of God; to those who fell, severity, but to you, God's kindness, if you continue in His kindness; otherwise you also will be cut off. 23 And they also, if they do not continue in their unbelief, will be grafted in; for God is able to graft them in again. 24 For if you were cut off from what is by nature a wild olive tree, and were grafted

contrary to nature into a cultivated olive tree, how much more shall these who are the natural *branches* be grafted into their own olive tree?

These verses contain an extended analogy comparing the people of God to an olive tree. The "rich root of the olive tree" (vvs. 16, 17) is clearly a reference to the Patriarchs with whom the Abrahamic covenant was made (11:1 and 11:28 and the following considerations). The physical nation Israel is likened to the natural branches of this cultivated olive (vvs. 14–16, 19, 24.) (Note also the Old Testament passages where Israel is compared to an olive tree: Jer. 11:16, 17; Hos. 14:6). Many, though not all (vvs. 5, 17), of these natural branches have been broken off, rejected from covenant blessing. Gentile Christians have been grafted into the tree contrary to nature. That is to say, they have been made partakers of covenant blessing (vvs. 17, 24). All of this points to the organic and covenantal unity of the people of God. There is one olive tree! It embraces the root, Abraham and the patriarchs, the natural branches, national Israel, and the ingrafted branches, Christian Gentiles. All these are included in the one olive tree. Most instructive also is what is not said by Paul. He does not say the wild olive becomes a cultivated olive. He does not say that with the *"church age"* a new olive tree or even a fig tree has been planted. Paul's teaching in this passage is a very hostile environment for the separation of the church and Israel taught by Dispensationalism.

Ephesians 2:11–19 is the third key passage.

11 Therefore remember, that formerly you, the Gentiles in the flesh, who are called "Uncircumcision" by the so-called "Circumcision," *which is* performed in the flesh by human hands—12 *remember* that you were at that time separate from Christ, excluded from the commonwealth of Israel, and strangers to the covenants of promise, having no hope and without God in the world. 13 But now in Christ Jesus you who formerly were far off have been brought near by the blood of Christ. 14 For He Himself is our peace, who made both *groups into* one, and broke down the barrier of the dividing wall, 15 by abolishing in His flesh the enmity,

which is the Law of commandments *contained* in ordinances, that in Himself He might make the two into one new man, *thus* establishing peace, 16 and might reconcile them both in one body to God through the cross, by it having put to death the enmity. 17 *and He came and preached peace to you who were far away, and peace to those who were near;* 18 for through Him we both have our access in one Spirit to the Father. 19 So then you are no longer strangers and aliens, but you are fellow citizens with the saints, and are of God's household,

In this passage we are once again and even more explicitly confronted with the unity and continuity which exists between the church and Israel. The teaching of this passage may be summarized under three assertions.

Gentiles were once afar off. Verse 11 makes clear that in this passage Paul is addressing Gentile Christians. Verse 12 describes the condition of the Gentiles as one of being:
- separate from Christ
- excluded from the commonwealth of Israel
- strangers to the covenants of promise
- those who have no hope
- without God in the world.

Gentiles are now made nigh. In verse 13, Paul does not explicitly reiterate what it is that Christian Gentiles have been brought near to. Two contextual considerations, however, put beyond doubt that to which Gentiles have been brought nigh. The *"bringing near"* of verse 13 must be defined in terms of the separation and exclusion of immediately preceding context in verse 12. The two verses are obviously related and mutually defining. It is the blessings enumerated in verse 12 to which the Gentiles have been brought nigh. This includes the blessings of Christ, hope, and God, but cannot exclude the blessing of being brought near, incorporated into, the commonwealth of Israel. The *"bringing near"* is also defined in the succeeding context. In verse 19 by way of conclusion.[14] Paul does explicitly fill in what Gentiles have been brought near to. They are now "fellow-citizens with the saints."

Saints, here, is obviously a designation of Jewish saints. *Fellow-citizens* is related to the root found in verse 12 in the word, commonwealth, in the phrase, *commonwealth of Israel.*[15] This makes clear the precise idea of verses 14 and 15. The uniting of Jew and Gentile does not occur via the creation of a new entity with no continuity with God's former covenant dealings. Jews and Gentiles are united as fellow citizens in the "new" Israel. The "one new man" of verse 15 is practically equivalent to the New Israel. Not in a church out of relation to Israel, but in the New Israel are Jew and Gentile united, united via the ingrafting or bringing near of the Gentiles.

The bringing near of the Gentiles occurs through the work of Christ (vvs. 13–18). Christ has demolished the separating wall that kept the Gentiles out of Israel. Any teaching that envisions the future revival of national Israel as God's covenant people is a virtual re-creation of this separating wall and an affront to the Christ who in the finality of His cross work demolished it. The finality and eschatological character of Christ's cross forbids any undoing of its effects.

As one contemplates Galatians 3, Romans 11 and Ephesians 2, one wonders how Paul could have more thoroughly or explicitly rejected the church/Israel distinction taught by Dispensationalism.

Sixth, the Scriptures teach the eschatological unity of the people of God. The ultimate fruition of history is, according to the Bible, one people of God. When the Scriptures are examined they teach that God's people are one in essence throughout the ages of history. Here, however, we raise the question: What of the eternal state, the future era, the age to come? Will there be two distinct peoples of God then? Several clear passages anser with a firm, *"No!"*

For example, Matthew 8:11 and 12 is clear in its answer to this question.

> 11 And I say to you, that many shall come from east and west, and recline *at the table* with Abraham, and Isaac, and Jacob, in the kingdom of heaven; 12 but the sons of the kingdom shall be cast out into the outer darkness; in that place there shall be weeping and gnashing of teeth.

Gentiles are saved and are drawn into the kingdom of heaven. Jews—the children of the kingdom—are cast out. This implies, of course, that saved Jews remain in. Gentiles and Jews are, thus, one with Abraham, Isaac and Jacob in the eschatological kingdom.

John 10:16 is also clear:

> 16And I have other sheep, which are not of this fold; I must bring them also, and they shall hear My voice; and they shall become one flock *with* one shepherd.

There shall be one fold of both Gentile and Jewish sheep. This is true *now* in the present age of the inaugurated kingdom. It is also true in the consummate kingdom of the age to come.

Hebrews 11:39–40 also teaches the very same thing:

> 39 And all these, having gained approval through their faith, did not receive what was promised, 40 because God had provided something better for us, so that apart from us they should not be made perfect.

The writer has enumerated many Old Testament heroes of the faith. He now states that while they gained approval, they did not receive what was promised. This is explained by the comment that God did not wish them to be made perfect apart from "us". This is clearly a reference to New Covenant believers. Being made perfect has reference to the "promise" or "goal" repeatedly mentioned in the preceding context (4:1; 8:6; 9:15; 11:3, 13, 17). Here, then, is an explicit statement that all of God's people in both the Old Testament and New Testament will enjoy the eternal inheritance together.

Revelation 21:9–14 is the climactic statement of the New Testament with regard to ultimate oneness of the people of God.

> 9 And one of the seven angels who had the seven bowls full of the seven last plagues, came and spoke with me, saying, "Come here, I shall show you the bride, the wife of the Lamb." 10 And he carried me away in the Spirit to a great

and high mountain, and showed me the holy city, Jerusalem, coming down out of heaven from God, 11 having the glory of God. Her brilliance was like a very costly stone, as a stone of crystal-clear jasper. 12 It had a great and high wall, with twelve gates, and at the gates twelve angels; and names *were* written on them, which are *those* of the twelve tribes of the sons of Israel. 13 *There were* three gates on the east and three gates on the north and three gates on the south and three gates on the west. 14 And the wall of the city had twelve foundation stones, and on them *were* the twelve names of the twelve apostles of the Lamb.

In the New Heavens and New Earth, there is one city, one bride. Its gates bear the names of the twelve tribes of Israel. Its foundations bear the names of the twelve apostles of the Lamb. Symbolism could not more clearly teach the eschatological unity of the people of God of the church and Israel.

Several lessons are forcibly underscored by the above demonstration that the church is the new and true Israel of God. There is a legitimate, direct application of Old Testament prophecy about the future of Israel to the church (Cf. Isa. 54:1–3 with Gal. 4:26ff.). The history of the Bible has a single theme, redemption. It may and ought to be read so. The doctrines of the New Testament must be understood and can only be rightly understood in light of their Old Testament origins. The dignity of the church is enhanced by the realization of its heritage in Old Testament Israel. It is the culmination of God's age-long purpose of redemption, one with and the heir of all His covenant dealings.

The Unity of the Church and Israel Defended
The Problem Displayed

We have seen that the church is regarded as the New Israel in the New Testament. But how can this be? How and why is it proper for the mainly Gentile church to be regarded as Israel, the New—the true—Israel of God? Granted that the New Testament does so regard Israel, how is this estimate to be defended in light of the Gentile character of the church?

The Problem Illustrated

Just in case the difficulty we are now facing is not clear enough already, it may be pointedly illustrated by a consideration of the Old Testament and New Testament data with respect to the New Covenant. In Jeremiah 31:31–34, the promise of a new covenant is repeatedly and emphatically addressed to Israel, to be specific, the House of Israel and the House of Judah. Jeremiah 31:31 affirms: *"Behold, days are coming," declares the LORD, "when I will make a new covenant with the house of Israel and with the house of Judah."* The New Testament just as repeatedly and just as emphatically claims these promises of the New Covenant as the church's. The cup of the new covenant is the cup that the church drinks in the Lord's Table (Matt. 26:28; 1 Cor. 11:23–25). The Apostle to the Gentiles and other ministers of the church are "servants of the new covenant" (2 Cor. 3:2–6). Jesus the mediator and high priest of the church is such in virtue of the new covenant (Heb. 8:6–13; 10:16–18; 13:7, 17; 13:20, 21).

All this is, of course, another proof of the unity of the church and Israel. If the promise made to Israel is fulfilled to the church, the church in some sense must be Israel. Otherwise the terms of the promise have been broken. These passages, therefore, disprove the so-called literal or national interpretation of the New Covenant and underscore a principle of biblical interpretation vital to proper eschatology. The New Testament interpretation of the Old Testament is the final authority on its proper interpretation. Any interpretation that ignores or contradicts the New Testament use of an Old Testament passage is wrong. It is surprising how many people have more confidence in their own interpretive principles than they do in those of the New Testament.

But the question is this. Granted that the New Covenant is fulfilled in and to the church, How can this be? How can the Apostle to the Gentiles call himself a minister of the New Covenant? How can promises made to Israel be fulfilled to a mainly Gentile church? How can this divine procedure be justified? How is it justifiable to regard the (mainly Gentile) church as the New Israel?

The Problem Solved
There are two lines of thought that explain and validate the New Testament identification of the church as the New Israel.

The first line of thought is that the promises made to Israel may be fulfilled to the church *because the nucleus of the church was and is the elect remnant of the nation Israel.*

The promises to the nation, Israel, contained a conditional element. Of course, they were not completely dependent on human obedience. The condition of human obedience was contained in the context of God's sovereign purpose. Yet while they are to be understood within the framework of divine sovereignty, the conditional element is clear (Exod. 19:5, 6). Only faithful Jews could lay claim to the promises. That there would be such the divine purpose would secure, but that all Jews would be faithful was no where certified (Rom. 11:3f).

Further, the promises to the nation were repeatedly fulfilled only to the remnant of faithful Jews. This was true of the Exodus generation. A whole generation to whom the promise of the land had been proclaimed died without receiving it. The generation of the Exile also illustrates this. The promise of a return to the land in Jer. 29:10–14 was not fulfilled to all, but only to some—a faithful remnant. Thus, too, the promise of the new remnant is given. The promise of the New Covenant is fulfilled only to a faithful remnant (Rom. 11:1–10; Isa. 59:20, 21).

Finally, it was prophesied that the promises of the New Covenant would be extended also to the Gentiles. Isaiah, as well as Jeremiah, prophesied the New Covenant (Isa. 54:8–10; 55:3). He clearly foretold that the blessing brought to Israel would overflow to the Gentiles (Isa. 19:25; 42:1–6; 49:5, 6; 52:13–15; 54:1–3; 56:1–8).

The second line of thought that justifies identifying the church as the New Israel is that *the head of the church was and is the Messiah of Israel.* Both in Gal. 3:6–29 and again in 2 Cor. 1:19, 20 the promises made to Israel are regarded as fulfilled in Christ. He is profoundly the seed and the Israel to whom the promises were made and fulfilled. He is the possessor as the epitome and embodiment of faithful Israel of all the promises. This is a most literal fulfillment of those promises since Jesus was Jewish.

2 Corinthians 1:19 For the Son of God, Christ Jesus, who was preached among you by us—by me and Silvanus and Timothy—was not yes and no, but is yes in Him. 20 For as many as may be the promises of God, in Him they are yes; wherefore also by Him is our Amen to the glory of God through us.

If, however, the promises belong by divine grant to Him, He may certainly share them with whomever He will. Or in other words, whoever is one with Christ in virtue of that possesses the promise. This is, of course, especially the point in Galatians 3:29:

And if you belong to Christ, then you are Abraham's offspring, heirs according to promise.

The teaching of the New Testament that the church is the New Israel of God is a quite literal fulfillment of the predictions of the Old Testament.

Chapter 18: Are Israel and the Church the Same?

The Superiority of the Church to Israel

IN THE LAST CHAPTER we emphasized the unity and continuity between Israel and the church. Now we must emphasize the differences and discontinuity between Israel and the church. We have been saying that the church is the New *Israel*. Now we must emphasize that the church is the *New* Israel. Though there is basic unity between the church and Israel, there is also the development, advancement, and superiority of the church over Israel. The church may be considered as the true Israel and as such the continuation of the Old Covenant people. It may also be considered to be the New Israel and as such a new beginning by God. The church as the New Israel, superior to the Old Israel, will be examined under two headings:

The Superiority of the New Israel Demonstrated
Two classic passages demonstrate the superiority of the church as the New Israel.

The first is Matthew 16:16–20. In verse 18 Jesus makes the famous statement, "You are Peter and upon this rock I will build my church." There is no necessity of entering into many of the difficult exegetical details with which this passage confronts us. For our purposes, it is enough to establish three points.

First, Peter and the rest of the apostles are the rock or foundation of the church. This is the most natural understanding of this

passage and is corroborated by Paul's reflection on Matt. 16:18 in
Eph. 2:20: "having been built upon the foundation of the apostles
and prophets, Christ Jesus Himself being the corner *stone*..."
Paul's interpretation of Matt. 16:18 makes clear that it is all the
apostles and not merely Peter who are the foundation of the
church. It is important to point out that "the prophets" of Eph.
2:20 are not Old Testament prophets. The order shows that they
are not. Paul does not say prophets and apostles. He says rather,
apostles and prophets. Apostles and prophets are mentioned twice
together in the succeeding context. Both Eph. 3:5 and 4:11 plainly
refer to New Testament prophets.

Second, the apostles are officially (and not personally) the
foundation of the church. In other words, it is their teaching
which forms this foundation. This is the real point of Matt. 16:18.
Peter is proclaimed the rock because of his momentous confession of the identity of Jesus in the immediately preceding context
(Matthew 16:16). It is as apostles, those who witness to Jesus'
Lordship, that they are the rock of the church (1 Cor. 3:10,11). The
Apostles founded the church as the repositories of the truth
brought by Christ to the world (John 1:14–18; Heb. 1:1, 2a).

Third, the future tense of Jesus' prediction must be emphasized: "I will build My church." If the apostles are the foundation
of the church that Christ *will* build, it must have begun *at least in
one sense*, during their lifetimes and ministries—and not before.

The second passage is Matt. 21:33–43. In verse 43 Jesus declares: "Therefore I say to you, the kingdom of God will be taken
away from you, and be given to a nation producing the fruit of
it." This passage clearly assumes the unity of Israel and the
church. It is the same *vineyard* or *kingdom* that is given to both the
old and the new vine-growers. Nonetheless, in a very pro-
nounced fashion it manifests that the church is a new beginning.
The old nation headed by its corrupt leaders is to be destroyed. A
new nation (with new leaders—the Apostles) is to be given the
kingdom. It is to be noted that the term, nation, here is not plural
i.e., it is not a reference to the nations or the Gentiles. The term is
singular and is thus a reference to the church as God's new nation, His new Israel (1 Pet. 2:9). This transfer of privilege was
prophesied in the Old Testament (Isa. 65:12–15; 62:1, 2).

The Superiority of the New Israel Illustrated

The New Testament doctrine of the relation of the church and Israel is certainly paradoxical. How can the church be as old as Adam and as new as Christ's advent at the same time? How can the church be the same as Israel yet different? The caterpillar in nature provides a wonderful illustration. There is a metamorphosis of an ugly, crawling worm into a beautiful butterfly. The butterfly has characteristics and abilities not possessed by the worm, but is fundamentally the same animal. Albertus Pieters writing during the Depression provides another illustration.

> Recently many banks have been closed for a time, have been re-organized, and have resumed business, sometimes under the same name, sometimes with new names. In such a case it is quite often appropriate to speak of the re-organized institution as a new bank. New capital has been subscribed, new rules adopted, new directors elected, a new president and new cashier have been appointed. It is a new institution. Yet, for other purposes, it is a continuation of the former bank, particularly so with regard to the assets. He who signed a promissory note payable to the bank before it was re-organized must make it good to the new bank. For such purposes it is the same old bank. Precisely so stands the case between Israel and the Church. It is not that the Church is the "spiritual Israel," but that it is re-organized Israel. When we call the Church the New Covenant Israel, we are not allegorizing or spiritualizing the prophecies as some maintain; we are simply recognizing the historic fact of this re-organization, whereby the Church, in strict legality and in unbroken continuation, took over the assets of the national Israel, said assets being the promises of God—not some of them, but all of them. It took over the assets of Israel because it was, for legal and prophetical purposes, Israel, the only group having a legitimate right to the title.[1]

In Hebrews 9:8–10, the Bible provides its own illustration of this speaking of a reformation of Israel.

The Superiority of the New Israel Described

Here we ask the question, In what ways is the church *new and improved?* To this question two fundamental answers may be given. There is, first of all, a new universality. That is to say, God's people now include all the nations. This is the subject of extended prophecy in the Old Testament (Psa.22:25–31; 72: 8–11, 17; Isa. 19:19–25; 42:1–6; 49:5, 6; 52:13–15; 54:1–3; 62:1, 2; 65:12–15; 56:1–8; 66:21). The New Testament regards the inclusion of the Gentiles in God's people as the fulfillment of prophecy (Acts 15:15–17; Rom. 15:7–12; Rom. 9:24–29). This characteristic of the New Israel is the subject of repeated comment by Paul (Gal. 3:23–29; Eph. 3:1–11; Col. 1:25–27; Rom. 16:25ff.). In these passages *the mystery* is seen to consist in this new universality. Classic Dispensationalism teaches that a mystery is something un-prophesied. It sees the church age as an unpredicted parenthesis in the history of the world. This is not the New Testament's definition of mystery. A mystery is something previously prophesied but not previously understood or experienced (Matt. 13:11–17; Rom. 16:25ff.).

In the New Israel there is also a new spirituality. There is a great stream of predictions beginning in the Old Testament continuing in the early parts of the New Testament and culminating in the day of Pentecost that forecast the coming of the Spirit in a new way to God's covenant people (Cf. Isa. 44:1–5; 59:20, 21; 11:1, 2; 42:1; Ezekiel, 36:26ff; 39:29; Joel 2:28ff.; Zechariah 12:10; Matt. 3:11 and its parallels). Both the language of the *baptism* and the *pouring out of the Spirit* imply the volume, deluge, or increased quantity of the Spirit (John 7:37–39; Acts 1:5, 8). All these predictions have their inaugural fulfillment in the coming of the Spirit on the day of Pentecost (Acts 2:5–47, esp. vvs. 16, 17 and the subsequent "*Pentecosts*" of the book of Acts). The signs of Pentecost signal the coronation of the Messiah (Acts 2:29–36) and indicate that an era of new spirituality had come upon the people of God. Upon the Old Testament Zion, the Spirit was sprinkled. His streams ran through her. Now the Spirit is to be poured out in abundance. Zion is to be literally plunged into and immersed in the Spirit. Mother Zion had been sprinkled, now she is to be baptized.

Surely the reality of the outpoured Spirit must exercise a formative and rejuvenating effect on our faith, hope, and aspirations for our lives, ministries, and churches. How it should hearten us to contemplate that we live in the time of the Spirit foretold by the prophets! The Spirit provides a new dynamic for missions. The outpouring of the Spirit is the dynamic of the new universality of God's people. It is the power of the Spirit that carries the church forward in its mission to all the nations (John 16:7–14; Acts 1:8; 2:3, 4). This points out to us the importance of the missionary task of the church. It is one of the peculiar tasks of the church in the New Covenant.

The new spirituality of the church and the outpouring of the Spirit is related to the unity of the church as the body of Christ. The Spirit now corporately indwells the people of God. The church is a spiritual temple (1 Cor. 3:16; Eph. 2:22; 1 Pet. 2:5). There is a new, pervasive spirituality about God's nation and temple. The Spirit had worked in individual Israelites, but now His work is corporate, church-wide. It is surely this new eschatological spirituality of God's people that lies behind Paul's phrase, the body of Christ. Such a phrase would automatically conjure up eschatological ideas in one acquainted with the Old Testament. "The body of the Messiah" would mean for Jews the eschatological people of God (Rom. 12:5; Col. 3:15; Eph. 4:3–7; 1 Cor. 11–13). Old Covenant Israel did not possess the spiritual unity, fellowship, and oneness of the body of Christ. The corporate spirituality, unity, and commonality of the church did not exist in Old Testament Israel. A Jonathan and David might hold sweet communion, but a Joab, Abner, and Saul also worshiped with them in the same congregation of Israel. There was a unity in the flesh, but not in the Spirit. There were regenerate Israelites, but never a regenerated Israel. Its constitution was fleshly, not spiritual. What a privilege fellowship in a true church is; the saints of the Old Covenant knew only its flashes and shadows![2]

Chapter 19: Has Christ Already Come?

ONE OF THE fundamentals of evangelical and orthodox Christianity is the doctrine of the bodily return of Christ to earth from heaven. It is essential to Apostolic Christianity that we believe that the unique, historical person known as Jesus of Nazareth, the Son of God, will one day return to this earth with the same resurrected but real human nature with which He departed. The classic and often cited proof of this doctrine is found in the words of the angels to the Apostles in Acts 1:11, "and they also said, 'Men of Galilee, why do you stand looking into the sky? This Jesus, who has been taken up from you into heaven, will come in just the same way as you have watched Him go into heaven'." This doctrine is confessed in the major creeds of the church and cannot be rejected without departing from the orthodox faith. It is not, therefore, the purpose of this section of our studies to argue for the bodily return of Christ. That doctrine is assumed. My purpose here is to take up the problems associated with what has become known as the imminence of Christ's return.

The New Testament clearly teaches the nearness and unknown time of the return of Christ and urges Christians to have an attitude of expectancy and alertness with regard to that return. When I speak of the imminence of Christ's return, that is what I am talking about. As professing Christians have struggled to understand and embrace this teaching, however, they have been tempted to doctrinal errors. A number practical excesses and doctrinal extremes in the history of the church have taken as their pretext the doctrine of the imminent return of Christ. It is my purpose to examine three such extremes in this section of our studies. These three extreme reactions to the New Testament doctrine of the imminence of Christ's return are *Hyper-Preterism, Pretribulationism,* and *Date-setting* (or, if you will, *Calculationism*). The first named of these views is the most serious and will be dealt with in the present chapter.

In order to understand Hyper-Preterism it is helpful to remind ourselves of the identity of preterism. Preterism was originally a method of interpreting the Book of Revelation originating within Roman Catholicism. Jesuits offered preterism as an alternative to the historicist method of interpretation that identified the Roman Papacy as the Beast or Antichrist. It is also to be contrasted with the system of interpretation known as futurism that was also presented by the Jesuits as an alternative to historicism. While futurism referred the events of the Revelation primarily to a future period of tribulation at the end of this age, Preterism declared that with very few exceptions its prophecies were fulfilled by or before the destruction of Jerusalem in A.D. 70. Much of postmillennialism has a strong preteristic tendency.[1]

In the present chapter, however, I am using the term, preterism, to describe more than a system of interpretation for the prophecies of the Revelation. Preterism has come to be promoted in recent years as a system of prophetic interpretation useful in explaining New Testament prophecy in general. That is to say, it tends to find in the events of A.D. 70 or before the fulfillment of *most* New Testament prophecies.

Hyper-Preterism, however, finds the fulfillment of *all* New Testament prophecy in those events. Hyper-Preterism is defended in a volume authored by J. Stuart Russell entitled *The Parousia*.[2] It is this thorough-going preterism which is our subject in this chapter.[3] In this rebuttal of Hyper-Preterism, we will first explain its assertions and then examine its arguments.

- **Preterism** teaches that *many* prophecies are fulfilled at the destruction of Jerusalem in 70 A.D.
- **Hyper-Preterism** teaches that *all* prophecies are fulfilled at the destruction of Jerusalem in 70 A.D.

Its Assertions

The Parousia attempts to examine every prophetic utterance not only in the Book of Revelation, but also in the entire New Testament. Russell may be allowed to state his amazing conclusions for himself.

> Our Lord affirms the same speedy coming of judgment upon the land and people of Israel; and He further connects this judgment with His own coming in glory, the Parousia. This event stands forth most prominently in the New Testament; to this every eye is directed, to this every inspired messenger points. It is represented as the nucleus and centre of a cluster of great events; the end of the age, or close of the Jewish economy; the destruction of the city and temple of Jerusalem; the judgment of the guilty nation; the resurrection of the dead; the reward of the faithful; the consummation of the kingdom of God. All these transactions are declared to be coincident with the Parousia.[4]

These assertions are so amazing that one might fail to take them literally. Suffice to say, that in the following pages of his conclusion and throughout the book, Russell makes clear that the parousia, resurrection, and judgment took place at the destruction of Jerusalem, though in "the region of the spiritual and invisible".[5] He even asserts that "Scripture prophecy guides us no further" than the events which took place at the destruction of Jerusalem.[6]

Its Arguments

An examination of Russell's closing summary in *The Parousia* reveals that there are two main arguments upon which he bases his bold system.[7] In the first place he bases his system on the language of imminence used in the New Testament with regard to the Second Coming. Such language is, of course, widespread. His contention is simply that taking such language seriously requires us to believe that Jesus' parousia actually took place during the lifetimes of at least some who originally were told to watch and wait for Christ's return because it was near. In the second place Russell builds his case on three passages which appear to assert that Christ would return within the lifetimes of at least some of his original disciples. Those passages are the following:

> Matthew 10:23 But whenever they persecute you in this city, flee to the next; for truly I say to you, you shall not finish *going through* the cities of Israel, until the Son of Man comes.

> Matthew 16:28 Truly I say to you, there are some of those who are standing here who shall not taste death until they see the Son of Man coming in His kingdom."

> Matthew 24:34 Truly I say to you, this generation will not pass away until all these things take place.

We will take up these arguments in reverse order.

The Argument from the Three Passages

Impressive as these references may seem at first glance, Russell's application of them to Christ's second coming or parousia cannot be sustained with regard to any of them.

Matthew 24:34 does refer to the then-living generation of Jews, but an examination of the context shows (as John Murray argues), that there is a contrast present with verse 36.[8] The "all these things" is contrasted with the "that day and hour" of verse 36. "That day and hour" is a reference to Christ's second coming. "All these things" must, therefore, be (as the use of similar phrases throughout the discourse suggests) a reference to the events surrounding the destruction of Jerusalem. It is not the Second Coming of Christ, but all the things connected with the destruction of Jerusalem that occurs during the lifetime of the generation of Jews living when Christ spoke these words.

Matthew 16:28 might seem an unambiguous statement that the second coming of Christ would take place during the lifetimes of Peter, James, and John. There are, however, a number of difficulties in the way of this plausible interpretation.

(1) Matthew 16:28 along with its parallel passages Mark 9:1

and Luke 9:27 each occur immediately prior to the account of the Transfiguration in their respective gospels. It is impossible to believe that this juxtaposition is coincidental. The language of Christ *coming in His kingdom* would appear, then, to be a reference to His transfiguration on the Mount which was a kind of precursor of His second coming in glory. Also suggestive of this identification is the reference to "some of those standing here" a clear reference to Peter, James, and John who accompanied Jesus up the Mount of Transfiguration.

(2) It might be argued that this identification contradicts the contextual reference in Matt. 16:27 to the fact that "the Son of Man is going to come in the glory His Father". Far from identifying the two comings the two verses are intended to contrast them by calling the one a coming in "the glory of His Father" and the other a "coming in His kingdom". It is significant that in the parallel passages in Mark and Luke the language of coming is not used with reference to the Transfiguration. This strengthens the view that there is an implied contrast with reference to Christ's glorious coming which is mentioned in each immediately preceding context. There is a contrast in Mark 8:38 and 9:1 between "the Son of Man...when He comes in the glory of His Father with the holy angels" and "seeing the kingdom of God after it has come with power." There is also a contrast in Luke 9:26 and 27 between "the Son of Man...when He comes in the glory of His Father with the holy angels" and "seeing the kingdom of God".

(3) Since Russell's book is named *The Parousia,* it is worth noting that in none of these passages (and certainly not in Matthew 16:28 and its parallels) is the word, parousia, used.[9] As we will see, this is a key exegetical fact.

Matthew 10:23's reference to "until the Son of Man comes" might again appear to be plausibly understood of Christ's second coming. The reference, "you will not finish going through the cities of Israel," seems to fit the preterist scheme that makes this coming take place at the destruction of Jerusalem in A.D. 70. Disagreement has, however, reigned over every aspect of the interpretation of Matthew 10:23. This itself should caution us against grounding our whole scheme of eschatology on such a text. The coming of the Son of Man referred to here has been explained as: (1) an afterwards unmentioned coming of Jesus to the cities of Israel during His earthly ministry (2) His transfiguration (3) His resurrection and/or outpouring of His Spirit (3) His coming in blessing by His Spirit on His apostles' ministries (4) His coming at the destruction of Jerusalem (5) His final coming in glory at the end of the age. Likewise the reference to the cities of Israel has been understood to refer to: (1) the literal cities of Israel of that day (2) any cities where Christ's ministers might flee for refuge to the end of the age, especially cities inhabited by professing members of God's people (3) the cities of a restored Israel during the great tribulation at the end of the age.

Such diversity of opinion among exegetes does not mean that a compelling interpretation of this text is impossible. The fact is, however, that I have no dogmatically held understanding of this text to offer. I can give my opinion, however, by way of several observations.

First, it is not necessary in order to avoid the extremes of Hyper-Preterism to maintain that all references to "the coming of the Son of Man" must refer to His final coming at the end of the age. We have already seen that Matthew 16:28 in all likelihood refers to the Transfiguration. There His coming is clearly a reference to His transfiguration on the Mount. Another such "coming" may be found in John 14:18 where the reference is probably to Jesus' post-resurrection appearances to His disciples or to the coming of His Spirit at Pentecost. We may be uncomfortable with the Bible using this terminology to refer to events beside the second coming of Christ in glory. It would certainly be simpler to dispose of Hyper-Preterism if we could argue that there is only one coming of Christ mentioned in the Bible, His coming in glory that takes place at the end of the age. We must remember, however, that the very idea of a *second coming* of Christ implies that there was a first coming (Heb. 9:27 and 28).

Here is the conclusion of the matter. If Matthew 10:23 did refer to a coming of Christ in judgment at the destruction of Jerusalem, this would not prove that such a coming was *the second coming*.

Second, the whole context of the statement in Matthew 10:23 appears to me limited and local. The commission given here to the twelve limits their ministry to Israel and tells them not go to Samaritans or Gentiles. This contrasts strikingly with the commission given them in Acts (Matt. 10:5, 6 with Acts 1:8). This does not mean that the commission of Acts 1:8 immediately abolished the commission of Matthew 10. Galatians 2:7–10 indicates that this commission to the Jews in some sense was assumed into the Great Commission to take the gospel to all the nations.

Third, there are striking parallels to Matt. 10:23 in Matt. 23:34 where again Jesus' disciples are warned that the living generation of Jews will "persecute [them] from city to city". This seems to confirm a limited reference for Matt. 10:23. This coming is, thus, to be contrasted with the coming of Christ in glory after the destruction of Jerusalem, the consequent captivity of the Jews, and the times of the Gentiles (Matt. 24:4–28 with Luke 21:24–28).

Fourth, the language of Matthew 10:16–22 is parallel in many respects to the language of the Olivet Discourse with reference to the days preceding the destruction of Jerusalem. Compare Matthew 23:34 and Mark 13:9 with verse 17; Mark 13:11–13 and Luke 21:12–17 with verses 19 through 22; and Matthew 24:9 and 13 with verse 22.

My conclusion is that the "coming" of Matt. 10:23 is a reference to His sending of judgment upon Jerusalem in A.D. 70 through the Roman armies. If we may trust the summary given of Stephen's ministry by the Jews in Acts 6:14, Stephen's teaching appears to confirm this conclusion. Thus, Matthew 10:23 does refer to the destruction of Jerusalem, *but it doesn't matter*. This *coming* must be distinguished from the coming of Jesus after the "times of the Gentiles". Luke's account of the Olivet Discourse makes this distinction absolutely clear. Luke 21:20–27 clearly teaches that the second coming in glory does not occur at the destruction of Jerusalem, but after the destruction of Jerusalem, the exile of the Jews into all the nations, the times of Gentiles, and the signs in the sky. All these things intervene between the destruction of Jerusalem and the second coming of Christ.

This study of the three foundational texts of Russell's Hyper-Preterist interpretation of Christ's parousia show how weak is the foundation upon which it is built. Against the house of Hyper-preterism a flood of biblical data regarding the parousia may be unleashed.

First, the word, parousia, itself means presence or arrival. A parousia of Jesus where He does not remain present in a renewed earth is biblically speaking really no parousia at all.

Second, the parousia brings with it the resurrection of the dead. A resurrection of the dead which is not visible, which takes place (to use Russell's words) only "in the region of the spiritual and invisible" is just no biblical resurrection at all (John 5:28 and 29). The biblical resurrection also carries with it the physical transformation of the world as the new home of the resurrected people of God (Rom. 8:19–23). Furthermore, It brings an end to the world of the ungodly and a new world in which righteousness dwells (2 Pet. 3:11–13). Clearly, the resurrection is not past already.

Third, the use of the word, parousia, in the New Testament is conclusive against a Hyper-Preterist interpretation of Christ's second coming. It occurs twenty-four times. There are six non-eschatological references to the arrival of men. It is used once of the eschatological arrival of the anti-Christ (2 Thess. 2:9). Its seventeen other occurrences refer to the parousia of Christ.

Fourth, Hyper-Preterism consistently carried out empties the New Testament of hope for the modern believer. If the rapture of the living saints, the resurrection of the dead saints, the coming of Christ are already past realities, if all prophecy is really fulfilled, then upon what do we base our hope for the future? The Hyper-Preterist has no hope to offer Christians for the future.

Fifth, Hyper-Preterism involves the supposition that hundreds of thousands of living saints were raptured into heaven at the coming of Christ in the destruction of Jerusalem. How could such a thing occur and there be no record of it? Furthermore, from whence did the continuing church spring if all believers were raptured from the world in A.D. 70? Must we assume that the church left on earth after that point were all hypocrites and unregenerates? Is the church today sprung from a congregation of hypocrites and false believers?

The Argument from Imminence

Russell also argues the necessity of his position from the language of imminence regarding Christ's return found in the New Testament. That argument brings us back to the overarching theme of this section of our studies, the imminence of Christ's return. Simply stated, Russell's question (and ours) is this: How could the New Testament assert the imminent return of Christ and command believers to be alert for that return if that return was at least 20 centuries in the future? Russell regards this problem as an impregnable fortress surrounding his Hyper-preterist castle.

It is necessary to introduce this discussion of *imminence* by saying something about the various definitions of the term, imminence. This has been a matter of no little importance in modern debates about prophecy.[10] Two different understandings of this word must be carefully distinguished.

There is, first, the definition assumed by R. H. Gundry. He comments as follows: "By common consent imminence means that so far as we know, no predicted event will necessarily precede the coming of Christ. The concept incorporates three essential elements: suddenness, unexpectedness or incalculability, and a possibility of occurrence at any moment."[11] He regards this definition as the standard one in the current debate about Pretribulationism. In this he is certainly correct. Gundry is not a Pretribulationist and does not believe in the idea that Christ's coming could occur at any moment. Thus, because he regards imminence as involving any-moment-ness, Gundry denies that the Bible teaches the imminence of Christ's return. He says, "The full force of the exhortations to watch for Jesus' return, then, does not require imminence of the Parousia."[12]

On the other hand, there is the perspective of the Reformed theologian, John Murray. John Murray believed that certain events had yet to occur before the parousia. Still, he could say, "there is in the New Testament a doctrine of imminence...."[13] For John Murray imminence simply means nearness. Gundry and Murray are, it is clear, working with two different definitions of imminence. It is *"any-moment-ness"* for Gundry, *"nearness,"* for Murray.

Two comments are appropriate. First, none of the common English versions ever use the words, imminent or imminence, of the second coming of Christ. The meaning of the English word cannot then be determined from the Bible. Since the word, imminence, is an English word, it is relevant and necessary to ask what its proper definition should be. Webster defines "imminent" to mean "likely to happen without delay; impending; threatening." This definition allows a meaning for the word that does not require that we regard imminence and *any-moment-ness* as equivalents.

Second, there seem to be good grounds upon which to maintain the use of the term, imminence. Thus, we will use the term as Murray does. It enshrines an important, New Testament emphasis on the nearness and in that sense the imminence or the *impending-ness* of the parousia.[14]

There is a doctrine of the imminence or the nearness of Christ's return, in the New Testament. The adjective, near, (engus) and its various relatives occur frequently in the New Testament with reference to Christ's return. It is this usage of the Greek word for *near* that is the primary foundation and regulative basis for affirming that the New Testament teaches the imminence of Christ's return. The relevant data may be classified under four headings.

1. The Adjective, Near
Matt. 24:33; Mark 13:29; and Luke 21:31 prophesy a time before the parousia when God's people will be able to know that it is near. Phil. 4:5 probably refers to the parousia, though there is a possibility that the reference is spatial rather than temporal. Both Rev. 1:3 and 22:10 contain the phrase, "the time is near," and include a reference to the parousia. although it is possible that certain preliminary signs may also be included.

2. The Perfect Tense of the Verb, Has Drawn Near
Here the key references are Romans 13:12; James 5:8; and 1 Peter 4:7. The meaning of the perfect tense in these passages is clear. In the past the parousia has drawn near and now in the present it remains in a condition of nearness.

3. The Present Tense of the Verb, Is Drawing Near
Here the references are Luke 21:28 and Hebrews 10:25. The "day," and with it "our redemption" are drawing near or approaching.

4. The Comparative, Nearer
The idea is that salvation was near when they believed, but that
now it is even more near The reference here is Romans 13:11.

The nearness of the consummation does not mean that there are
no preceding signs. According to Romans 13:11 something that
was near can become nearer. The present tenses of Luke 21:28
and Heb. 10:25 imply the same thing. The point of these passages
is surely not that since time has passed salvation must be nearer.
This is too trite to need saying. Rather the comparative and the
present tenses point to the observable occurrences and developments of certain signs of the parousia. The use of the phrase, "as
you *see* the day approaching" (Heb. 10:25) is particularly clear in
this regard. The teaching of the New Testament, then, regarding
the nearness of the parousia may be summarized as follows: (1) It
is drawing near. (2) It has come near. (3) It is now near. (4) It is
coming nearer.

There is a great and pressing question that such teaching raises. How consistently with the claims of truth and reality could
the New Testament and its writers believe that the parousia was
near at least 1900 years before the event? This is the question that
the Hyper-Preterists thinks cannot be answered by the one who
believes that Christ's coming is yet future. The answer to this
question is provided by five inter-related considerations.

1. The Inaugurated Eschatology of the New Testament
With the first advent of Christ the age of fulfillment, the consum-
mating era of world history, has dawned. The age to come, as we
have seen, has broken in, the present age is passing away (Heb.
6:5; 1 John 2:8; 1 Cor. 2:6; 1 Cor. 10:11; Heb. 9:26). The phrase, *"last
days,"* is without exception in the New Testament used of the era
between the inauguration and the consummation of the kingdom. The New Testament views our era as the relatively brief final era of history before the Day of the Lord. This requires that
terminology like that of "near", "nearer", be seen in the context of
the long, historical perspective.

2. The Delay Character of the Present Era

There is considerable evidence in the Olivet Discourse for a long delay before Christ's return (Matt. 24:48; 25:5; 25:14, 19; Luke 21:20–28). In the rest of the New Testament there is also evidence for a delay of a long, but undetermined length in Christ's return. Rev. 10:1–7 identifies the present gospel age as a period of divine delay for the purpose of preaching the gospel. This period of patient delay is in part what is meant by the mystery of God (Col. 1:26ff.; 1 Cor. 2:6–8; Eph. 3:6; Rom. 16:25–27).

This problem of delay is addressed explicitly in 2 Peter 3. It is the problem raised by the denial of Christ's return by the false teachers. Note verses 3 and 4.

> Know this first of all, that in the last days mockers will come with *their* mocking, following after their own lusts, and saying, "Where is the promise of His coming? For *ever* since the fathers fell asleep, all continues just as it was from the beginning of creation."

Because of the mocking of the false teachers, in verses 8 through 10 of this passage the problem of delay is addressed.

> 8 But do not let this one *fact* escape your notice, beloved, that with the Lord one day is as a thousand years, and a thousand years as one day. 9 The Lord is not slow about His promise, as some count slowness, but is patient toward you, not wishing for any to perish but for all to come to repentance. 10 But the day of the Lord will come like a thief, in which the heavens will pass away with a roar and the elements will be destroyed with intense heat, and the earth and its works will be burned up.

Here we are advised that the apparent slowness of the promised coming must be considered in light of three considerations. First, the divine perspective (v. 8) must be considered. Jesus is God. One day with Him is as a thousand years. In light of this the delay should not discourage us. Second, the momentous purpose of Christ's delay must be considered (vvs. 9, 15). The purpose is nothing less than the salvation of men. Such a momentous purpose means that even a long delay is understandable. Finally, the delay should be understood in light of the predictions of the Lord Himself (v. 10). The reference to the Lord coming like a thief alludes to the Olivet Discourse (Matt. 24:43). It reminds us that the Lord predicted that His coming would be long enough delayed that men may fall asleep waiting for Him and that wicked servants may doubt his return at all Matt. 24:43 and 48).

The predictions of the nearness of the Lord's return must not be divorced from the indications of delay that occur side by side with them in the New Testament. The nearness of Christ's return is a nearness consistent with some possible delay.

3. The Uncertain Timing of the Parousia

The uncertain timing of the parousia is spoken of frequently in the New Testament (Matt. 24:36, 42; 25:13; cf. Mark 13:32). These references are found in the Olivet Discourse. Thus, in the very discourse in which the nearness of the parousia is most explicitly asserted Jesus most emphatically asserts the unknown time of the parousia. The coming of Christ is not near in any sense that makes its time known. It is near, but its time is still unknown.

4. The *Sign-Character* of the Present Age

While distinct signs or precursors occur immediately prior to the second advent, the whole inter-adventual period is full of processes and developments which lead directly to the parousia. Living in the midst of such processes, how can we view the advent as anything but near? Around us the final developments, the closing processes of history are heightening to their climax in Christ's return. Two such processes are the world-wide preaching of the gospel (Matt. 24:14) and the mystery of iniquity (2 Thess. 2:7). It is in this light that Heb.10:25's statement that we "see the day approaching" is probably to be understood.

5. The Climactic Character of the Parousia

The events surrounding Christ's return are by far the most important events of history (2 Pet. 3:1–16). In general the more important an event is, the farther it casts its shadow of nearness.

Christmas in comparison to other holidays casts a longer shadow of expectation. The Bicentennial Fourth of July cast a much longer shadow of expectation than other Fourth of July's before or after 1976. Helpful illustrations may be drawn from the arena of geographical nearness. There is the fact that the signs stating the distance to major cities are placed farther out from them than those for smaller cities. I remember a sign on the interstate in Arizona near the Grand Canyon. It had two distances on it. Williams 27 miles. Los Angeles 459 miles. No Interstate would have a sign for Williams, Arizona, at a distance of 459 miles. Los Angeles deserved such a sign because it was bigger and more important. Los Angeles *is near* at a much further distance than Williams. There are the looming Rocky Mountains which because of their great size begin to look near as you drive towards them on the plains of Colorado long before a smaller hill would even be visible. Even so, the inconceivably more glorious event of the parousia must so attract our attention and preparations that all between pales into insignificance. John Murray remarks on Rom. 13:12:

> It is the nearness of prophetic perspective and not that of our chronological calculations. In the unfolding of God's redemptive purpose the next great epochal event correlative to the death of Christ, His resurrection and ascension, and the outpouring of the Holy Spirit at Pentecost is Jesus' advent in glory. This is the event that looms on the horizon of faith. There is nothing of similar character between the present and this epochal redemptive event.[15]

These considerations thoroughly justify the orthodox view that the second coming of Christ could be truly spoken of as near almost 2000 years ago. In this way they destroy the argument of the Hyper-Preterists based on the imminence of Christ's return. The New Testament nearness of Christ's return does not require that He return in the first century or at the destruction of Jerusalem in 70 A.D.

Chapter 20: Can the Date of Christ's Coming Be Calculated?

ON THE SHELF in my study not far from where I am sitting as I write this are two books which are representative (sadly) of a much larger body of literature. These books purport to calculate or predict the time of Christ's return. One purports to predict His return in 1988, the other in 1994. It is my purpose in this chapter to address the question of setting dates for Christ's return. Why do I take the time to deal with this subject? There are two reasons. First, there is the reality that calculating the time of Christ's return has been a recurrent problem in the history of Christian eschatology. Second, there is a reasonable forecast that date-setting fever will continue among professing Christians in the years following the dawn of the new millennium. The remedy for this is *Christ's Declaration that the Time of His Return Is Unknown* found in Matt. 24:36.

I am assuming two things in this chapter. First, the Bible predicts the yet future bodily return of Christ (Acts 1:9; 3:19, 20). Second, this return of Christ will not be secret, but public, glorious, visible, and universal (Matt. 24:24–27; 1 Thess. 5:1–4; 2 Thess. 1:6–10). My rejection of setting dates for Christ's second coming in no way means that I do not believe that Christ is coming.

Matthew 24:36 is the classic biblical rebuttal of the tendency of calculating the time of Christ's return. I intend to expound this text under three headings:

Its Brief Exposition

Matthew 24:36 reads as follows:

> But of that day and hour no one knows, not even the angels of heaven, nor the Son, but the Father alone.

By way of a brief or preliminary exposition of this passage, I want to say two things. First, when Christ refers to "that day and hour", he is referring to the day and hour or time of His second coming. The entire context puts this beyond doubt. Jesus has been speaking of His second coming in the preceding context (24:27, 30, 31). He goes on to speak of this event in the immediately succeeding context (24:37). He uses this exact language to speak of His second coming in the following context (24:42, 44, 50).

Second, Christ asserts here that knowledge of the time of His second coming is hidden from every intelligent creature. Of the time of His coming, Christ says, *"no one knows, not even the angels of heaven, nor the Son, but the Father alone."* Now this statement is from one viewpoint quite perplexing. It raises the question, If Christ is God and, therefore, omniscient or all-knowing, how can there be anything he does not know?

The solution to this question is suggested by *The 1689 Baptist Confession.* In Chapter 8, paragraph 2, it echoes the historic, orthodox doctrine of the person of Christ. There the Confession states that the Son of God possessed a "whole, perfect, and distinct" human nature. Thus, the Bible speaks of Him as a man physically or bodily. He was hungry, thirsty, and grew tired. The Scripture also speaks of him as a man spiritually or mentally. He grew and matured intellectually (Luke 2:40, 52; Heb. 5:8). Therefore, when we come to Matt. 24:36 there should be nothing surprising to us in Christ's assertion that there were some things He did not know. If we are not stumbled when we hear the Son of God say, "I thirst," there is no reason why we should be stumbled when we hear Him say that there is something He does not know. If we are not stumbled when the Scripture says that he grew in wisdom, then there is no reason for us to be stumbled when the Scripture declares that not even the Son knows the time of

His second coming. Jesus is speaking here as a man. He is not declaring to us the contents of the divine mind, but of His human intellect.

Christ here asserts that neither He, nor any other man, nor even the angels of heaven knew the time of His second coming. Think about the implications of that statement. Jesus' statement implies that God had not revealed the date of the end of the world to any of the men or angels by which God communicated to men in the Old Testament. It also implies that He had not revealed it to the Son by which He brought that revelation to conclusion in the New Testament. All of God's special revelation is brought to us either by the angels and men through whom God spoke in the Old Testament or through His Son and the other men through whom He spoke in the New Testament (Hebrews 1:1–2). Jesus is, thus, plainly teaching that the time of His coming is not a part of the revelation God chose to give men in the Word of God. Therefore, no amount of scholarship or genius, not even a whole life-time of study dedicated to the study of typology, numerology, or prophecy will ever find in Scripture some secret, figurative, mysterious revelation of the time-period of Christ's return. It has not been put in the Scriptures and no amount of searching will find it there.

Its Foolish Perversion

The "date-setters" are ready with an answer to this verse. They argue that, though we cannot know the day or hour of Christ's return, we can know the week, month or year. Speaking of Matt. 24:36 one has said, "However, this does not preclude or prevent the faithful from knowing the year, the month, and the week of the Lord's return".[1] Another has said, "Not surprisingly, when we have completed our study we will know much about God's timetable for the history of the world. But we will not know the day and hour of the actual end of the world when Christ is to come the second time".[2] Having said this the same author later concludes that the last day and return of Christ would be, if his calculations are correct, between Sept. 15 and Sept. 27, 1994.[3]

Now, frankly, such dealing with Scripture would be laughable, if it were not so serious. Can we read this passage of God's Word and conclude that Christ actually means to say that we cannot know the day or hour, but we can know the year, month, and week of Christ's return? Yet for the sake of displaying the decisive, biblical evidence against giving a timetable for Christ's return, the time must be taken to further confirm the meaning of this text.

It should be plain that the Bible nowhere clearly predicts the time of Christ's return. If it were plain, Christians would not need Bible teachers to write 500 page books unpacking the mysteries of biblical prophecy and numerology to show them the time. It should also be plain that the "date-setters" have been wrong hundreds and probably even thousands of times in such predictions. Thus, the burden of proof is on any person who after all this is going to tell us that we can know the week, month, or year of Christ's return. We want to know where the Bible anywhere teaches this. The whole drift of biblical teaching is plainly against such predictions. The date-setter, therefore, is obligated to show us why he believes we can know the week, month, or year. The burden of proof is on him. The fact is that he cannot prove that any such predictions of Christ's return are biblical. Before he wastes our time and emotions as servants of the Master, he has to prove this foundational assumption of his whole system. The fact is that he cannot.

Its Contextual Confirmation

False teachers have always quoted Scripture (2 Peter 3:16). The problem with their quoting of Scripture is that they quote it out of context. One of the great marks of false teaching is that it quotes Scripture, but without regard to its context.

This is also true of the perversion of Scripture that we are now considering. It quotes and interprets Matt. 24:36 without regard to its biblical context. It is, therefore, my purpose to show you very carefully what this verse means within its context. We will look at the immediately preceding context, the immediately succeeding context, and the broader New Testament context.

The Immediately Preceding Context

The significant thing that we learn about verse 36 when we read the preceding context is that it is a part of a contrast. Notice verses 34 through 36. What is the contrast?[4] There is a contrast between the "all these things" of verse 34 and "that day and hour" of verse 36. If "that day and hour" refers, as we have seen, to the second coming of Christ, to what does the phrase, "all these things," refer? To answer this question look at Matt. 24:1–3, for clearly, in their questions, the disciples were in danger of confusing two distinct events: the destruction of Jerusalem and the second coming of Christ. The contrast of verses 34 through 36 is intended to clear up this confusion for them. "All these things," therefore, refers to all those events associated with the destruction of the temple and Jerusalem. "That day and hour" refers to the events associated with the second coming of Christ proper.

Here we come to the crucial point for our purposes. How does Christ contrast these two events? The answer is plain. He gives a time-sign for the destruction of Jerusalem. He gives no time-sign for the second coming of Christ. Notice: "This generation will not pass away until all these things take place...but of that day and hour no one knows...." He says that the destruction of Jerusalem would take place within the life-time of the then living generation of Jews.

Now do you understand the contrast Jesus makes in these verses? He contrasts the giving of a time-sign for the destruction of Jerusalem with the giving of no time-sign for His Second Coming. He gives a very broad time-sign for the destruction of Jerusalem—this generation. The destruction of Jerusalem, he says, will occur sometime in the next forty years, but I give you no time-sign at all for my own coming.

What does this mean for our interpretation of Matt. 24:36? Is Jesus saying, what the date-setters assert, that we cannot know the day or hour, but we can know the week, month, or year? *Obviously not!* The contrast is not between the day and the month, but between a broad time-sign encompassing a period of forty years and no time-sign at all. Jesus determined the date of the destruction of Jerusalem to within forty years, but He gives no time-sign for His coming at all. What nonsense this makes of the claims of the date-setters to know even the year of Christ's coming! Far from knowing the week, month, or year, we do not even know the generation of Christ's coming!

The Immediately Succeeding Context
In the following context Jesus calls upon his disciples to be constantly alert for His return (Matt. 24:42–44, 50; 25:13). These commands to be alert for His coming assume that even then the timing of His coming was unknown. If only the week and month of Christ's return could be known, as the date-setters suggest, then we would not have to be constantly alert. Clearly, then, when Jesus says that you do not know the day or hour of my return, He means to say that its timing is completely unknown, therefore you must be always ready.

The Broader New Testament Context
The first passage that must be considered here is Luke 17:20–21.

> 20 Now having been questioned by the Pharisees as to when the kingdom of God was coming, He answered them and said, "The kingdom of God is not coming with signs to be observed; 21 nor will they say, 'Look, here *it is!*' or, 'There *it is!*' For behold, the kingdom of God is in your midst. "

The meaning of this passage has been disputed. The question concerns what Jesus means by the kingdom of God in verse 20. Not a few have thought that by the kingdom of God he meant the present, spiritual phase of the kingdom of God. Hence, they have interpreted the passage to mean that the kingdom of God does not come with observation because it is spiritual in character. Though that is a common interpretation, I do not believe that it is the right interpretation.

The correct interpretation begins by observing that verses 20 and 21 are closely connected with the following speech of Jesus. What is Jesus talking about in that following speech? Clearly, He is talking about His second coming. That is the time when the kingdom of God will come in power and glory at a future period.

It seems clear to me, therefore, that when Jesus speaks of His kingdom in verse 20 that He is referring to the future, glorious coming of the kingdom. Furthermore, it was clearly about this coming of the kingdom that the Pharisees were thinking in verse 20, when they raised the issue. I believe that what Jesus is saying is what one Greek lexicon says. It paraphrases: The kingdom of God is not coming "in such a way that its rise can be observed."[5] In other words, its appearance will be abrupt, sudden, and dramatic. This is the sense of v. 21b: *For behold, the kingdom is in your midst.*

Now a key word must be examined more closely. The Greek word, observation, found in verse 20 is translated *"signs to be observed"*. It comes from a verb that means to watch carefully. It is used of the Jews watching Jesus to see if He would heal on the Sabbath (Mark 3:2; Luke 6:7; 14:1). It is used of the spies who watched Jesus carefully to catch Him in His words (Luke 20:20). It is used of the Jews who plotted against Paul in Damascus and watched the gates carefully to ambush him when he left the city (Acts 9:24). It is used in Gal. 4:10 of the careful, superstitious observation of religious holy days. What then is its force here? Jesus is saying that no amount of careful observation or scrutiny will enable anyone to predict the time of Christ's return. No observation of history, no watching of the skies, no scrutiny even of the holy book will give any clue as to the time of Jesus glorious return.

The second passage to be considered as part of the broader New Testament context is Acts 1:6–7:

> 6 And so when they had come together, they were asking Him, saying, " Lord, is it at this time You are restoring the kingdom to Israel? " 7 He said to them, "It is not for you to know times or epochs which the Father has fixed by His own authority;

When the disciples asked about the restoration of the kingdom to Israel, their question was rooted in Old Testament prophecy. The Old Testament had, indeed, predicted "the time...when the saints...(would take)...possession of the kingdom" (Dan. 7:22). Now it may be that the disciples still had too carnal and national-istic an idea of what the restoration of the kingdom to Israel would mean, but it is clear that their hope for such a restoration was firmly built on biblical basis (Acts 3:21; Matt. 19:28). This restoration occurs, of course, in conjunction with the glorious appearance of the Messiah in His second coming.

Thus, the disciples are raising here the same question that Jesus answered in Matt. 24:36. It is not surprising, therefore, that Jesus answers them in language which is clearly dependent upon, and refers back to, Matt. 24:36. He refers to the Father just as He did in Matt. 24:36. There he said, "But of that day and hour no one knows, not even the angels of heaven, nor the Son, but the Father alone". Here He says, "it is not for you to know times or epochs which the Father has fixed by His own authority". The statements are clearly parallel, but there is one key point at which Jesus enlarges upon and interprets what He said in Matt. 24:36. You will notice that He does not speak of "the day and the hour". Now He speaks of "times or epochs".

Whatever these words more exactly mean, they plainly confirm the meaning that we have attached to the words of Jesus in Matt. 24:36. Thus, they plainly condemn the date-setters. When Jesus denies that we can know the day or hour, He is not contrasting this with the week, month, or year. Rather, He is denying that we can have any knowledge of the date of Christ's arrival. Not the day, nor the hour, nor the time, nor the epoch is within our grasp, and therefore not the week, month, or year.

The third passage is 1 Thessalonians 5:1–4:

> 1 Now as to the times and the epochs, brethren, you have no need of anything to be written to you. 2 For you yourselves know full well that the day of the Lord will come just like a thief in the night. 3 While they are saying, "Peace and safety!" then destruction will come upon them suddenly like birth pangs upon a woman with child; and they shall not escape. 4 But you, brethren, are not in darkness, that the day should overtake you like a thief;

The meaning of this passage is plain itself and also plain in light of Matt. 24:36 and Acts 1:6, 7. Paul here uses the same two words used in Acts 1:6–7: "times and epochs". He plainly says that there is no need to write them about such things because they already know that the day of the Lord is coming like a thief in the night. The phrase, *"thief in the night"*, is drawn from Matthew 24. The idea is plainly that Christ's coming is sudden and unexpected. This is confirmed by verse 3. That verse pictures the ungodly world as promising itself peace and safety when sudden and inescapable judgment overtakes them through Christ's return. Thus, Paul is plainly saying that he need not write them about the time of Christ's return, because they already know that its timing is unknown.

Its Concluding Application

The "date-setters" make predictions that time after time prove to be false. Thus, they are very akin to false prophets, and we may apply to such false teachers the warnings of Deuteronomy 18:20ff.

Deuteronomy 18:22 addresses the people of God regarding the false prophet with the command, "You shall not be afraid of him." These are the last words of Deuteronomy 18. They are perfectly applicable to the modern date-setters. Don't be afraid of them! Don't be worried by them! Don't be rattled by them! Don't be moved by them! Don't be made cautious by them! Don't give respect to their forecasts in any way! They may speak with a show of great learning. They may speak with amazing dogmatism. Still, don't be afraid of them.

Deuteronomy 18:20 commands of the false prophet: *"That prophet shall die."* False prophets in the Old Testament were to be put to death. We live no longer in the Old Testament economy. While we should not literally kill these false prophets, we should do everything we can to kill their influence. We should rebuke them, denounce them, warn people against them; and exercise church discipline against them.

Why is this an important duty for us to take to heart? Such false teachers give Bible-believing Christianity a bad name. They deceive and lead into sin immature believers. They bring scorn on the very doctrine they pretend to uphold, the second coming of Christ. People hear of such date-setting for the second coming of Christ and say to themselves, "Those crazy Christians are at it again!" We must tell people that we agree that the people who write and believe such books are terribly wrong, but we must tell them that this is so because the Bible itself condemns them.

Deuteronomy 18 also contains a command about the true prophet in verse 19: "Whoever will not listen to My words which he shall speak in My name, I Myself will require it of him." In Old Testament Israel the presence of false prophets did not mean that there were not true prophets to whom they had to listen. Similarly in our day the presence of false predictions of Christ's return does not mean that we may ignore all that Bible does teach about Christ's return. We must not allow all the extremism to steal from us the "blessed hope" of the appearing of our great God and Savior, Christ Jesus.

Chapter 21: Will Christ Come Before the Final Tribulation?
Arguments Against Pretibulationism

SUPPOSE YOU suddenly had no Bible and had to judge what the teachings of the Bible were from the shelves of Christian bookstores. From the many shelves of books containing manuals on the Pretribulation rapture and from the many popular novels sensationalizing this theory (with titles like *Left Behind!*), you would conclude that prominent among the teachings of the Bible was the Pretribulation rapture. You would certainly be surprised when—upon recovering your Bible—you searched and discovered that there was not one text supporting the Pretribulation rapture theory in all the Bible! You would be even more surprised to find many texts that seemed to strongly contradict it.

Pretribulationism, or the secret rapture theory, is the teaching that Christ will come for the church before the Great Tribulation at the end of the age. It is a distinctive feature of Dispensationalism. The teaching that Christ will come both before (secretly) and after (gloriously) a future tribulation (whatever terminology may be used for these *two comings*)[1] is justified by and based upon the church/Israel distinction of Dispensationalism. As we will see, only the strict separation of the church and Israel assumed by Dispensationalism can justify and ground this theory.

There are many reasons why a study of Pretribulationism is both necessary and important. First, the dogmatism with which this theory is believed and the divisive consequences of this dogmatism demand it. Its wide-spread incorporation into statements of doctrine in Fundamental and Evangelical churches excludes believers who reject this theory from membership or leadership in such churches. Second, since it is so widely believed, most pastors will almost certainly be confronted with the necessity of publicly or privately refuting it and defending their rejection of it. Third, and as we shall see, in a very real sense it is the source of many of the practical, destructive tendencies of the modern, popular eschatology. Finally, Pretribulationism must be examined because of its theological interest. It is the outgrowth and result of the view of the imminence of Christ's return at work in the resurgent Premillennialism of the 19th Century. Here the observation of Sandeen is helpful:

> But perhaps more important was the continually reiterated argument of the pretribulationists that the hope of Christ's return had to be an imminent hope or it was not hope at all. If one believes that a period of tribulation must first take place before the coming of Christ, they said, then he cannot look forward to the second advent but must wait only for greater suffering. Regardless of the question of scriptural justification for one point of view over the other, the pretribulationist position was certainly more likely to appeal to that portion of American Christendom which was attracted by the millenarian message.[2]

Though Pretribulationism is justified by means of the Dispensational church/Israel distinction, in all likelihood the doctrinal force which created this view was what Sandeen calls above "the imminent hope" of the 19th century Premillennialists.

We will follow a straightforward procedure. In this chapter we will present *Arguments Against Pretribulationism*. In the next chapter we will consider *Arguments for Pretribulationism*.

Arguments against Pretribulationism Presented

The Unity of the Church and Israel
In an earlier chapter the forceful, biblical reasons for rejecting the church/Israel distinction of Dispensationalism were examined.

Not withstanding the clear element of superiority in the church, the fundamental principle of the unity and continuity of the church and Israel was clearly established. We saw beyond any doubt that the church is the new and true Israel of God. If the church is the new Israel, this completely undermines Pretribulationism. This is so for three reasons.

First, it destroys the foundation of Pretribulationism, the alternate dealings of God with the church and Israel. The stiff division of time between the *Church Age* and the *Great Tribulation* can only be maintained in conjunction with a stiff division between the church and Israel. But such a division between the church and Israel is not taught in the Bible.

This Dispensational structure of the alternate dealings of God with Israel and the church is annihilated if the Bible teaches that the church is the continuation of Israel, or, in other words, the new Israel of God.

Second, if the Bible teaches the unity of the church and Israel, the whole rationale for the secret rapture theory is destroyed. One of the main props of Pretribulationism is the argument that the church will be taken out of the world before the *Great Tribulation*. This temporal deliverance is the practical rationale for the Pretribulation theory. It would be a mistake to assume, however, that this implies that no true saints will be on earth during the seven year tribulation. As a matter of fact, Pretribulationists hold that many people will be saved during the *Great Tribulation*. Unless, however, you believe in the strict church/Israel distinction, such saints belong to the church. If they belong to the church, then this destroys the whole practical rationale for a Pretribulational rapture—the deliverance of the church from the Tribulation! Without the Dispensational church/Israel separation, the whole point of the Pretribulation rapture is nullified.

Third, the unity of the church and Israel destroys the only hermeneutical defense of Pretribulationism. In other words, only the sharp division of the church and Israel allow Pretribulationists to explain many passages of Scripture in a way consistent with their theory.

Luke 17:22–37 plainly speaks of the Second Coming of Christ

and may be used to illustrate this assertion. This passage obviously does not have in view a Pretribulational rapture. The coming is universally visible (vvs. 23, 24). It brings immediate destruction to the wicked (vvs. 28–30). It is the coming that concerns Christ's disciples (v. 22, cf. vvs. 31–35).

Pretribulationists realize all this. Thus, they explain that Christ wasn't speaking to His disciples as representatives of the church, but as representatives of the saved Jewish remnant of Israel. (Pretribulational exegesis usually regards the disciples of Christ in the Gospels as representative of Israel and not the church.) Many obvious objections may occur to the reader with reference to this explanation. One point, however, is unavoidable. If no separation between the church and Israel exists, the only possible explanation of the passage from a Pretribulational standpoint is destroyed.

The Obvious Relation Between the Coming, Rapture, and Tribulation in Those Passages Where They Are Explicitly Related

Now I must explain that this argument is to some degree *ad hominem*. What I mean is that I do not accept the identification of the tribulation in a couple of these passages with the *"little season"* (Rev. 20:3) or final tribulation at the end of the age. Nonetheless most, if not all, Pretribulationists would, and therefore the argument holds against them.

If the Pretribulationists are correct, we would expect that we would find passages in the Bible where the Pretribulational order of events is clear. This order would be the coming of Christ and rapture of the saints[3] first and then the final tribulation. Interestingly, we find no passages where such an order is presented. Rather, we find several passages where the opposite order is clear.

Matthew 24:29–31 is a good example of this problem. Pretribulationists identify the tribulation of Matthew 24:14–28 as what they call *the Great Tribulation*. This presents a problem for them because there is no mention of a coming or rapture prior to this tribulation. The order of the passage is clear. There is the tribula-

tion and after that in verses 29 through 31 there is the gathering of
the saints at the coming of Christ.

The entire book of Revelation, chapters 1 through 22, presents
a similar difficulty for Pretribulationists. The typical Dispensational and Pretribulational understanding of Revelation is as
follows:

Chapters 1–3	Chapters 4–18	Chapter 19	Chapter 20	Chapters 21–22
Church Age	Tribulation	2nd Advent	Millennium	Eternal State

Again assuming for the sake of argument that this presentation is
correct, the clear order is the *Church Age (with no mention of a
Pretribulational rapture)*; the Tribulation, the Second Advent *(issuing in the* first *resurrection)*. Again the order is not at all Pretribulational.[4]

It is evident that 2 Thessalonians 2:1–12 creates the most intense difficulty for the Pretribulational rapture theory. I accept
the identification of the events of this chapter with the final tribulation or little season at the end of the age. Again, however, the
order is explicit. Tribulation *(the apostasy and the revealing of the
man of lawlessness)*, occurs first. Following that there is the rapture *(the coming of Christ and the gathering of the saints to Him)*[5]; this
is clearly the meaning of verses 1 through 3 in particular.

> 1 Now we request you, brethren, with regard to the coming
> of our Lord Jesus Christ, and our gathering together to
> Him, 2 that you may not be quickly shaken from your com-
> posure or be disturbed either by a spirit or a message or a
> letter as if from us, to the effect that the day of the Lord has
> come. 3 Let no one in any way deceive you, for *it will not
> come* unless the apostasy comes first, and the man of law-
> lessness is revealed, the son of destruction,

Certainly these passages, the only ones in the New Testament
where coming and rapture and tribulation are explicitly related
would seem to leave little doubt on this issue. At the very least,
they create an immense presumption in favor of Posttribulation-

ism, the view that Christ's coming and the rapture of the saints occurs after the final tribulation.

Paul's Systematic Teaching on the Subject to the Thessalonians

The clear teaching of 1 and 2 Thessalonians together provide us with extensive teaching on the return of Christ. This teaching is, however, plainly and pointedly at odds with the Pretribulational theory.

We will consider Paul's teaching in these two epistles at some length. There are a number of good reasons to lay this sort of emphasis on it. First, even the most extreme Dispensationalists accept 1 and 2 Thessalonians as authoritative for the church. Second, 1 Thessalonians 4:13–18 is supposed by Pretribulationists to be the classic passage on the rapture. Third, 1 and 2 Thessalonians contain the most detailed, systematic, and continuous presentation of Paul's teaching on the subject. Granted, much of significance is conveyed elsewhere. 1 Corinthians 15 is especially rich in this subject. Yet 1 and 2 Thessalonians taken together as Paul's doctrinal instruction to a single church is of unparalleled importance and clarity. The teaching of Paul on this subject to the Thessalonians ought to be understood as a whole, and when it is, tremendously clarifies our subject. In examining this teaching we will take up in order the three major passages where it occurs.

The first of these passages, 1 Thessalonians 4:13–5:11, may be examined by means of the discussion of five exegetical issues.

The first of these issues may be called *the problem of the Thessalonians*. The theme of this passage in general is clearly to comfort and encourage the Thessalonian believers concerning believing loved ones who had died. This is the theme with which it begins and with which it concludes (4:13, 18; 5:11). This raises the question: What precisely was the doctrinal problem that resulted in their "grieving like the rest who had no hope"? In answering this question, we must be careful not to twist the clear aspects of the passage to fit a speculative answer about the exact problem Paul now addresses.[6]

Nevertheless, if a clear picture of the misunderstanding that troubled the Thessalonians can be formed, it will certainly assist our understanding of the passage. Is it possible to form such a picture? If we examine carefully Paul's first and last statements in the passage, such a clear picture does emerge. According to verse 13, the problem centered on the condition of those believers who die before Christ's return. Paul's first words in verse 14 are to the effect that such will be brought with Christ, i.e., brought again from the dead at Christ's coming because of their union with Christ. Paul proceeds to assure the Thessalonians that so far from their death being a cause of grief, it is, if anything, a promotion (vvs. 15, 16). After digressing in the early verses of chapter 5, Paul returns to the opening theme of the passage in verse 10, where he repeats his assurance that whether we are awake or asleep at Christ's return resurrection-life with Christ will be ours. All this suggests that some doubt was entertained by the Thessalonians about the very resurrection of dead believers.

It has seemed unlikely to some that the Thessalonian problem could center on the resurrection of believers. They reason, *Surely such a fundamental doctrine could not have been doubted.* There are, however, reasons to reject this reasoning and adopt the more natural understanding of Paul's terminology. (1) Paul's teaching at Thessalonica, though effective, was brief and violently interrupted (Acts 17:1ff.). (2) Any but the most clear teaching on this issue would be subject to misinterpretation or doubt because of the intellectual hostility of the Greek world to the idea of bodily resurrection (Acts 17:32). (3) As a matter of fact, Paul's word in 1 Thess. 4:13 rules out any minimizing of the problem. He says explicitly, "we do not want you to be uninformed that you may not grieve *as do the rest who have no hope.*" This statement is unambiguous. In solving the Thessalonians' problem and supplying their lack of information, Paul makes clear that, while the coming *(parousia)* of Christ, the resurrection of dead Christians and the rapture of living believers occur in a definite order, they also occur in immediate succession.

The second of these issues may be called *the sounds of the descent.* Every Pretribulationist believes, and must believe, that 1 Thessalonians 4:13–18 speaks of the Pretribulational rapture of the church. This rapture, so they say, is secret. If this is so, Paul certainly gives a misleading presentation of the subject in verse 16. The shout of the Lord, the voice of the archangel, and the trump of God seem more calculated to wake the dead than to encourage secrecy. Furthermore, when one examines the biblical backgrounds of these matters, more evidence for a posttribulational viewpoint accumulates. Gundry supplies this background:

> Posttribulationism gains nevertheless, in the parallel between the "great (i.e. loud) trump," in which the emphasis lies on the publicity of the posttribulation advent (Matt. 24:27–31), and the "voice" and the "trump" in 1 Thess. 4:16. And there is good reason to connect the "voice of the archangel" (presumably Michael, the only archangel named in the Bible) with the resurrection of Old Testament saints. Michael is specially associated with Israel in Dan. 10:21 and 12:1, 2, in the latter reference in close juxta-position with the resurrection. If the resurrection and translation of the Church will occur simultaneously with the resurrection of Old Testament saints as indicated by the "voice of the archangel," the rapture will occur after the tribulation, for the resurrection of Old Testament saints will not occur till then (Isa. 25:8; 26:19; Dan. 12:1–3, 13).[7]

The third issue may be called *the meeting in the air*. Verse 17 contains Paul's famous assertion that believers will *meet the Lord in the air*. Pretribulationists assume that statement implies that after this meeting, Christ and the church return together to heaven. Actually, this is neither stated, nor implied. In fact the word in the original (*apantesis*) implies exactly the opposite. F. F. Bruce says:

> When a dignitary paid an official visit or parousia to a city in Hellenistic times, the action of the leading citizens in going out to meet him *and escorting him on the final stage of his journey* was called the apantesis....[8]

Gundry aptly comments on the implication of this word: "This connotation points toward our rising to meet Christ in order to escort Him immediately back to earth."[9] This meaning of meeting (*apantesis*) is confirmed by its two other uses in the New Testament. Matt. 25:6 speaks of the ten virgins who were waiting to go out and meet the bridegroom and then return with him to the wedding feast. Even more clearly Acts 28:15 speaks of how the brethren came out to meet Paul and accompanied him on the final leg of his journey to Rome. If this is the meaning and implication of the word, then it is utterly inconsistent with the Pretribulational theory.

The fourth issue may be described as *the connection with chapter 5*. I refer, of course, to the close connection between the teaching of 4:13–18 and that of 5:1–11. The uninspired chapter division has created the impression for some that 5:1ff. takes up a different subject than 4:13–18. This idea has been defended by some and (as will become clear) is necessary to a Pretribulational interpretation of 4:13–18. Such an interpretation cannot, however, be defended for several reasons.

(1) The articles in 5:1 prevent this division and tie 5:1ff. to the foregoing. Paul refers to "*the* times and *the* epochs." The articles obviously indicate that Paul is continuing to speak of Christ's parousia. It is the times and the epochs of the events just being discussed to which Paul refers. The article is clearly used here as Dana and Mantey say, "to denote previous reference".[10]

(2) The typical division between 4:13–18 and 5:1ff. is to the effect that the first passage deals with parousia and the second with the Day of the Lord. The implication is that these are distinguishable events. The day of the Lord, however, designates precisely that event described in 4:13–18. Note that the fivefold use of Lord in 4:13–18 leads up to and anticipates the phrase, the day of the Lord in 5:2.

(3) The supposed implication of this distinction between the parousia and the Day of the Lord is that the church does not have to do with the Day of the Lord because the Pretribulational rapture removes the church from the world before the day of the Lord. This, however, is not the teaching of 5:4–6. Paul's language is careful, "you brethren, are not in darkness that the day should *overtake* you like a thief." The warning of verse 6 to be alert and sober implies that believers must await with expectation the

Day of the Lord. The Day of the Lord comes like a thief to both believers and unbelievers, but it does not *overtake* believers like a thief. The result is that one must identify the Day of the Lord with the parousia of 4:13–18. This, however, is devastating for Pretribulationism. It is to say that the same parousia which brings resurrection and rapture to the church brings "sudden destruction" (v. 3) to the wicked and *overtakes* the wicked like a thief in the night (v. 2).

The fifth and final issue may be called *the timing of the Day*. Paul comments in 1 Thessalonians 5:1–2 that the Thessalonians do not stand in need of written instruction concerning the timing of the parousia. No doubt, this was because of the previous oral instruction he had given them during the time of his ministry in Thessalonica. Thankfully, Paul does not leave us in doubt about what he had taught them during that time. He elaborates what it is that they know already in verses 2 through 4. These verses tell us two bits of information concerning the timing of the Day of the Lord.

(1) Verses 2 and 3 indicate that the day will be wholly unexpected by the wicked and will catch them in a state of carnal security. The analogy of a thief in the night indicates this. It occurs in a similar context in Matthew 24:36–44 (note esp. vvs. 37–39). 1 Thessalonians 5:3 conveys a similar impression. Note that they are *saying* (not crying out for) *peace and safety*. (cf. Jer. 6:14 and 8:11.) In other words, verse 3 does not speak of people crying out in fear and terror for peace and safety. It rather speaks of carnal people congratulating themselves on the peace and safety of their condition.

(2) Verse 4 indicates that the church will be alert and ready for the day of the Lord. *But you, brethren, are not in darkness, that the day should overtake you like a thief.* Thus, they will not find the day to be like a thief to them (Matt. 24:42–44).

The second of the major passages that make up Paul's systematic teaching on the Second Coming to the Thessalonians is 2 Thessalonians 1:4–10. This passage is often overlooked on the question of Pretribulationism. In the context of verse 4, Paul is commending the Thessalonians for their faith in the midst of persecution.

Verse 5 adds Paul's encouragement that such sufferings are a mark of their future inheritance of glory. Verses 6 and 7a then proceed to describe in what the righteous judgment of God mentioned in verse 5 will consist. It will consist in God's repaying with affliction those who afflict the Thessalonian believers (v. 6). It will also consist in God's giving relief to His afflicted people including the Thessalonians as well as Paul and his helpers (1 Thess. 1:1).

The crucial point is reached in verse 7b where Paul tells us explicitly when all this will happen. It will be "when the Lord Jesus shall be revealed from heaven with His mighty angels in flaming fire." Paul's plain meaning is that the event that brings relief to God's afflicted church is the revelation of Jesus Christ bringing immediate destruction to the wicked. There is no conceivable way this can be squared with Pretribulationism. (1) Most Pretribulationism acknowledges Christ's "*revelation*" to be Posttribulational (for the obvious reason that a revelation can scarcely be a "secret rapture"). (2) Christ's revelation means immediate and eternal destruction for those afflicting Christ's people (v. 8ff.). (3) Christ's revelation brings relief from affliction to the church (vvs. 6, 7, 10). Thus, the church is still on earth and still being afflicted up to the point of Christ's revelation. Every escape route for Pretribulationism is cut off.

2 Thessalonians 2:1–12 is the last of the three major passages that constitute Paul's systematic teaching to the Thessalonians. Paul states the *general subject* of this passage in verse 1 in the words: "the coming of our Lord Jesus Christ, and our gathering together to Him." The parousia of Christ and the gathering of Christians to Christ are here viewed as one event occurring at one time. Four considerations demand this. (1) In 1 Thess. 4:13–18 Paul has taught in the most explicit terms possible that the *parousia* of Christ and the rapture and resurrection of Christians occur in immediate succession and are certainly not divisible by seven years of time. The word for *coming* used here in 2 Thessalonians 2:1 is *parousia*. (2) A single article introduces and connects the coming and gathering. The single article "means that the two things are closely connected...two parts of one great event".[11] (3) Unless the gathering is identified with the parousia, Paul does

not discuss or mention the gathering again in the passage. Paul, however, tells us that he intends to discuss this very subject in verse 1. This again points toward the two being viewed as a single occurrence. (4) The order is significant: parousia, then gathering. This is the order of 1 Thess. 4:13–18.

The idea that the parousia occurs after, but the gathering before the tribulation is contradicted by this. The point of all this for the subject under discussion is clear. In this passage the one, inseparable event of parousia and gathering is clearly placed after the great apostasy (v. 3) and the appearance of the Antichrist (v. 8), events that Pretribulationists believe occur during the final tribulation.

The *precise occasion* of this instruction is mentioned in verse 2. The words of this chapter were penned to counter aberrations that were beginning to trouble the church at Thessalonica. There was a practical aberration related to a doctrinal aberration. The practical aberration is identified in the words, "that you may not be shaken from your composure or disturbed." The problem seems to have been an inordinate excitement leading to the undisciplined life rebuked in 2 Thessalonians 3:6–12.

The related doctrinal aberration becomes clear in verse 2 also. The source of this doctrinal problem was the rumor that Paul had taught or was now teaching, "that the Day of the Lord has come". Much discussion has been devoted to the precise meaning of the verb, has come, in this verse. Does it mean "is at hand" or "has come"? The meaning is clearly the latter. (1) It is in the perfect tense. This demands the understanding that the action of the verb has happened in the past even though it has standing results in the present. (2) In its other occurrences in the New Testament it always designates something already present and is often contrasted with things about to come. Note the contrast in 1 Cor. 3:22 and Rom. 8:38. (3) Paul could not be refuting the notion that the day was at hand, because this would have contradicted his own teaching that the day was at hand (Phil. 4:5; Rom. 13:11, 12).

This interpretation, however, raises a problem. How could the Thessalonians have taught or believed that the day had come in the absence of the things Paul had taught them were to be associated with it from 1 Thessalonians 5:1?

The false teaching must have been that the parousia or the Day of the Lord was certain to occur in the immediate future. It had come in the sense of being certainly in the immediate future. The false teachers affirmed that it would only be a few more days, weeks, or months at most. This understanding makes sense of the reaction of some in Thessalonica who apparently gave up their normal employment in wild anticipation of the parousia (2 Thess. 2:2 with 3:6–14). It avoids making the day of the Lord encompass preceding events in a way that contradicts 1 Thessalonians 5:2 and 3. It also distinguishes the Thessalonian error from Paul's own teaching that the day of the Lord was near (Romans 13:11 and 12).

Tragically, there are modern counterparts to the Thessalonian fanatics. Those who affirm that Christ's coming will take place at a specific date in the near future certainly commit the same doctrinal blunder and promote the same practical error. Any emphasis on a "soon" coming which could be "any moment" approaches the error of the Thessalonians and also tends toward the practical error of the Thessalonians.

Paul next gives some very *clear teaching* calculated to correct these aberrations in the Thessalonian church. Verse 3 declares: *(It will not come) unless the apostasy comes first and the man of lawlessness be revealed.* Paul here refutes the fanatics, by clearly asserting that the Day of the Lord could not be in the immediate future because two events must first occur. Several observations are warranted.

(1) The doctrine that imminence means any moment-ness is clearly refuted by Paul's words. Paul did not believe either that no prophesied event remained before the parousia or that it could be at any moment. In fact he exposes such teaching as in seed form the Thessalonian error.

(2) Paul clearly assumes that "the apostasy and the revelation of the man of sin" would be clearly observable and identifiable events to the generation of Christians living when they occur. This militates against identifying these events with any that have occurred so far in church history! No event has given rise to such a consensus.

(3) The presumption is that the events described in verse 3 occur shortly before the parousia. Once they do occur, Paul implies, and only then, will the statement that the Day of the Lord has come be appropriate. The fact that the man of lawlessness is destroyed by the parousia is a further indication of this (v. 8).

Though the teaching of this passage plainly refutes Pretribulationism, interpretations have been advanced in an attempt to blunt its force. These must now be addressed.

Some Pretribulationists have identified "the apostasy" of verse 3 with the rapture. English, Wuest, and others have attributed the meaning *departure* to apostasy (*apostasia*) deriving that meaning from the cognate verb meaning literally to stand from and sometimes depart (*aphistemi*). This interpretation would neatly insert a reference to the Pretribulational rapture into this chapter.[12]

There is no example in the entirety of the Koine Greek writings (including, of course, the 40 occurrences in the Septuagint and the one occurrence in the New Testament) of this word designating anything other than political revolt or religious apostasy. As Gundry comments, "It is unthinkable that Paul would use for the rapture a word the connotation of which overwhelmingly has to do with civil and religious defection".[13]

Other Pretribulationists have identified the *"restrainer"* (vvs. 6 and 7) with the Holy Spirit in the church.[14] This allows them to assert that, when the Holy Spirit is taken out of the way, the church whom He indwells is also taken out of the world. In this way they find a Pretribulational rapture in this passage. Several comments show the unsatisfactory character of this view: (1) Any identification of the restrainer must be established on the strongest exegetical grounds, since Paul himself did not explicitly identify the restrainer. (2) Even the identification of the restrainer with the Holy Spirit does not entail the idea that it is the Holy Spirit *in the church and removed in the rapture* that is the Restrainer. (3) A more likely identification of the restrainer and the restraint is that of an angel and his angelic power. Nothing can be urged against such identification. Angels are viewed as in conflict with the powers of darkness in closely parallel passages

(Dan. 10:10–13; Rev. 20:1ff.; 13:7ff.). Since the mystery of iniquity is the product of (fallen) angelic operation, one might expect for reasons of parity or analogy that its restraint would be angelic. (4) Unanswerable objections can be raised against the restrainer being the Holy Spirit in the church.[15] For instance, the giving of the Holy Spirit at Pentecost was the accomplishment of the work of Christ. Such a withdrawal of the Spirit amounts to a reversal of an infallible result of Christ's death—the outpouring of the Spirit.

Chapter 22: Arguments for Pretribulationism Answered

THIS CHAPTER examines two arguments for Pretribulationism.

The Argument from the Imminence of Christ's Return

R. H. Gundry provides us with the definition of imminence assumed by Pretribulationists: "By common consent imminence means that so far as we know, no predicted event will necessarily precede the coming of Christ. The concept incorporates three essential elements: suddenness, unexpectedness or incalculability, and a possibility, of occurrence at any moment."[1]

The argument which Pretribulationists derive from this understanding of imminence may be stated in a syllogism:

> *Major Premise*: The church is taught to expect Christ's coming as imminent (one that could occur at any moment).

> *Minor Premise*: If predicted events such as the tribulation must occur before Christ's coming it cannot be imminent (one that could occur at any moment).

> *Conclusion*: No predicted events such as the tribulation can occur before the coming of Christ. Thus, it is and must be pretribulational.[2]

If the truth of its premises is granted, this syllogism appears valid. The problem is, however, with its major premise that Christ's coming is imminent in the sense of possibly occurring at any moment. Two lines of argument refute the doctrine of the any moment return of Christ.

First Argument

The first argument against an any moment return of Christ is that the New Testament evidence used to prove "any-moment-ness" neither teaches nor implies it. Three different New Testament ideas are used to support the idea of an any-moment coming of Christ: the idea of *expectancy* regarding Christ's return, the idea of the *nearness* of Christ's return, and the idea of *alertness* for Christ's return.

The terminology of *expectancy* does not imply any-moment-ness. The New Testament often uses language which teaches that Christians should live in expectation of Christ's return.

A number of observations show the futility of using this terminology to prove any-moment imminence. First, the idea of expectancy conveyed by these words does not necessarily imply the thought that what we expect may come at any moment. Common sense reveals that we may wait for and expect things that we know cannot come at any moment. These words occur in all branches of Greek literature with reference to events that cannot take place at any moment. For instance, one of the most important new Testament words meaning expectancy is used in the sentence, "Let Lucia wait until the year expires."[3]

Second, each of the words conveying expectancy is used of eschatological events that the Pretribulationist himself admits cannot occur at any moment. "The appearing of the glory of our great God" (Tit. 2:13), "the revealing of the sons of God" (Rom. 8:19), "the revelation of Jesus Christ" (1 Cor. 1:7), "the early and later rains" (Jas. 5:7), "the coming of the day of God, on account of which the heavens will be destroyed by burning, and the elements will melt with intense heat!" (2 Pet. 3:12), "new heavens and a new earth, in which righteousness dwells" (2 Pet. 3:13) and "the appointed time" of the Posttribulational coming of Christ (Mark 13:33)—all of these events are Posttribulational according to Pretribulationists themselves, and the terminology of expectancy is used of all of them.

The *terminology of nearness* does not imply any-moment-ness.

Perhaps the most obvious proof of this is that it is regularly used of Jewish feasts being near. Such feasts—far from occurring at any moment—fell on set days during the year (John 2:13; 6:4; 7:2; 11:55). This terminology is used of an obviously posttribulational advent in Luke 21:28 and 1 Peter 4:7. It is also used of the seasons of the year (Matt. 21:34; 24:32; Mark 12:38; Luke 21:30).

The *terminology of alertness* does not imply any-moment-ness. It does not in itself contain any necessary implication of the *any-moment-ness* of whatever it is for which we are remaining awake and sober. I have been told that a friend of mine stayed awake all night before his plane was to return to the USA from a time of overseas' ministry. His staying awake did not imply that his plane might leave at any moment, but only that he feared he would oversleep. Wakefulness and sobriety do not necessarily contain the idea of any-moment-ness.

Furthermore, the terminology of alertness is used of eschatological events that cannot occur at any moment. It occurs frequently, for instance, in the Olivet discourse. The point is, of course, that the coming described in that discourse is admitted by Pretribulationists to be Posttribulational. Clearly, such terminology does not imply "any-moment-ness" there. The terminology of alertness is used in 1 Pet. 1:13 and 4:7 of "the revelation of Jesus Christ" and "the end of all things"—events which are also plainly Posttribulational from a Pretribulationist's perspective. Thus, it is impossible to deduce any-moment-ness from the terminology of alertness.

Second Argument

A second argument also refutes the any-moment view of imminence. The New Testament states that there must and will be a necessary delay before the Second Coming of Christ. This delay completely undermines any-moment imminence. Any-moment-ness is frequently affirmed by saying that no predicted event needs to occur before the rapture. The problem is that many predicted events that occur prior to the Second Coming are mentioned in the New Testament: (1) There was to be a delay of undetermined length before Christ's return (Matt. 24:45–51; 25:5,19; Luke 18:7; 19:11–27). (2) The carrying out of the great commission demanded

some delay (Matt. 24:14; 28:18–20; Acts 1:8; 22:21; 23:11; 27:24).
(3) The death of Peter *in old age* required many years of delay
(John 21:18, 19; 2 Peter 1:14). (4) The destruction of Jerusalem and
the carrying of the Jews captive into all the nations until the times
of the Gentiles are fulfilled must occur first (Luke 21:23–38). Since
most of the New Testament was written before that destruction,
at least those parts of the New Testament cannot encourage believers to an any-moment expectation. (5) The commission of
Paul to take the gospel far away to the Gentiles and the prediction that he would bear witness at Rome involved some delay in
the second coming (Acts 9:15; 22:21; 23:11). (6) 2 Thess. 2:1–12
contains Paul's explicit teaching that the signs of the apostasy
and the man of sin must occur "first" and connect these events
with a period just prior to the second coming of Christ. If the
Apostles taught such things, they could not have taught an any-
moment expectation of Christ's return.

The view that the imminence of Christ's return might be at
any moment has seemed attractive to many, but when it is examined closely, it is clearly an extremist interpretation of imminence. It runs it into insoluble conflict with the clear teaching of
the rest of the New Testament. It misunderstands the meaning of
the New Testament terminology upon which the doctrine of the
imminence of Christ's return is based.

The Argument based on the Church's Salvation from Wrath

What is the argument for Pretribulationism based on the church's
salvation from wrath? Again, it may best be summarizes by
means of a syllogism.

> *Major Premise*: The church is saved from the wrath of God.
>
> *Minor Premise*: The tribulation is the wrath of God.
>
> *Conclusion*: The church is saved from the tribulation.[4]

I believe that the syllogism presented above is formally valid.
The conlusion, in other words, follows from the premises as they
are stated. There can also be no doubt that its major premise is

biblical. The problem is with the minor premise in which the tribulation is equated with the wrath of God. Consider a number of problems with this premise.

First, the passages used to support the idea that the church is saved from the wrath of God have nothing to do with the so-called tribulation judgments. Often, 1 Thessalonians 5:9 ("For God has not destined us for wrath, but for obtaining salvation through our Lord Jesus Christ.") is cited by Pretribulationists as a promise that the church will not go through the final tribulation.[5] This interpretation of the text is simply wrong. The context restricts the meaning here to God's eternal wrath beginning with the Day of the Lord after the tribulation (1 Thess. 5:1–4; cf. 2 Thess. 2:1–3). The contrast with salvation in 1 Thess 5:9 demands the meaning of eternal wrath. The salvation mentioned is clearly eternal salvation not salvation from tribulation (1 Thess. 1:9, 10; 2 Thess. 1:6–10; 2:10–14). The contrast is clearly eternal salvation and eternal wrath. The usage of the word, wrath, dictates the meaning of eternal wrath. While it is twice used of the wrath of God in the destruction of Jerusalem (Luke 21:23; 1 Thess. 2:16), it is never used of tribulation judgments. It most frequently refers to final destruction (1 Thess. 1:9–10). Consistency demands that if such passages teach the deliverance of the church from the tribulation, they also teach the deliverance of every saved person from the tribulation (including the tribulation saints). The reasons given in 1 Thess. 5:9, 10 for the salvation of those delivered from the wrath of God is that Christ died for them. This raises the question, "Did not Christ die for and thus save the so-called 'tribulation saints' from the wrath of God?"[6]

Second, presence in the tribulation does not imply participation in the wrath of God. Tribulation is the portion of God's people, but this clearly does not mean that they experience the wrath of God (1 Thess. 3:4; Acts 14:22). The same events may be wrath for some and chastisements for others. Revelation 7:1–3 speaks of some who are protected in the midst of the tribulation. The analogy of Israel in Egypt illustrates protection from God's wrath in the midst of tribulation. Since the seven plagues of the Revelation are reminiscent of the ten plagues on Egypt, this illustration has a pointed relevance.[7]

Third, Revelation 3:10 is often cited in support of the idea that the church is delivered from going through the tribulation. This verse states that the church of Philadelphia will "be kept from the hour of testing", but it does not teach or imply a pretribulational rapture. The key words are "I also will keep you from the hour of testing."

Several things show that the use that Pretribulationists make of this text is misguided. The Greek preposition, *from* (ek), contradicts the use they make of the verse. It always conveys the idea of "emergence from within" in John's writings. The idea is, then, of emergence from tribulation rather than previous removal (Rev. 7:14).[8] The verb, *keep* (tereo), means to guard. Such keeping is unnecessary if the church is removed to heaven before the tribulation. Who needs protection in heaven? The only other occurrence of the Greek phrase, *keep from* (tereo ek), in the New Testament shows that it conveys the exact opposite of removal from danger. It implies preservation while in danger. John 17:15 reads, "I do not ask Thee to take them out of the world, but *to keep them from* the evil *one*." The problem is obvious, is it not? *Take them out of the world* would be a very apt way of describing the concept of the Pretribulation rapture. Yet keeping them from the evil one *is contrasted with* taking the disciples out of the world.[9]

It is possible that the "hour of testing" may not be a reference to the tribulation at all. It may refer to the outpouring of judgment at Christ's Second Advent. Thus, Revelation 3:10 would not teach a Pretribulational rapture, but only a pre-*"hour of testing"* rapture (Luke 21:34–36; Matt. 24:37–40; Luke 17:28–30).

By way of conclusion to this chapter, several important warnings about the theory of the Pretribulational Rapture are appropriate.

First, Pretribulationism fits well into and is often part of the system of "easy Christianity" so prevalent in our day. This view permeates many evangelical churches today. Easy Christianity includes the teachings of (1) eternal security as opposed to the perseverance of the saints (2) easy believism (3) the carnal Christian theory (4) an imbalanced view of God as mainly love (5) entertainment-worship (6) judgment according to decision rather than works. The teaching of Pretribulationism that assures men that God would never allow His church to go through the *Great Tribulation* fits perfectly with this mentality.

Second, Pretribulationism tends to leave men unprepared. Paul warned men of coming tribulation to prepare them. Pretribulational teaching taken seriously tends to leave professing Christians unprepared for such tribulation (1 Thess. 3:4).

Third, the clearly unbiblical character of Pretribulationism shows the biblical ignorance of much of modern evangelical thought. One reason that this theory has survived and prospered in evangelical churches is tragic lack of biblical knowledge.

Fourth, Pretribulationism raises false hopes of immunity from tribulation in this world.

Fifth, it tends to the Thessalonian error by teaching an any-moment view of imminence. There is only a small and slippery step from saying that the Lord is coming at any moment (the Thessalonian error) to saying that the Lord may come at any moment.

Sixth, Pretribulationism teaches an incipient *Second-Chance-ism*. It necessarily teaches that men will be saved after Christ's return for His church. Such teaching clearly tends to the practical effect of lessening the urgency of turning to Christ now. Thus, it is a threat to the souls of men.

SECTION 3:
QUESTIONS RELATED TO THE RESURRECTION

Chapter 23: What Does the Bible Teach About the Resurrection?

THE RESURRECTION of the dead is one of those core truths held in common by all orthodox Christians. It is appropriate, therefore, to allow the 1689 Baptist Confession of Faith (echoing here its famous grandmother, the Westminster Confession of Faith) to guide our thinking through of this subject. Its statements provide a very helpful tool with which to examine this important issue.

> 2 At the last day, such of the saints as are found alive, shall not sleep, but be changed; and all the dead shall be raised up with the selfsame bodies, and none other; although with different qualities, which shall be united again to their souls forever.

> 3 The bodies of the unjust shall, by the power of Christ, be raised to dishonour; the bodies of the just, by his Spirit, unto honour, and be made conformable to his own glorious body.[1]

The theme of these two paragraphs is *the final change*. Their structure provides a helpful outline as we think our way through the subject of the resurrection in this chapter.

I. The Fact of the Final Change

Clearly, 1 Thess. 4:13–17 (especially v. 17); 1 Cor. 15:50–53; and 2 Cor. 5:1–4 teach that only saints physically survive the Second Coming of Christ. Without passing through death they receive the glorified body and existence.

After teaching the transformation of all living saints, the Confession affirms the doctrine of the general resurrection of all men. This is clear enough from the statement of paragraph two that "all the dead shall be raised." This general statement is, however, made even more explicit in paragraph 3 when it is explained further that "all the dead" means both "the bodies of the unjust" and "the bodies of the just."

The Scriptures plainly assert this doctrine of a general resurrection of all the dead at the last day. The three classic witnesses to it are Daniel 12:2; John 5:28, 29; Acts 24:15. Such a general resurrection is also strongly implied in a number of passages which describe the general judgment and its everlasting consequences (Revelation 20:11–15; Matthew 25:31–46; Romans 2:5–16).

II. The Character of the Final Change

In the words, "with the selfsame bodies, and none other, although with different qualities," the Confession grapples with an important question in the doctrine of the resurrection. What is the relation of the resurrected body to our present body? The Confession presents its answer by paradoxically asserting two things. It asserts, first, that the resurrection body is the identical body which we now possess. It is this body. Second, it asserts that it is this identical body with a difference. It is this body with different qualities than it now possesses. As Hodge says, it is "not a new body substituted for the old, but the old changed into the new."[2]

The differences between our present body and the resurrection body will be discussed later in this chapter. Here we will focus is on the elements of continuity that permit the Confession to speak of the resurrection body as being the selfsame body.

What does this mean practically? It means that the very body that dies and is buried must and will be raised from the dead. There is no resurrection where the body committed to the ground does not come up from it. The final change is not a merely spiritual resurrection. When Jesus was raised from the dead, this meant that the tomb and the grave-clothes were empty of the body that they had contained (John 20:1–8). So also, when Jesus summons the dead in the day of the resurrection, that action entails that those "in the tombs...shall come forth" (John 5:28–29). This same basic fact is conveyed in the analogy of a seed used by the Apostle Paul which beautifully epitomizes both the continuity and discontinuity of the resurrection body to this one (1 Cor. 15:35–38). It is the physical body committed to the ground in the seed which springs up in the plant which grows from it. The existence of the plant means that there is no longer a dead seed buried in the ground.

One implication of this is that the resurrection body is a physical body. The resurrection life is bodily and material. This must be so if it is to be in any sense the continuation of the old body. *The new body is not heavenly or spiritual in the sense of being immaterial.*

Many misunderstand the language of the Apostle Paul in relation to this issue. The phrase, "heavenly body," (1 Cor. 15:48) has seemed to designate a non-physical body to some. This is, however, to read Greek or Platonic ideas into biblical language. Paul has described some very physical, heavenly bodies in the immediately preceding context (1 Cor. 15:40–42).

Some also mistake the phrase, "spiritual body," (1 Cor. 15. 44) to mean a body composed of spirit. This is, again, a complete misunderstanding of Paul's meaning. Hoekema's able comments clear the mistake.

> One of the difficulties here is that the expression "a spiritual body" has led many to think that the resurrection body will be a nonphysical one—spiritual is then thought to be in contrast with physical.
>
> That this is not so can be easily shown. The resurrection body of the believer, we have seen, will be like the resurrection body of Christ (cf. 1 Cor. 15:48, 49). But Christ's resurrection body was certainly a physical one; he could be touched (John 20:17, 27) and he could eat food (Luke 24:38–43). Further, the spiritual...does not describe that which is

nonmaterial or nonphysical. Note how Paul uses the same contrast in the same epistle, chapter 2:14–15: "Now the natural...man receiveth not the things of the Spirit of God: for they are foolishness unto him; and he cannot know them, because they are spiritually judged. But he that is spiritual...judgeth all things, and he himself is judged of no man" (ASV). Here the same two Greek words...are used as in 15:44. But spiritual...here does not mean nonphysical. Rather, it means someone who is guided by the Holy Spirit, at least in principle, in distinction from someone who is guided only by his natural impulses. In similar fashion, the natural body described in 15:44 is one which is part of this present, sin-cursed existence; but the spiritual body of the resurrection is one which will be totally, not just partially, dominated and directed by the Holy Spirit.

...Our future existence...will be an existence completely and totally ruled by the Holy Spirit, so that we shall be forever done with sin. Therefore the body of the resurrection is called a spiritual body. Geerhardus Vos is correct when he insists that we ought to capitalize the word spiritual in this verse (Hoekema refers to 1 Cor. 15:44—SW.), so as to make clear that the verse describes the state in which the Holy Spirit rules the body."[3]

Some also have misunderstood the language of verse 50 in the same way: "Now I say this, brethren, that flesh and blood cannot inherit the kingdom of God; nor does the perishable inherit the imperishable." Paul's point here is not that the resurrection body is immaterial, but that it is imperishable (v. 50b). The phrase, "flesh and blood," is used to describe the weak and mortal character of our present bodies that are as such unfit for the future kingdom of God. In Luke 24:39 Jesus stated that his resurrection body was "flesh and bones." The language of verses 51 through 54 confirms that what we have here is not immaterial bodies, but imperishable ones. The body is not abolished. It is "changed." It is raised "imperishable." It puts on "immortality."

III. The Permanence of the Final Change

The Confession clearly states that the change brought about by the resurrection is final and permanent. These bodies "shall be united again to their souls *for ever.*" Reasons to believe in the endless character of this condition will be given in the next chapter. Daniel 12:2 and Matthew 25:46 are, however, the most relevant passages. No further alteration in the physical or spiritual condition of any human being is conceivable after the final change wrought by the resurrection of the dead.

IV. The Time of the Final Change

Paragraph 2 begins with the phrase, "at the last day," and asserts that both the righteous and the wicked are raised "at the last day". This phrase indicates, therefore, that the resurrection is general. The change of the living saints, the resurrection of the righteous, and the resurrection of the unrighteous—all of these events occur at the same time, *at the last day.*

In this language the Confession simply reflects the natural force of various Scriptures which we have already considered. There are three passages (and only three) that mention together the resurrection of both the righteous and the unrighteous (Dan. 12:2; John 5:28, 29, and Acts 24:15). Every one of them conveys the natural impression that the resurrections of the righteous and the unrighteous occur at the same time. Before one reads his system of biblical prophecy into such texts, he should stop and ask himself why it is that it is not found in at least one of them.

The point is that the doctrine of a general resurrection is impossible to reconcile with any form of premillennialism. If both the righteous and the wicked are raised and judged at Christ's second coming and at that point in the words of Matt. 25:46 "go away into eternal punishment" or "into eternal life," then who is left to populate the millennium that is supposed to take place for the next thousand years?

V. The Contrast in the Final Change

The Resurrection of the Unrighteous

The resurrection is a mysterious matter, and this is especially true of the resurrection of the unjust. It is the subject of far less biblical comment than that of the righteous. Daniel 12:2 speaks of it as a resurrection to disgrace (or shame) and everlasting contempt. John 5:28, 29 speaks of it as a resurrection of judgment rather than of life. It brings a man face to face with judgment in the sense of divine wrath and the second death.

The contrast stated in John 5:28–29 where the resurrection of the unjust is contrasted with a "resurrection of life," is instructive. It explains why the Bible so frequently speaks only of the resurrection of the righteous. Though the unjust are raised, theirs is a very strange and paradoxical resurrection. Though they are raised physically, they are not raised to "life", but to "death." In the highest sense, theirs is not a resurrection—a restoration to true life—at all.

Unconverted friends should never think of death as an escape from divine wrath. Even death is no refuge from God. Even from there the mighty arm of divine wrath can draw them and make them stand before His awful throne in the last day. Even if men blow themselves to bits, or burn themselves to ashes, God will re-assemble them so that they must face His great, white throne!

The Resurrection of the Righteous

The Confession contrasts the resurrection of the just with that of the unjust at three points. There is a contrast as to its pattern, its agent, and its character.

Christ's resurrection body is *the pattern* for our own. The glory of the resurrection body consists, first of all, in this: it is made like Christ's glorious body (Phil. 3:21; 1 Cor. 15:20–23, 48, 49; Rom. 8:17, 29, 30; Col. 1:18; 3:4; 1 John 3:2; Rev. 1:5). Scripture teaches, therefore, that what we know of Christ's resurrection body will be true of ours.

While the Confession remarks in general that the unjust are raised by the power of Christ, in distinct contrast to this it asserts that *the agent* in the resurrection of the righteous is His Spirit. We have seen that, when Paul describes the new body as a Spiritual body (1 Cor. 15:44–46), the term, *Spiritual*, should be capitalized because it is a reference to the Spirit of God. This affirms an intimate relation between the resurrection body and the Spirit of God. It is a body ruled, indwelt, and energized supremely by the Spirit of God. All of this clearly implies the agency of the Spirit of Christ in the resurrection of the righteous. Many other passages contain this same thought (Rom. 8:11; 2 Cor. 3:18; 1 Cor. 15:45; Rom. 8:23; 2 Cor. 1:22; 5:5; Gal. 6:8). Each of these passages speaks of the Spirit's agency in the resurrection of the righteous as part of His saving work. The resurrection of the righteous is a part of the salvation of the righteous, while the resurrection of the unjust has nothing to do with salvation.

The Confession states that there is a contrast in the Confession as to the character of the resurrection of the righteous. The unjust are raised to dishonor, the just to *honor*. Paul elaborates on what the Confession calls the "honor" of the resurrection body in 1 Cor. 15 by means of several contrasts.

THE CONTRASTS OF 1 COR. 15
Between the Present Body and The resurrection body

Adam	Last Adam
Living Soul	*Life-giving Spirit*
1. Earthy	1. Heavenly
2. Soulish	2. Spiritual
3. Perishable (Mortal)	3. Imperishable (Immortal)
4. Dishonor	4. Glory
5. Weakness	5. Power

The difference between the present body and the resurrection body is the difference between bearing the image of Adam and bearing the image of the Last Adam. Paul, however, brings in this difference by way of supporting the contrast between the "soulish" body and the "Spiritual" body. This contrast is closely related to the next one which contrasts the "earthy" and the "heavenly" (1 Cor. 15:47). Since these first two contrasts are closely related, they will be treated together.

The contrasts between *soulish and Spiritual* and also that between *earthly and heavenly* do not describe a body composed of spirit. The term, Spiritual, rather describes the new body as ruled and energized by the Holy Spirit. Similarly the term, heavenly, when contrasted with earthy characterizes the new body as associated with God and reflecting divine virtue and power in a way surpassing the earthy body. The contrast between soulish and Spiritual, and also that between earthy and heavenly, is not merely a contrast between the fallen body of Adam and the glorified body of Christ, but between Adam in his un-fallen condition and Christ's resurrected condition. In 1 Cor. 15:45 an Old Testament text (Genesis 2:7) referring to Adam in an un-fallen condition is cited. It was no shame or depravity on Adam's part that he was "from the earth, earthy." That was simply how God had created him (Gen. 2:7).

This is the clue to understanding the meaning and significance of these two contrasts. Both reflect on the fact that man as originally created, though innocent and righteous, had not attained a state of matured, moral purity. Adam was capable of sinning and falling from the divine favor. There was a test to pass before a mature and perfected ethical integrity could be achieved. The bodily manifestation of that perfected condition would also have to wait. The condition of attaining the full outward and bodily manifestation of glory was the coming of mankind to a place where his loyalty to God was tested, perfected, and impeccable. Genesis 2:16, 17 states the condition of continued life with God.

> 16 And the LORD God commanded the man, saying, "From any tree of the garden you may eat freely; 17 but from the tree of the knowledge of good and evil you shall not eat, for in the day that you eat from it you shall surely die.

Genesis 3:22 implies that either for good or for ill mankind was to attain an endless life. In a condition of perfected righteousness this would be a great blessing, while in a condition of matured depravity it would be a terrible curse. Thus, God takes action to prevent Adam from eating from the tree of life in a fallen condition.

22 Then the LORD God said, "Behold, the man has become like one of Us, knowing good and evil; and now, lest he stretch out his hand, and take also from the tree of life, and eat, and live forever"

Genesis 3:22 implies that all men will be raised to endless bodily life and that for the unrighteous such life will be a terrible curse.

Though, of course, the power of heaven and the might of the Spirit of God were responsible for the original creation of Adam, the highest expression of the power of heaven and the energy of the Spirit of God awaited the ethical perfection and maturation of man. This moral perfection was necessary before mankind could be endowed with the full measure of power and virtue God had in store for the human race. When Adam fell, his loss of ethical innocence and righteousness resulted in an initially radical and afterwards progressive loss of even that measure of power and ability he originally possessed. When the Last Adam successfully fulfilled the divine will, He did not simply regain what Adam loss, He attained that higher condition which Adam failed to attain. The ideas of Spiritual body and heavenly body, then, describe the physical condition of one who has come to complete union and fellowship with God; who has attained matured, ethical perfection; and, thus, is given the fullest measure of the wise, mighty, and holy operations of the Spirit of God which a creature may know.

Perishable and imperishable (1 Corinthians 15:42, 50, 52, 53, 54) contrast that which is subject to decay, to withering, to dissolution, to deterioration, to destruction and to ruin with that which is not subject to such decay. Flesh may and will decay (Gal. 6:8). Seed may deteriorate and the grass which springs from it wither (1 Pet. 1:23). Beauty may decay (1 Pet. 3:4). Food may rot and will certainly be destroyed and consumed when eaten (Col. 2:22). Even thus, the present body will deteriorate, die, and decay. The resurrection body is not subject to such decay. That body and the whole future inheritance of which it is a part is incorruptible or imperishable (1 Pet. 1:4, Rom. 2:7).

Mortal and immortality (used in parallel with the previous words in 1 Cor. 15:53, 54) contrast that which is subject to death with that which will not and cannot die. What is immortal is not just alive, it is incapable of dying.

Dishonor and glory (v. 43 with vvs. 40, 41) contrast a body characterized by disgrace and shame with a body which by its brightness, splendor, and radiance attests the fame, renown, honor, and excellence of the one who possesses it. Dishonor is used to describe perverse, sexual desires (Rom. 1:26), men with long hair (1 Cor. 11:14), evil reports and reproach (2 Cor. 6:8, 11:21), and household vessels used for unpleasant functions (2 Tim. 2:20). All such dishonor characteristic of our present bodies, which are subject to decay and the curse brought about by sin, and, thus, subject to the reproach and dishonor which sin rightly deserves, will be forever abolished by the glory of the new body.

Glory refers to manifested excellence. The physical splendor of the new body will attest the excellence and virtue of the son of God, and will demand the acclaim and secure the fame of its possessor (vvs. 40, 41). The shining splendor of the sun manifests its nature, so also the resurrection body manifests the excellence of the child of God.

Weakness and power (v. 43) contrast a body subject to infirmity, dysfunction, sickness, disease, and the ultimate manifestation of bodily inability, death, with a body not subject to such things. Such a powerful body is able without difficulty, hindrance, or breakdown to fulfill the holy desires of its possessors.[4] The new body will never experience the weakness, tiredness, and infirmity that is so often in us a temptation and an occasion of sin.

Paul tells us that he rejoiced in hope of the glory of God. That is what we should do in response to such truths. Think of the honor and glory of the resurrection life! The new body is one of great power. It does not confront, because of weakness, the continual frustrations that our present bodies do. It serves God tirelessly and powerfully in the redeemed creation. The new body is one of glory. The very bodily appearance of the resurrected son of God is a continual vindication of God's delight in him. To himself and to the created universe his very body attests the excellency of His character and shuts the mouth of any conceivable reproach or slander. The new body is imperishable. It is the body of one whose character by the grace of God has been brought to perfect, irreversible, moral holiness and righteousness. It is, therefore, a body that never grows weak, is never blemished, is always as powerful and as beautiful physically as it ever was.

Most blessed of all, perhaps, the new body is the sign and seal of that condition in which fellowship with God has been perfected. It is indwelt, ruled, and energized to the highest degree by the Spirit of God. Its union with God in Christ, its possession of the highest divine favor is unchangeable, immutable, and irreversible. It is a Spiritual and heavenly body.

SECTION 4:

QUESTIONS RELATED TO THE ETERNAL STATE

Chapter 24: Endless Punishment

WITH THIS CHAPTER we come to the eternal state—the final and eternal condition of all things. This chapter will take up the eternal state of the wicked and deals with the doctrine of endless punishment. The next chapter takes up the eternal state of believers.

The doctrine of endless punishment has come under intense attack in our age. In such a climate, it is important to remember that this doctrine has been one of the core truths about eschatology that the whole church has held in common since its beginning. Epitomizing the central place this doctrine has held in the church historically is its position in the major creeds of the Reformation period. Chapter 32 of the *1689 Confession of Faith* (echoing the teaching of the *Westminster Confession of Faith*) bears emphatic testimony to the doctrine of eternal punishment.

1 God hath appointed a day wherein he will judge the world in righteousness, by Jesus Christ; to whom all power and judgment is given of the Father; in which day, not only the apostate angels shall be judged, but likewise all persons that have lived upon the earth shall appear before the tribunal of Christ, to give an account of their thoughts, words, and deeds, and to receive according to what they have done in the body, whether good or evil.

2 The end of God's appointing this day, is for the manifestation of the glory of his mercy, in the eternal salvation of

the elect; and of his justice, in the eternal damnation of the reprobate, who are wicked and disobedient; for then shall the righteous go into everlasting life, and receive that fulness of joy and glory with everlasting rewards, in the presence of the Lord; but the wicked, who know not God, and obey not the gospel of Jesus Christ, shall be cast aside into everlasting torments, and punished with everlasting destruction, from the presence of the Lord, and from the glory of his power.

3 As Christ would have us to be certainly persuaded that there shall be a day of judgment, both to deter all men from sin, and for the greater consolation of the godly in their adversity, so will he have the day unknown to men, that they may shake off all carnal security, and be always watchful, because they know not at what hour the Lord will come, and may ever be prepared to say, *Come Lord Jesus; come quickly.* Amen.

No less than three times in paragraph two the Confession reiterates its commitment to the doctrine of the endless torment of the wicked. It speaks of "eternal damnation," "everlasting torments," and "everlasting destruction." To my knowledge no one has ever seriously questioned whether such language in the Confession is intended to teach the doctrine of the endless torment of the wicked. Interestingly enough, many have challenged the idea that the biblical language to which such phrases allude was intended to teach the doctrine of endless torment. The best rebuttal of challenges to the doctrine of endless torment is the natural force of Scripture itself. The Scriptural support for endless torment may be categorized into three classes: *Its Positive Assertions; Its Emphatic Negations; Its Miscellaneous Expressions.*

The Positive Assertions of Scripture

The Scriptures positively assert that the sufferings of the damned are eternal. The biblical testimonies to this are many.

Matthew 18:8 And if your hand or your foot causes you to stumble, cut it off and throw it from you; it is better for you to enter life crippled or lame, than having two hands or two feet, to be cast into the eternal fire.

Matthew 25:41 Then He will also say to those on His left, 'Depart from Me, accursed ones, into the eternal fire which has been prepared for the devil and his angels;

Matthew 25:46 And these will go away into eternal punishment, but the righteous into eternal life.

2 Thessalonians 1:9 And these will pay the penalty of eternal destruction, away from the presence of the Lord and from the glory of His power,

Hebrews 6:2 of instruction about washings, and laying on of hands, and the resurrection of the dead, and eternal judgment.

Jude 1:6 And angels who did not keep their own domain, but abandoned their proper abode, He has kept in eternal bonds under darkness for the judgment of the great day.

Revelation 14:10 he also will drink of the wine of the wrath of God, which is mixed in full strength in the cup of His anger; and he will be tormented with fire and brimstone in the presence of the holy angels and in the presence of the Lamb. 11 And the smoke of their torment goes up forever and ever; and they have no rest day and night, those who worship the beast and his image, and whoever receives the mark of his name.

Those who deny the doctrine of endless torment have frequently objected to it by arguing that *the terms translated by the words, eternal or everlasting, in these passages may in some cases designate limited or finite duration.* To this objection several responses may be made:

(1) Granting only for the sake of argument, that in some instances this language may be used of finite duration, it still cannot be

denied that, if the biblical writers wished to express the idea of eternal duration, these were the best and only words available to them. Says Hodge,

> The strongest terms which the Greek language affords are employed in the New Testament to express the unending duration of the penal torments of the lost. The same words (aion, aionios, and aidios) are used to express the eternal existence of God (1 Tim. 1:17; Rom. 1:20, 16:26), of Christ (Rev. 1:18), of the Holy Ghost (Heb. 9:14), and the endless duration of the happiness of the saints...[1]

(2) In the vast majority of its uses, such language means that endless duration. When used of the age to come and not this age, it universally refers to endless duration. Shedd says,

> In by far the greater number of instances, aion and aionios refer to the future infinite age, and not to the present finite age; to eternity, and not to time. Says Stuart, "...In all the instances in which aionios refers to future duration it denotes endless duration..."[2]

(3) The language that refers to the eternal blessedness of the righteous is strictly parallel to that which refers to the eternal torment of the wicked. Thus, any argument that denies the eternality of the punishment of the wicked also undercuts the eternal duration of the blessedness of the righteous. Matthew 25:46 is the classic statement of this. "And these will go away into eternal punishment, but the righteous into eternal life."

(4) The adjective, eternal, (aionios) must be distinguished from the noun, eternity, (aion). The standard lexicons recognize that the noun sometimes merely refers to an age-long period of time. They do not recognize this in reference to the adjective. Of the 69 uses of the adjective in the New Testament 67 are translated by means of eternal or some synonym. In all sorts of ways the meaning of endless duration is made clear in such passages. It is used constantly of eternal life (Matthew 19:16): "And behold, one

came to Him and said, "Teacher, what good thing shall I do that I may obtain eternal life?" It is used of eternal punishment as contrasted with eternal life (Matthew 25:46): "And these will go away into eternal punishment, but the righteous into eternal life." It is used to describe a sin for which one can never be forgiven (Matthew 12:32): "And these will go away into eternal punishment, but the righteous into eternal life." It is used of that water of eternal life after the drinking of which we will never thirst (John 4:14). "But whoever drinks of the water that I shall give him shall never thirst; but the water that I shall give him shall become in him a well of water springing up to eternal life." The food of eternal life is contrasted with the food that perishes (John 6:27). "Do not work for the food which perishes, but for the food which endures to eternal life, which the Son of Man shall give to you, for on Him the Father, *even* God, has set His seal." Having eternal life means never perishing (John 10:28): "and I give eternal life to them, and they shall never perish; and no one shall snatch them out of My hand." It is used of the eternal God (Romans 16:26): "but now is manifested, and by the Scriptures of the prophets, according to the commandment of the eternal God, has been made known to all the nations, *leading* to obedience of faith". It is used of God's eternal dominion (1Timothy 6:16): "who alone possesses immortality and dwells in unapproachable light; whom no man has seen or can see. To Him *be* honor and eternal dominion! Amen." It is used of the eternal electing purpose of God (2 Timothy 1:9): "who has saved us, and called us with a holy calling, not according to our works, but according to His own purpose and grace which was granted us in Christ Jesus from all eternity". It is used of the eternal being of the Spirit of God (Hebrews 9:14): "how much more will the blood of Christ, who through the eternal Spirit offered Himself without blemish to God, cleanse your conscience from dead works to serve the living God?" It is used of the endless duration of the New Covenant (Hebrews 13:20), "Now the God of peace, who brought up from the dead the great Shepherd of the sheep through the blood of the eternal covenant, *even* Jesus our Lord...."

Only two of the sixty-nine uses of this adjective are not translated by eternal or a synonym in the NASB, and these should be.

In Romans 16:25 it is translated with the words, *long ages past.* "Now to Him who is able to establish you according to my gospel and the preaching of Jesus Christ, according to the revelation of the mystery which has been kept secret *for long ages past....*" The Greek, however, may be literally translated, *for times eternal.* This is a perfectly intelligible translation which informs us that from everlasting God had kept the gospel secret. It is further commended to us by the contextual use of the same adjective, eternal, in the next verse. There it must be translated, eternal. Romans 16:26 reads, "but now is manifested, and by the Scriptures of the prophets, according to the commandment of the eternal God, has been made known to all the nations, *leading* to obedience of faith." The thought seems to be that the eternal God because of His eternal plan kept this matter secret from eternal times.

The other usage not translated by means of eternal or a synonym is found in Titus 1:2: "in the hope of eternal life, which God, who cannot lie, promised long ages ago...." The adjective occurs twice in this verse. Once it is translated, eternal. Once it is translated as a part of the phrase, *long ages ago.* The Greek may literally be rendered, *from times eternal.* The parallel with Romans 16:25 suggests this translation. The use of the adjective to refer to eternal life in the same verse also makes this translation attractive. It would form a kind of contrast and say that the future eternal life has been promised from the past eternal times. But what can it mean for God to have promised eternal life from all eternity? To whom could He have promised it in eternity past? The mention of the ones chosen of God in Titus 1:1 gives the clue to answer this question. God chose His people in Christ (Eph. 1:4). In what has been called the covenant of redemption between the Father and Son in eternity past He may be said to have promised eternal life for them to His Son.

> 2 Timothy 1:9 "who has saved us, and called us with a holy calling, not according to our works, but according to His own purpose and grace which was granted us in Christ Jesus from all eternity,

> 1 Corinthians 2:7 …but we speak God's wisdom in a mystery, the hidden *wisdom*, which God predestined before the ages to our glory;

There is, thus, not a single case in the sixty-nine uses of the adjective in the New Testament that does not bear the meaning, eternal. In light of this evidence the theories which attempt to escape the biblical witness regarding eternal punishment by attributing a different meaning to the biblical terms must be regarded as futile.

The Emphatic Negations of Scripture

Another class of passages teaches the doctrine of eternal punishment. I refer to those statements of Scripture which speak of the torment of the wicked as ceaseless or endless.

> Luke 3:17 And His winnowing fork is in His hand to thoroughly clear His threshing floor, and to gather the wheat into His barn; but He will burn up the chaff with unquenchable fire.

> Mark 9:43 And if your hand causes you to stumble, cut it off; it is better for you to enter life crippled, than having your two hands, to go into hell, into the unquenchable fire…

> Mark 9:48 …where *their worm does not die, and the fire is not quenched.*

> Matthew 3:12 And His winnowing fork is in His hand, and He will thoroughly clear His threshing floor; and He will gather His wheat into the barn, but He will burn up the chaff with unquenchable fire.

The Miscellaneous Expressions of Scripture

Various expressions are used in the Bible which convey in many different ways the utter hopelessness and endlessness of the torments of hell.

Matthew 13:41 The Son of Man will send forth His angels, and they will gather out of His kingdom all stumbling blocks, and those who commit lawlessness, 42 *and will cast them into the furnace of fire; in that place there shall be weeping and gnashing of teeth.*

Matthew 24:51 *...and shall cut him in pieces and assign him a place with the hypocrites; weeping shall be there and the gnashing of teeth.*

Matthew 25:30 And cast out the worthless slave into *the outer darkness; in that place there shall be weeping and gnashing of teeth.*

Such expressions must be placed alongside of the solemn warnings of Scripture to avoid at all costs ever coming into such judgment. Consider, for instance, the warning about the unpardonable sin in the gospels (Matt. 12:31, 32 and Mark 3:29).

Matthew 12:31 Therefore I say to you, any sin and blasphemy shall be forgiven men, but blasphemy against the Spirit shall not be forgiven. 32 And whoever shall speak a word against the Son of Man, it shall be forgiven him; but whoever shall speak against the Holy Spirit, it shall not be forgiven him, either in this age, or in the *age* to come.

Matt. 26:24 and Mark 14:21 convey the same doctrine by speaking of those for whom it would have been better if they had never been born.

Matthew 26:24 The Son of Man *is to* go, just as it is written of Him; but woe to that man by whom the Son of Man is betrayed! It would have been good for that man if he had not been born.

The state of man after the resurrection is everywhere in the Bible viewed as the final and eternal human condition. The Bible clearly states that the wicked will be raised bodily for the purpose of enduring divine wrath (Dan. 12:1, 2; John 5:29, Acts 24:15). Why would God raise the wicked from the dead, if punishment is not eternal or if the wicked were simply to be annihilated?

Two Contemporary Challenges to the Doctrine of Eternal Punishment

Such evidence puts beyond any doubt the scriptural support for the doctrine of the endless torments of the wicked. Two heresies, however, have challenged this evidence. It is necessary to present certain additional arguments against them.

Universalism teaches that all men without exception will one day be saved. Against this stands the uniform witness of Scripture that there are two contrasting destinies for men. Remember the passages cited above that teach the resurrection of the wicked. Universalism also involves the patent absurdity that Satan himself will be saved. (The damned suffer only the same fate as the devil and his angels, Matt. 25:41.) Universalism also must ignore or deny the statement of Christ that for some men it would have been better if they had never been born (Matt. 26:24). If Universalism is true, then it is always better to have been born. The evidence cited in favor of Universalism is terribly weak when seriously considered. Universalists cite the universal language of Scripture (all men, the world etc.). It is a simple fact that such language in Scripture often does not designate all men without exception, but rather all the elect or mankind as a whole. The elect can be saved, and in them the world as a whole, without each and every man being saved.

Annihilationism (or Conditional Immortality) is probably the more popular heresy in our day. It teaches that at some point, after a period of punishment in hell, both the bodies and the souls of the wicked will be extinguished into non-existence. The punishment for sin, death and the second death, is viewed as final extinction or absolute annihilation.

Several considerations show the folly of this position. First, it cannot be reconciled with the statement of Christ that for some it would have been *better if they had never been born*. It must say that ultimately their condition will be *exactly as if they had never been born*.

Second, Annihilationism foolishly equates the biblical language of destruction with the philosophical idea of annihilation. Destruction in the Bible, however, never means to put something into complete non-existence. Rather,it means to ruin (2 Thess. 1:9; 2 Pet. 3:11).

Third, Annihilationism perverts the biblical teaching regarding the penalty for sin. When Jesus vicariously and substitutionarily took upon Himself the penalty for our sins, He was not annihilated or extinguished. He was punished with suffering and torment both of body and soul. He was not annihilated.

Any doctrine of the love of God that casts doubt on eternal punishment is a false doctrine. It is a doctrine that emasculates God by under-estimating His perfect justice and by minimizing the radical evil of sin. We must not confuse firm insistence upon the doctrine of eternal punishment with sadistic delight in it. It was the one who could say of Himself that He was gentle and humble (Matt. 11:29) who in the Scriptures most frequently and insistently and vividly warned of the danger of eternal fire.

Chapter 25: Heaven on Earth?

THIS IS THE concluding chapter of this attempt to simply explain the gospel eschatology of the Bible. In it we turn our attention to the eternal state of the righteous. Where will believers in Christ spend eternity? The answer to this question brings us to consider *the doctrine of the redeemed earth*. Biblical prophecy looks forward to a redeemed world and a renewed earth as the eternal inheritance of God's true people. This doctrine is crucial both to a proper understanding of Christian eschatology and to a proper appreciation of the Christian hope.[1]

The Biblical Necessity of the Doctrine

The Bible is a book of redemptive history. Its theme is the historical unfolding of God's redemptive plan for the world. Redemption and its biblical synonyms, salvation and reconciliation, each imply the restoration—the buying back—of that which is saved and redeemed and reconciled.

Christianity from its inception has understood that what was lost and forfeited in the fall was more than simply individual spirits or souls. Among the earliest heresies that Christianity vigorously rejected were Docetism and Gnosticism. Both these heresies in typical Greek fashion exempted the flesh—the physical side of humanity—from participation in redemption. This rejection of the spiritualizing tendency of Gnostic thought is thoroughly grounded even in the earliest biblical presentation of redemption.

The Beginnings of Redemption in Moses

Genesis begins with the account of the creation of the heavens and the earth by the immediate activity of God. There is the constant refrain that this physical creation was good (1:4, 10, 12, 18, 21, 25). This culminates on the sixth day with the statement of Genesis 1:31: "And God saw all that He had made, and behold, it was very good."

In this same account the creation of mankind is closely linked with this physical creation. Genesis 1:26–28 reads:

> Then God said, "Let Us make man in Our image, according to Our likeness; and let them rule over the fish of the sea and over the birds of the sky and over the cattle and over all the earth, and over every creeping thing that creeps on the earth." ...And God blessed them; and God said to them, "Be fruitful and multiply, and fill the earth, and subdue it; and rule over the fish of the sea and over the birds of the sky, and over every living thing that moves on the earth."

The same relationship between man and the physical creation are confirmed by Genesis 2:4–25. That account emphasizes the physical as well. The creation of man's body is described. His vocation and responsibility to care for the Garden of Eden is stressed. The creation of the woman suited to his needs is emphasized. Even the physical nakedness of the first married couple is brought out.

It is not surprising, then, that the fall of man recorded in Genesis 3 brings disastrous consequences for man physically and for the physical creation. Adam confesses shame over his physical nakedness. Physical pain in childbirth for the woman results. Physical death—returning to the dust—is another awful result.

The seed-promise of redemption contained in Genesis 3:15 implies the reversal of these curses. It is a promise of the victory over the seed of the serpent given to the seed of the woman. The bruising of the serpent's head must surely imply the undoing of the evil done to physical body and to his physical domain—the earth.

The later development of God's redemptive purpose in the books of Moses confirms all this. The promise of the land is a constant theme in God's covenantal dealings with Abraham (Gen. 12:1; 15:7, 18; 17:8). This promise is not annulled by the later developments in the history of redemption. The farthest horizons of the books of Moses hold out the land as the final inheritance of God's people. In Deut. 30:1–10 it is still the promised land that is held out as their inheritance. The later references to the land in the history of redemption show that the promise of the land is not annulled but broadened or universalized into the promise of a new earth.

The Pictures of Redemption in the Prophets
The rest of the Old Testament everywhere assumes that the land or earth is the sphere of redemption and the final inheritance of God's people. The textual evidence for this is as massive: (Psalm 10:16; 25:13; 37:9, 11, 22, 29, 34; Proverbs 2:21, 22; 10:30; Isaiah 14:1, 2; 49:8; 57:13; 60:21; 62:4; Jeremiah 32:41; 33:11; Ezekiel 36:28; 37:14, 25; 39:26; Psalm 2:8; 21:10; 34:16; 104:35; 109:15; 112:2; 119:119; Proverbs 11:31; Isaiah 11:9; 42:4; 58:14; 62:7; Jeremiah 33:15; Daniel 2:35; Daniel 2:44; 7:23; Zechariah 14:9, 17)

These texts put beyond doubt that salvation and redemption is an earthly matter both in terms of the sphere of its operation and the sphere in which its results will be enjoyed. Some, however, may ask: *Are not the prophets simply speaking of heavenly matters by means of imagery drawn from the world? Does not this raise doubt about whether these earthly images can really be the basis for a doctrine of a redeemed earth?*

It is true that some of the prophetic images found in the Old Testament may be explained in this way. This cannot, however, explain all of this language. The emphasis on the earth and land is too pervasive and too deeply rooted in the biblical doctrine of creation itself to be explained away on this basis. To dismiss all of the emphasis on the earth in favor of a more "spiritual" view of the eternal state raises serious questions. On what basis do we conclude that the eternal state cannot involve the earth? This conclusion needs to be examined to see if it is derived from a mindset inherited from Greek philosophy. The assumption that the eternal state cannot be earthly must be grounded in the New Testament itself. It must not be imported into it from the prejudices of our own minds.

The Predictions of Redemption in the New Testament

When we turn to the New Testament, however, we do not discover any tendency to spiritualize this Old Testament emphasis on the earth as the sphere of redemption. There are a number of key New Testament passages that are very significant here.

Matthew 5:5 Blessed are the gentle, for they shall inherit the earth. This verse is a quotation of Psalm 37:11. The terms, "meek" (or gentle), "inherit," and "earth," are the precise words used in the Greek translation of Ps. 37:11. The context of Matthew 5:5 and in particular the other "Beatitudes" shows that the inheriting of the earth spoken of in verse 5 is, at least primarily, an eschatological event. In verses 3–9, 19, 20 a future, eschatological receiving or entering the kingdom of heaven is mentioned in a synonymous or parallel way. This shows that Psalm 37:11 must also have reference to an eschatological event. Jesus shows no signs in this verse of spiritualizing the Old Testament emphasis on the earth. There is a universalizing of the emphasis,[2] but no spiritualizing.

Matthew 6:10 Thy kingdom come. Thy will be done, on earth *as it is in heaven.* The Lord's Prayer itself connects the doing of the Father's will on earth with the coming of His kingdom. Clearly, the consummate coming of God's kingdom involves the perfect doing of His will on earth. There is no sign here of a spiritualizing of the earthly expectations of the Old Testament. Rather the coming of God's kingdom involves precisely the moral transformation of the earth.

Matthew 13:38–41 and the field is the world; *and as for the good seed, these are the sons of the kingdom; and the tares are the sons of the evil one; and the enemy who sowed them is the devil, and the harvest is the end of the age; and the reapers are angels. Therefore just as the tares are gathered up and burned with fire, so shall it be at the end of the age. The Son of Man will send forth His angels, and they will gather out of His kingdom all stumbling blocks, and those who commit lawlessness.*

and will cast them into the furnace of fire; in that place there shall be weeping and gnashing of teeth. "Then the righteous will shine forth as the sun *in the kingdom of their Father. He who has ears, let him hear.* Jesus interprets the symbols of the Parable of the Tares in perfect accord with the earthly expectation of the Old Testament. The field in which is planted the Word of God is the world. This world-field is then identified in verse 41 as the kingdom of the Son of Man. The return of Christ brings not the annihilation of this world-field, but its purification. With its purification it becomes the kingdom of the Father in which the righteous shine in resurrection glory. This parable assumes that the scene of the eternal kingdom is the transformed and purified world.

Matthew 19:28 And Jesus said to them, "Truly I say to you, that you who have followed Me, in the regeneration *when the Son of Man will sit on His glorious throne, you also shall sit upon twelve thrones, judging the twelve tribes of Israel. And everyone who has left houses or brothers or sisters or father or mother or children or farms for My name's sake, shall receive many times as much, and shall inherit eternal life."*

The key word here is *regeneration.* This word is used twice in the New Testament. In Titus 3:5 it is used of the spiritual rebirth of individual Christians. Matthew 19:28 uses it of the rebirth of the world. Verse 29 provides a further contextual indication of the meaning of the word, regeneration, by describing the condition in view in verse 28 as "eternal life." This passage clearly affirms, then, the earthly expectations of the Old Testament and teaches us that God's intention is not merely to regenerate individuals, but also to regenerate the world.

Acts 3:21 whom heaven must receive until the period of restoration *of all things about which God spoke by the mouth of His holy prophets from ancient time.* In this passage there is an explicit reference to the predictions and expectations of the Old Testament prophets. They are said to have spoken of "the period of the restoration of all things." This period is viewed as yet future. It commences at the time of Jesus' return from heaven (Acts 3:19, 20). The term, restoration, then, is very clear. Christ's return brings not the annihilation of all things, but the restoration of all things. What are the "all things" of which verse 21 speaks? This phrase may refer to either the entire world or to all the things associated with the theocratic kingdom of Israel. It is possible that the phrase, "all things," has special reference to the theocratic kingdom. At Christ's Second Coming, the theocratic kingdom, destroyed in the days of Nebuchadnezzar, will be restored and glorified in a redeemed earth. Note also Acts 1:6, 7. Even if this is the proper reference, the restoration of the world is still assumed. The theocratic kingdom cannot be restored without the restoration of the world of which it is a part. This assumption is all the more necessary since the context speaks of what "the prophets" and "all the prophets" predicted. It is clear (as we have seen) that they did predict the restoration of the earth.

Romans 8:18–23 For I consider that the sufferings of this present time are not worthy to be compared with the glory that is to be revealed to us. For the anxious longing of the creation *waits eagerly for the revealing of the sons of God. For* the creation *was subjected to futility, not of its own will, but because of Him who subjected it, in hope that* the creation *itself also will be set free from its slavery to corruption into the freedom of the glory of the children of God. For we know that* the whole creation *groans and suffers the pains of childbirth together until now. And not only this, but also we ourselves, having the first fruits of the Spirit, even we ourselves groan within ourselves, waiting eagerly for our adoption as sons, the redemption of our body.* In Romans 8:18–23 we come to one of the most plain and important testimonies to the doctrine of the redeemed earth. This doctrine is so alien to the thinking of many interpreters that considerable diversity of opinion has arisen even over such a plain passage. John Murray has ably silenced the multitude of conflicting voices with regard to the identity of what Paul here simply calls "the creation" or "the whole creation." Here are his remarks:

> The word "creation" denotes the creative act in 1:20. Here it must refer to the product. The question is: How much of created reality does it include? It must be observed that it is delimited by verses 20 through 23. And the best way to arrive at the denotation is to proceed by way of exclusion in terms of this delimitation. *Angels* are not included because they were not subjected to vanity and to the bondage of

corruption. *Satan* and the *demons* are not included because
they cannot be regarded as longing for the manifestation of
the sons of God and they will not share in the liberty of the
glory of the children of God. The children of God are not included because they are distinguished from "the creation"
(vss. 19, 21, 23)—there would be no purpose, for example,
in saying "and not only so, but ourselves also" (v. 23) if believers were included in the groaning predicated of creation in the preceding verse. *Mankind in general* must be excluded because it could not be said of mankind that it "was
subjected to vanity, not of its own will"—mankind was
subjected to all the evil it is called upon to endure because
of the voluntary act of transgression. The *unbelieving* of
mankind cannot be included because the earnest expectation does not characterize them. Even those who are at
present unbelieving but will be converted are excluded because they will be comprised in the children of God who, as
partakers of the glory to be revealed, are distinguished
from "the creation" (vss. 19, 21). We thus see that all *rational*
creation is excluded by the terms of verses 20 through 23.
We are restricted, therefore, to non-rational creation, ani-
mate and inanimate.[3]

This passage, therefore, teaches in the most plain and literal language that the physical creation will enter into and enjoy the glory of the sons of God. This glory is plainly identified in verse 23 as
the redemption of the body. The glorious transformation at the
return of Christ transforms the bodies of Christ's people, but will
also transform physical creation delivering it from the slavery to
corruption in which it now lies. A resurrected earth will be the
context for the enjoyment of the resurrected bodies of the sons of
God.

John 3:17 For God did not send the Son into the world *to judge the*
world, *but that the* world *should be saved through Him.* John 3:17
teaches that the salvation of the world is the intended result of
the sending of the Son of God to the world. The world in this context must, of course, be primarily a reference to the great multitude no man can number which will be saved by Christ's death

and one day constitute a redeemed race. That reference, however, witnesses to the corporate character of the redemption achieved by the Lord. Such a corporate salvation of humanity is insepara- ble from the idea of the restoration of the physical creation over which humanity was to rule. The purpose of Christ is not, in oth- er words, to salvage a few individuals from a ruined world and take them to heaven. It is to save the world, and this implies the salvation also of the physical creation from ruin.

Colossians 1:15–23 And He is the image of the invisible God, the first-born of all creation. For by Him all things were created, both in the heavens and on earth, visible and invisible, whether thrones or domin- ions or rulers or authorities—all things have been created by Him and for Him. And He is before all things, and in Him all things hold togeth- er. He is also head of the body, the church; and He is the beginning, the first-born from the dead; so that He Himself might come to have first place in everything. For it was the Father's good pleasure for all the ful- ness to dwell in Him, and through Him to reconcile all things to Him- self, having made peace through the blood of His cross; through Him, I say, whether things on earth or things in heaven. And although you were formerly alienated and hostile in mind, engaged in evil deeds, yet He has now reconciled you in His fleshly body through death, in order to present you before Him holy and blameless and beyond reproach—if indeed you continue in the faith firmly established and steadfast, and not moved away from the hope of the gospel that you have heard, which was proclaimed in all creation under heaven, and of which I, Paul, was made a minister. Colossians 1:15–23 is an extended hymn of praise to Christ. It exalts Him as the head both of the old cre- ation (vvs. 15–17) and the new creation (vvs. 18–23). It plainly teaches the redemption of creation by our Lord. He is "the first- born of all creation...all things have been created by Him and for Him." If the world was created for Christ, and He is its first- born or heir, can we think that God will allow it to be finally de- stroyed as a result of Satan's machinations? The answer is, of course, no. The passage goes on, however, to make clear that Christ has redeemed the world made for Him. The "all things" "both in the heavens and on earth" which were created for Him (v. 16) are reconciled to God by Him (v. 20). This must not be un- derstood to support the heresy of universal salvation. It must, however, mean something. The terms used cannot be satisfied without the preservation and transformation of the physical creation.

Revelation 5:10 And Thou hast made them to be a kingdom and priests to our God; and they will reign upon the earth.4 This future reign clearly awaits the Second Coming of Christ in glory. Just as clearly, that return of Christ does not result in the evacuation of Christians from the earth forever. Rather, it results in their eternal reign upon the earth. Again, the Old Testament earthly perspective is not spiritualized, but universalized and affirmed.

Revelation 11:15 And the seventh angel sounded; and there arose loud voices in heaven, saying, "The kingdom of the world *has become the kingdom of our Lord, and of His Christ; and He will reign forever and ever."* The implication of this verse is plainly that the world is conquered by Christ and that He reigns (with His people, Rev. 5:10) in it and upon it forever and ever.

Revelation 21:24—And the nations shall walk by its light, and the kings of the earth *shall bring their glory into it.* Revelation 21 begins with a reference to the new heavens and new earth (vvs. 1–4). The implication of this phraseology will be considered below, but Rev. 21:24 points already in the right direction with regard to its interpretation. The new earth does not bring the destruction of the present earth or its rightful inhabitants. The nations and kings of the earth bring their glory into the city of God even in the new heavens and new earth.

The Significant Objections to the Doctrine

Stating and answering three of the most significant objections to the doctrine of the redeemed earth will broaden our understanding of the biblical evidence for it.

The Bible Teaches the Future Annihilation of the Present Heavens and Earth

The objection is that the Bible teaches the total destruction or annihilation of the present heavens and earth. It is true that the Bible teaches in a number of places the destruction of the world and the coming of a new heaven and new earth (Isaiah 65:17;

66:22; Matthew 24:35; 5:18; Mark 13:31; Luke 16:17; 21:33; 2 Peter 3:7,10, 13; Revelation 20:11; 21:1).

There are a number of reasons to reject the concept of total annihilation. First, the New Testament, as we have seen, explicitly and directly asserts that the earth will be redeemed and renewed. It is simply obstinate to insist on interpreting these passages in such a way as to contradict those plain assertions. If another satisfactory interpretation is available that avoids such contradictions it must be adopted.

Second, the analogy of the resurrection body of believers contradicts the idea that the earth will be annihilated and a completely new universe created. Hoekema says:

> Previously we pointed out that there will be both continuity and discontinuity between the present body and the resurrection body. The differences between our present bodies and the resurrection bodies, wonderful though they are, do not take away the continuity: it is *we* who shall be raised, and it is *we* who shall always be with the Lord. Those raised with Christ will not be a totally new set of human beings but the people of God who have lived on this earth. By way of analogy, we would expect that the new earth will not be totally different from the present earth but will be the present earth wondrously renewed.[5]

Hoekema is exactly right. Is the new body completely new, or is it the resurrection of this body from destruction? Our Confession asserts properly that it is the self-same body but with new qualities. It is the same body. In spite of the fact that the old body is destroyed by death, there is continuity and identity between this old body and the new one. It is just the same with the new earth. It is the present earth resurrected from the destruction of the last day.

The fact that the destruction of the world does not mean its total annihilation is plain in several of the very passages cited above. We have already seen the implication that the earth is not totally destroyed in Revelation 21:24 where even after the passing of the old earth, the nations and the kings of the earth are mentioned. Even more significant is the context of the statements quoted from 2 Peter 3. Perhaps, if any passage might appear to teach the annihilation of the present earth, it would be this one. Yet it must be remembered that the destruction of the now world and the coming of the new world has a plain contextual parallel in 2 Peter 3. The old world was destroyed before the coming of the now world. 2 Peter 3:6–7 says, "through which the world at that time was destroyed, being flooded with water. But the present heavens and earth by His word are being reserved for fire, kept for the day of judgment and destruction of ungodly men." The destruction of the old world did not mean its utter annihilation. So also the destruction of the now world does not imply its annihilation.

Third, the theology of redemption requires the rejection of the doctrine that the earth is annihilated at the last day. Many passages in the New Testament teach that creation as a whole has been redeemed and reconciled to God (Col. 1:15–23; Eph. 1:10). Hoekema states the matter clearly.

> If God would have to annihilate the present cosmos, Satan would have won a great victory. For then Satan would have succeeded in so devastatingly corrupting the present cosmos and the present earth that God could do nothing with it but to blot it totally out of existence. But Satan has been decisively defeated. God will reveal the full dimensions of that defeat when he shall renew this very earth on which Satan deceived mankind and finally banish from it all the results of Satan's evil machinations.[6]

The Phrase, New Heavens and New Earth, Has Reference to the Millennial Reign of Christ (Isa. 65:17–25)

It is not uncommon for both postmillennialists and premillennialists to apply many of the passages that speak of the future glory of the people of God on the earth to the millennium as they understand it. Many objections may be brought against such an interpretation of these passages. We have seen throughout our study multiplied reasons to reject both postmillennialism and premillennialism. If there is no future millennium, then, of course, these passages cannot refer to such a period. Many of these passages really speak not of a temporary or millennial reign, but of an eternal kingdom on earth. The passages under discussion assume the perfection or sinless-ness of this future kingdom. The millennium is not a perfected kingdom on anyone's interpretation. It cannot, therefore, be that to which these passages refer.

Isaiah 65:17–25 is the most problematic of such passages and speaks of the new heaven and new earth in terms that at first glance seem to fall short of perfection.

> 17 "For behold, I create new heavens and a new earth; And the former things shall not be remembered or come to mind. 18 But be glad and rejoice forever in what I create; For behold, I create Jerusalem *for* rejoicing, And her people *for* gladness. 19 I will also rejoice in Jerusalem, and be glad in My people; And there will no longer be heard in her the voice of weeping and the sound of crying. 20 No longer will there be in it an infant *who lives but a few* days, Or an old man who does not live out his days; For the youth will die at the age of one hundred And the one who does not reach the age of one hundred Shall be *thought* accursed. 21 And they shall build houses and inhabit *them;* They shall also plant vineyards and eat their fruit. 22 They shall not build, and another inhabit, They shall not plant, and another eat; For as the lifetime of a tree, *so shall be* the days of My people, And My chosen ones shall wear out the work of their hands. 23 They shall not labor in vain, Or bear *children* for calamity; For they are the offspring of those blessed by the LORD, And their descendants with them. 24 It will also come to pass that before they call, I will answer; and while they are still speaking, I will hear. 25 The wolf and the lamb shall graze together, and the lion shall eat straw like the ox; and dust shall be the serpent's food. They shall do no evil or harm in all My holy mountain," says the LORD.

Verses 20 through 23 seem to apply the language of "a new heaven and a new earth" to a period in which death is still a reality. It speaks of great longevity and remarkable freedom from early death for the people of God, but this language seems to assume that in the end death is still a reality. Because of this language, this passage has been a classic proof-text for those who believe in some form of millennial golden age.

Several conclusive arguments may be brought forward against the millenarian interpretation of this passage. First, all the other uses of the phrase, "New Heaven and New Earth," in the Bible have reference to the eternal state and the perfectly redeemed earth (Isa. 66:22–24; 2 Pet. 3:13, and Rev. 21:1). Second, the condition described in Isaiah 65 appears to be permanent not millennial (vvs. 17b, 18). Third, the New Testament applies this passage to the eternal state. Verse 19 reads, "I will also rejoice in Jerusalem, and be glad in My people; And there will no longer be heard in her the voice of weeping and the sound of crying," This anticipates Revelation 21:4: "and He shall wipe away every tear from their eyes; and there shall no longer be *any* death; there shall no longer be *any* mourning, or crying, or pain; the first things have passed away." Only the perfectly redeemed (and not the millennial) earth brings about the cessation of weeping and crying.

Fourth, the perfection of the conditions described in Isaiah 65 contradict the millennial interpretation. Isaiah 65:25 says, "'The wolf and the lamb shall graze together, and the lion shall eat straw like the ox; and dust shall be the serpent's food. They shall do no evil or harm in all My holy mountain,' says the LORD." Only the eternal state brings the end of all evil and harm in God's holy mountain.

How do we deal with the statements in this passage which assume the continuation of death in the New Heavens and New Earth? We must remember an important principle in the interpretation of Old Testament prophecy. Old Testament prophecy often predicts God's coming, glorious kingdom by things familiar to the people of God. Even we cannot understand what an earth without death would be like. This was even more true in the Old Testament shadows. Thus, the Prophets spoke of the age to come as the highest possible happiness in the world as we know it. Such happiness is pictured by a world where all the greatest sorrows and deepest tragedies of our world are unknown. Thus, this passage does not speak of the absence of death. It speaks rather of great longevity and the absence of premature death. The unknown is revealed in terms of the known and the future in terms of the past.

Ezekiel's prophecy of the wonderful temple illustrates this (Ezekiel 40–48). In particular, the prediction of sin offerings by a levitical priesthood within that temple must be explained on this basis (43:18–27). A woodenly literal interpretation of these chapters flatly contradicts the New Testament teaching on the finality and superiority of Christ's sacrifice and the final abolition of the old sacrifices by Christ's work (Remember Ephesians 2 and the Book of Hebrews).

The Bible Teaches Us To Look to Heaven, Not Earth, as Our Hope or Final Inheritance

There is a strong tendency throughout much of modern Christianity to think and speak of heaven as the place to which Christians should aspire. The Christian used to thinking of heaven as his destiny may wonder what to make of the many passages about heaven in the Bible which seem to support this viewpoint.

There are, indeed, a vast amount of references in the Bible to heaven. Many of them appear to point the Christian to heaven as his reward. Entering the kingdom of heaven is to be his aspiration. Having treasure in heaven is to be the goal of his earthly effort. A heavenly country and city are to be his hope. He has a heavenly calling (Matthew 5:3, 10, 12; 6:20; Philippians 3:20; Colossians 1:5; 2 Timothy 4:18; Hebrews 3:1; 11:16; 12:22.) Such texts seem a massive and air-tight case for heaven as our hope and destiny. Obvious as such a conclusion might seem, it is seriously misguided.

First, the kingdom of heaven is not the kingdom that has for its sphere or realm heaven. As observed in Chapter 8, kingdom in the Bible refers primarily to a reign and not a realm. The kingdom of heaven is not the realm of heaven. It is the kingdom ruled over by heaven. Heaven is the throne of God. Matthew 5:34 remarks, "But I say to you, make no oath at all, either by *heaven*, for it is the throne of God." Thus, the kingdom of heaven includes the earth and its inhabitants and may be entered and dwelt in by them while still on the earth. Consider the following New Testament statements in proof of this:

> Matthew 8:11 And I say to you, that many shall come from east and west, and recline *at the table* with Abraham, and Isaac, and Jacob, in the kingdom of *heaven;*
>
> Matthew 11:11 Truly, I say to you, among those born of women there has not arisen *anyone* greater than John the Baptist; yet he who is least in the kingdom of *heaven* is greater than he.
>
> Matthew 11:12 And from the days of John the Baptist until now the kingdom of *heaven* suffers violence, and violent men take it by force.
>
> Matthew 13:24 He presented another parable to them, saying, "The kingdom of *heaven* may be compared to a man who sowed good seed in his field.
>
> Matthew 16:19 I will give you the keys of the kingdom of *heaven;* and whatever you shall bind on earth shall be bound in *heaven,* and whatever you shall loose on earth shall be loosed in *heaven."*
>
> Matthew 23:13 But woe to you, scribes and Pharisees, hypocrites, because you shut off the kingdom of *heaven* from men; for you do not enter in yourselves, nor do you allow those who are entering to go in.

Second, it must be remembered that the term," heavenly," refers to the source of something not its nature or sphere. The heavenly man is the *man from heaven* (1 Cor. 15:47, 48). The heavenly vision consisted of *light from heaven* (Acts 26:13, 19). The heavenly calling is not a calling to heaven, but a *calling from heaven.* The heavenly country is not a country in heaven, but a *country from heaven* as well. The heavenly kingdom is the *kingdom from heaven* and not the kingdom in heaven. The heavenly city is a city that comes down out of heaven from God.

Third, it must be remembered that the treasure stored up for the

people of God in heaven descends from heaven at the return of Christ.
Though heaven is the happy abode of the disembodied righteous
during the present age, in the age to come heaven comes to earth.
Our inheritance is only reserved in heaven until the last day. Our
treasure is only temporarily stored up in heaven. Consider the
many assertions of the New Testament to this effect.

1 Thessalonians 1:10 …and to wait for His Son from *heaven,*
whom He raised from the dead, *that is* Jesus, who delivers
us from the wrath to come.

1 Thessalonians 4:16 For the Lord Himself will descend
from *heaven* with a shout, with the voice of *the* archangel,
and with the trumpet of God; and the dead in Christ shall
rise first.

2 Thessalonians 1:7 …and *to give* relief to you who are afflicted and to us as well when the Lord Jesus shall be revealed from *heaven* with His mighty angels in flaming fire,

1 Peter 1:4 …to *obtain* an inheritance *which is* imperishable
and undefiled and will not fade away, reserved in *heaven*
for you,

Revelation 3:12 He who overcomes, I will make him a pillar
in the temple of My God, and he will not go out from it anymore; and I will write upon him the name of My God, and
the name of the city of My God, the new Jerusalem, which
comes down out of *heaven* from My God, and My new
name.

Revelation 19:11 And I saw *heaven* opened; and behold, a
white horse, and He who sat upon it *is* called Faithful and
True; and in righteousness He judges and wages war.

Revelation 19:14 And the armies which are in *heaven,*
clothed in fine linen, white *and* clean, were following Him
on white horses.

Revelation 21:2 And I saw the holy city, new Jerusalem,
coming down out of *heaven* from God, made ready as a
bride adorned for her husband.

Revelation 21:10 And he carried me away in the Spirit to a great and high mountain, and showed me the holy city, Jerusalem, coming down out of *heaven* from God,

The Practical Conclusions from This Doctrine

This doctrine enables us to answer the best argument of both pre- and postmillennialists.
What is this argument? It is the countless Old Testament and New Testament prophecies that clearly prophesy a future, earthly kingdom. In the past, those opposing millenarianism often failed to satisfactorily interpret such passages. They attempted to apply them to the church in the present age or to heaven. Such interpretations did not make sense to many good people. They shouldn't have! They were wrong. Only the doctrine of the new earth provides a proper interpretation of such passages.

This doctrine enables us to appreciate the life to come.
One of the biggest hindrances we have in obeying the biblical commands to "rejoice in hope of the glory of God" is our unbiblical views of the life to come. We think of it as a timeless, spaceless, heavenly existence completely unlike our present life. Since we cannot grasp such an existence, we cannot look forward to it? Far better was the method of the Spirit who encouraged the people of God to think of the life to come in terms of this life glorified and redeemed. I am a little uneasy with certain hymns. Hoekema aptly remarks:

> One gets the impression from certain hymns that glorified believers will spend eternity in some ethereal heaven somewhere off in space. The following lines from the hymn "My Jesus, I Love Thee" seem to convey that impression: "In mansions of glory and endless delight/I'll ever adore thee in heaven so bright." But does such a conception do justice to biblical eschatology?[7]

This doctrine enables us to properly exalt the work of Christ.
Every Christian rejoices in the work of Christ, but only to the
degree that he understands it. Defective views of what He did
will diminish our ability to exalt Him. The Arminian thinks
Christ's work only makes salvation possible. Certain Calvinists
think that Christ's work saves only a small group from the general destruction of the world. The result of Christ's work will be
nothing less than a New Heaven and a New Earth. Isaiah 66:22–
23 asserts, "For just as the New Heavens and New Earth which I
make will endure before me.... All mankind (a redeemed world!)
will come to bow down before me."

Notes

Chapter 2; But How Could Everyone Be So Wrong?

1. In the interest of accuracy it must be said that there are some who claim to be Dispensationalists, but who do not hold to the secret rapture theory. Because they do not hold the Church-Israel distinction foundational to it, there are no Historic Premillennialists that hold the secret rapture theory. At least, I am not aware of any. It is also true, I think, and this is what the charts indicate, that the characteristic view of Dispensationalism is the secret rapture theory.

2. Dr. Charles Feinberg, *Premillennialism or Amillennialism*, (Zondervan, Grand Rapids, 1936), p. 27, cf. p. 202.

3. Papias, Fragments, IV, V, VI; This may be found in the *Ante-Nicene Fathers*, vol. 1, (New York, Scribner's, 1905), pp. 153, 154.

4. Pastor Mark Sarver, *The Historical Genesis and Development of Dispensationalism*, (An Unpublished Paper), p. 10.

5. Iain Murray, *The Puritan Hope*. (The Banner of Truth Trust, London, 1971), p. 200.

6. Ibid., p. 259.

Chapter 3: A Matter of Interpretation

1. See, for instance, Keith Mathison's fine summary in *Postmillennialism, An Eschatology of Hope*, (Presbyterian and Reformed, Phillipsburg, 1999), pp. 245–248.

Chapter 4: The Bible's Own System

1. George Eldon Ladd, *The Theology of the New Testament*, (Eerdmans, Grand Rapids, 1974), p. 47.

2. This flawed premise permeates the prophetic interpretation of Keith Mathison in his *Postmillennialism, An Eschatology of Hope*. See pp. 84–

93 and 107. This defective view may also be illustrated from the pages of J. Stuart Russell's *The Parousia*, (Baker Book House, Grand Rapids, 1985), pp. 527, 549, 550.

Chapter 6: The Bible's Own System—The Enhanced Scheme

1. Geerhardus Vos, *Pauline Eschatology*, (Eerdmans, Grand Rapids, 1972), on p. 38 provides a chart that suggested to me the illustrations here presented. The concepts and chart presented by Vos in this section of *Pauline Eschatology* are nothing less than epochal in their significance for the history of eschatological thought.

Chapter 7: The Dividing Line

1. There is nothing novel about this thesis. It is clearly the doctrine of the *1689 Baptist Confession of Faith* (32:1–3), which in turn reflects the *Westminster Confession of Faith* (33:1–3).

2. In *A Modern Exposition of the 1689 Baptist Confession of Faith* (Darlington, England: Evangelical Press, 1989), pp. 415–419, I take the same basic approach, but in a more simple and popular way. I make the same point utilizing seven of the major passages on the judgment in the New Testament.

3. This view of the structure of Romans 1:18–3:8 is supported by the following considerations: (1) 1:16 speaks of Jews and Greeks. There is no narrowing of the scope in v. 18 where those considered are called men, i.e., men in general. (2) 1:18-32 is not concerned with Gentiles only. Verse 23 alludes to Ps. 106:20 and Jer. 2:11 which passages speak directly of Jews. (3) There is nothing to indicate a change of scope in 2:1. The language is universal: "every man of you who passes judgment." The language is consequential. The *"therefore"* that begins verse 1 connects this with the foregoing. The language of passing judgment, though appropriate to Jews, is also applicable to Gentiles (2:15). (4) Both Jews and Greeks are considered in the body of 2:1-16. Cf. especially 2:6-15. How inappropriate to put these verses, then, in a passage supposed to be dealing with Jews only! (5) Note the occurrence of the term, men, in both 1:18 and 2:16. Its occurrence brackets the section and suggests that in its entirety it deals with men in general. (6) The transition or shift to Paul's treatment of Jews in particular is clearly marked. Note v. 17: "But if you bear the name, "Jew"." Throughout 1:18-3:8 this is the only clear transition or shift in the scope of reference.

4. J. Marcellus Kik, *An Eschatology of Victory*, (Presbyterian and Reformed, 1971), p. 5. See also Iain Murray's *Puritan Hope*, (Banner of Truth Trust, London, 1971), p. 250.

5. *The Scofield Reference Bible*, p. 1349; *The New Scofield Reference Bible*, pp. 1341, 1372.

6. *The New Scofield Reference Bible*, p. 1341.

Chapter 8: The Comng of the Kingdom Introduced

1. Raymond O. Zorn, *Church and Kingdom*, (Presbyterian and Reformed, Philadelphia, 1962), p. 48; cf. also Herman Ridderbos, *The Coming of the Kingdom*, (Presbyterian and Reformed, Philadelphia, 1975), pp. 22, 23.

Chapter 9: The Coming of the Kingdom in Christ's Parables

1. Ladd, *The Theology of the New Testament*, p. 95.

2. Ridderbos, *The Coming of the Kingdom*, p. 123. Ridderbos sees that this is the question when he says that the problem addressed in these parables is the "modality of the coming of the Kingdom of God."

3. None of this means that John's prophecy was fallible. What John prophesied was perfectly accurate. It was his private understanding of this prophecy and application of it that were mistaken. This is why Jesus warns him about not being stumbled at Him (v. 6).

4. Ladd, *The Theology of the New Testament*, p. 98.

Chapter 11: The Coming of the Kingdom in John's Vision

1. Harold Camping, *1994?*, (Vantage Press, New York, 1992)

2. R. C. Sproul, *Knowing Scripture*, (Intervarsity Press, Downers Grove, Illinois, 1979), p. 49.

Chapter 12: The Coming of the Kingdom in John's Vision—The Millennium on Earth

1. The translation, disrobed, is suggested by the *Dictionary of New Testament Theology* and supported by it with cogent arguments (vol. 1, p. 315) (Zondervan, Grand Rapids, 1986).

2. William Hendriksen, *More Than Conquerors*, (Baker, Grand Rapids, 1983), pp. 187, 188.

3. Hendriksen, *More Than Conquerors*, p. 185f..

4. Hendriksen, *More Than Conquerors*, p. 195.

Chapter 13: The Coming of the Kingdom in John's Vision—The Millennium in Heaven

1. The aorist of the verb, to live, may be translated either "lived," or "came to life." Either translation is possible, and both are consistent with the interpretation I will give. I will assume that the word means *come to life* and is intended to refer to *a kind of resurrection.*

Chapter 14: What the Bible Teaches About Heaven

1. Wilbur M. Smith, *Biblical Doctrine of Heaven*, (Moody Press, Chicago, 1968), p. 50.

2. Loraine Boettner, *Roman Catholicism*, (Philadelphia, Presbyterian and Reformed Publishing Company, 1962), pp. 218–234.

Chapter 15: Sheol, Hades, and Hell

1. In the NASB the Hebrew root (which has some unrelated meanings) is translated by Sheol 67 times, 60 of these 67 times hades is used to translate sheol in the Septuagint.

2. Harry Buis, *The Doctrine of Eternal Punishment*, (Philadelphia: Presbyterian and Reformed, 1957), p. 18ff.

Chapter 16: The Earthly Prospects of the Church

1. John Murray, *Collected Writings of John Murray*, vol. 2: Systematic Theology, (Banner of Truth Trust, Edinburgh, 1977), pp. 387ff.

Chapter 17: Are Israel and the Church Distinct Peoples of God?

1. C. C. Ryrie, *Dispensationalism Today*, (Chicago, Moody Press, 1965), pp. 44–48.

2. In making this statement I recognize that I run the risk of being accused of over-simplification. It is true that a great deal of discussion is going on today within circles that are historically Dispensational. I would still maintain, however, that at the end of the day there are two and only two basic positions which one may hold on this matter.

3. Albertus Pieters in *The Ten Tribes in History and Prophecy*, (Eerdmans, Grand Rapids, 1934) on pp. 77, 78 cites John Darby as follows, "The direct connection between the Millennium and the Old Testament is much closer than ours. It is the fulfillment of the New Covenant there promised." Jon Zens in *Baptist Reformation Review*, (Autumn 1973, Vol. 2, Number 3), in his article entitled, "Dispensationalism: A Reformed Inquiry into its Leading Figures and Features," on p. 33ff. cites numerous other Dispensationalists to this effect: John Darby, E. W. Bullinger, J. H. Brookes, C. I. Scofield, L. S. Chafer, John Walvoord, J. Dwight Pentecost, and Ernest Pickering.

4. Consult here the treatment of this subject in Chapter 2.

5. See especially Justin Martyr's *Dialog with Trypho the Jew*, ch. XI, CXX, CXXIII, CXXV, CXXXV. The quotation that follows is from chapter XI.

6. This is chapter 26 paragraph 1 of the 1689 Baptist Confession of Faith. The Westminster Confession of Faith makes a statement in chapter 25, paragraph 1 that is almost identical.

7. Iain Murray, *The Puritan Hope*, (The Banner of Truth Trust, London, 1971), pp. 258–260.

8. Jon Zens, *Baptist Reformation Review*, vol. 2, number 3, "Dispensationalism: A Reformed Inquiry...", p. 26f.; Cf. also Macpherson, *The Unbelievable Pre-Trib. Origin;* Clarence Bass, *Backgrounds of Premillennialism.*

9. Cf. the (Old) Scofield Reference Bible, p. 999ff.

10. The New Scofield Reference Bible, p.997.

11. C. C. Ryrie, *Dispensationalism Today,* (Chicago, 1965), pp. 44–48. Cf. also Jon Zens, Baptist Reformation Review, (2:3), p. 37.

12. The (Old) Scofield Reference Bible, pp. 93, 1002, 115; C. C. Ryrie, *Balancing the Christian Life,* (Moody Press, Chicago, c1969).

13. Charles Hodge, *An Exposition of 1 and 2 Corinthians,* (Associated Publishers and Authors Inc., Wilmington, Delaware, 1972), p. 111.

14. Note the strong concluding emphasis in the double conjunction (ara oun).

15. The Greek word (sumpolitai) is clearly reminiscent of *politeias* in verse 12. Hence, Paul here explicitly states that Gentiles have been incorporated into the ancient covenant (politeia, state or citizenship) of Israel. The idea of incorporation is made explicit in the prefix and in the subsequent phrase (NIV "and members of God's household").

Chapter 18: The Superiority of the Church to Israel

1. Albertus Pieters, *The Ten Tribes in History and Prophecy,* (Eerdmans, Grand Rapids, 1934), pp. 81.

2. The new spirituality of the Church must be considered with regard to the recipients of baptism. Suffice to say here, the new spirituality of the people of God is the reason the physical seed of the people of God is no longer included in the people of God. God's people are spiritual, not physical. The people of God after the reformation of all things are propagated by spiritual not physical birth (John 1:12, 13). Thus, in contrast to the carnality and ignorance of Old Testament Israel every true Israelite now knows the Lord, has his sins forgiven, and has God's law written in His heart (Jeremiah 31:31–34). It is not my purpose to go into detail. If you want that detail, you can obtain my book on biblical baptism. It is entitled *Biblical Baptism: A Reformed Defense of Believers' Baptism* (Truth For Eternity Ministries, Grand Rapids, 1998).

Chapter 19: Has Christ Already Come?

1. Cf. for example, David Chilton's *Days of Vengeance* (Dominion Press, Fort Worth, 1987).

2. J. Stuart Russell, *The Parousia,* (Baker, Grand Rapids, 1985).

3. Thorough-going Preterism has been the subject of hot debate in recent years. Postmillennialists are particularly embarrassed by it as it

tends to caricature their preteristic interpretations of many prophecies. C. Jonathin Seraiah in his *The End of All Things* (Canon Press, Moscow, Idaho, 1999) illustrates their reaction to it. Thorough-going Preterism as a result of this debate has become known by a variety of names. I have chosen the name, *Hyper-Preterism*, because this explains it in terms of its more well-known and orthodox sister, Preterism. It is called *Pantelism* because it teaches that all prophecy has been fulfilled. It is called Hymenaeanism by some after the man in 2 Timothy 2:17 and 18 who taught that the resurrection was past already.

4. Russell, op. cit, p. 538, 539.

5. Russell, Ibid., p. 547.

6. Russell, Ibid., p. 549.

7. Russell, Ibid., pp. 538ff.

8. John Murray, *Collected Writings of John Murray*, vol. 2 (Edinburgh: Banner of Truth Trust, 1977), pp. 387ff.

9. It might be argued against this that in 2 Pet. 1:16 the word, parousia, is used of the transfiguration. What Peter actually says, however, is this: "For we did not follow cleverly devised tales when we made known to you the power and coming (parousia) of our Lord Jesus Christ, but we were eyewitnesses of His majesty." It is unlikely that this is intended to identify the transfiguration as Christ's parousia. Christ's parousia is identified as a future event in 2 Pet. 3:4. It is more likely, then, that Peter intends to say that his eyewitness of the majesty of Christ confirms that what he has taught them about the power and coming of the Lord Jesus Christ is not a cleverly devised tale.

10. The meaning of imminence is not just important because of the very recent debates about Hyper-Preterism. One of the key arguments for Pretribulationism involves their understanding of imminence.

11. R. H. Gundry, The Church and the Tribulation, (Zondervan, Grand Rapids, 1973), p. 29.

12. Gundry, loc. cit., p. 43.

13. John Murray, *Collected Writings*, vol. 2, (Banner of Truth Trust, Edinburgh, 1977), p. 400. In other places Murray rejected the terminology of imminence—probably because he assumed the truth of Gundry's definition.

14. John Murray, *Collected Writings*, vol. 2, p. 399ff.

15. John Murray, *Romans*, (Eerdmans, Grand Rapids, 1968), vol. 2, p. 168.

Chapter 20: Can the Date of Christ's Coming Be Calculated?

1. Edgar C. Whisenant, *88 Reasons Why Christ Will Come in '88*, (Whisenant, 1988), p. 3.

2. Harold Camping, *1994?*, (Vantage Press, New York, 1992), p. 332

3. Harold Camping, *1994?*, pp. 525, 531.

4. See Chapter 16.

5. William F. Arndt and F. Wilbur Gingrich, *A Greek-English Lexicon of the New Testament and Other Early Christian Literature*, (The University of Chicago Press, Chicago, 1971), p. 628.

Chapter 21: Will Christ Come Before the Final Tribulation?—Arguments Against Pretribulationism

1. Many different distinguishing phrases have been used to make this distinction. The "two" comings have been distinguished by means of the phrase, "the rapture and the revelation." They have also been contrasted with the phrase "Christ's coming *for* His saints and coming *with* His saints."

2. Ernest Sandeen, *The Roots of Fundamentalism*, pp. 220, 221.

3. I am using the term, *rapture*, in this context to refer to the translation of the living saints without death into their glorified bodies. Many, I understand, use the term, *rapture*, to refer to the secret rapture. This is not my meaning here. Nor is it the necessary reference of the term.

4. Some Pretribulationists have recognized this difficulty. They have, therefore, sought in some figurative, typical, or spiritual fashion to identify the reference to the *door standing open in heaven* and the call to John in Revelation 4:1 to *come up here* as the secret rapture. This is desperate exegesis indeed!

5. A more lengthy treatment of this passage is given later in this chapter.

6. Robert H. Gundry, *The Church and The Tribulation*, (Zondervan, Grand Rapids, 1973), p. 100.

7. Gundry, *The Church and The Tribulation*, p. 104.

8. Gundry, *The Church and The Tribulation*, p. 104.

9. ibid.

10. Dana and Mantey, *A Manual Grammar of the Greek New Testament*, (Macmillan, New York, 1967), p. 141 and p. 137.

11. Leon Morris, *The First and Second Epistles to the Thessalonians*, (Eerdmans, Grand Rapids, 1959), p. 214.

12. Gundry's thorough destruction of this thesis should be consulted. Gundry, *The Church and The Tribulation*, pp. 114–118.

13. Gundry, Ibid., p. 117.

14. Gundry, Ibid., p. 125.

15. Gundry, Ibid., p. 126ff.

Chapter 22: Will Christ Come Before the Final Tribulation?—Arguments for Pretribulationism Answered

1. Gundry, *The Church and The Tribulation*, p. 29. I have argued in Chapter 20 that another definition of imminence and one that does not imply Pretribulationism is possible.

2. The book, *Things to Come*, by J. Dwight Pentecost, (Zondervan, Grand Rapids, 1974), a standard Dispensational work on eschatology, on pp. 202–204 provides this argument for the Pretribulational rapture position.

3. Gundry, *The Church and The Tribulation*, p. 30.

4. For this argument compare Gundry, *The Church and The Tribulation* p. 44; and Pentecost, *Things to Come*, pp. 216ff.

5. J. Dwight Pentecost, *Things to Come*, (Zondervan, Grand Rapids, 1974), p. 217.

6. Gundry, *The Church and The Tribulation*, pp. 44ff.

7. Note Rev. 16:1ff; Gundry, op. cit., p. 47.

8. Gundry, *The Church and The Tribulation*, pp. 55–56, says, "There is but one other place in Biblical Greek (LXX and NT) where [these Greek words] occur together, John 17:15.... The parallels between John 17:15 and Rev. 3:10 are impressive. Both verses appear in Johannine literature. Both come from the lips of Jesus. A probability arises, therefore, of similar usage and meaning. In John 17:15 the words "take out of"...mean to *lift* or *raise up* and *remove*. The expression gives an exact description of what the rapture will be, a lifting up and removal. Yet it is this expression against which Jesus throws [the phrase in Greek] in full contrast and opposition. How then can [the Greek phrase in question] refer to the rapture or to the result of the rapture when in its only other occurrence the phrase opposes an expression which would perfectly describe the rapture?"

9. Gundry, Ibid., p. 58ff.

Chapter 23: What Does the Bible Teach About the Resurrection?

1. This is Chapter 31, paragraphs 2 and 3 of the *1689 Baptist Confession of Faith*. It follows the *Westminster Confession* very closely at this point.

2. A. A. Hodge, *The Confession of Faith*, (Edinburgh, Banner of Truth Trust, 1869) p. 387.

3. Anthony Hoekema, *The Bible and the Future*, (Grand Rapids, Eerdmans, 1979) pp. 249, 250.

4. 2 Cor. 11:23–30 and 12:7–10 give a biblical description of weakness.

Chapter 24: Endless Punishment?

1. A. A. Hodge, *The Confession of Faith*, (Edinburgh, The Banner of Truth Trust, 1869, 1958), p. 393.

2. William G. T. Shedd, *The Doctrine of Endless Punishment*, (Minneapolis, Klock & Klock Christian Publishers, 1886, 1980), pp. 87, 88.

Chapter 25: Heaven on Earth?

1. Anthony Hoekema, *The Bible and the Future*, (Eerdmans, Grand Rapids, 1979), pp. 254ff. My thinking on this subject owes a great deal to this excellent treatment by Anthony Hoekema.

2. If one prefers to translate Psalm 37:11 with the word, land, and Matt. 5:5 with the word, earth, Jesus would be universalizing the Old Testament teaching.

3. John Murray, *The Epistle to the Romans*, vol. 1, (Eerdmans, Grand Rapids, 1965), pp. 301, 302.

4. There is a textual variant in Revelation 5:10. Some manuscripts have the present tense of the verb, reign, and should be read, "they reign on the earth." In this case, however, no doubt should be entertained as to the correct reading. First, the external evidence of the ancient manuscripts is clearly in favor of the future tense. Second, the internal evidence of the context also clearly favors the future tense. It is emphatically not the viewpoint of the Book of Revelation that believers were at that time reigning on the earth. They were suffering on the earth. The whole perspective of the Book of Revelation requires in this case the future tense.

5. Hoekema, *The Bible and the Future*, pp. 280, 281.

6. Hoekema, *The Bible and the Future*, p. 281.

7. Hoekema, *The Bible and the Future*, p. 274.